HANNIBAL

HANNIBAL

Ernle Bradford

DORSET PRESS
New York

This edition published by Dorset Press,
a division of Marboro Books Corporation.
1991 Dorset Press

ISBN 0-88029-667-4

Printed in the United States of America

M 9 8

CONTENTS

ACKNOWLEDGEMENTS

The author and publishers wish to thank the following who have kindly given permission for the use of copyright material:

Doubleday & Co. Inc. for an extract from *The Odyssey* translated by Robert Fitzgerald;

Evans Brothers Ltd. for an extract from *Enemy of Rome* by L. Cottrell;

Robert Hale Ltd. for an extract from *Carthage* by B. H. Warmington;

The Loeb Classical Library (William Heinemann Ltd.: Harvard University Press) for extracts from the Foster translation of Livy and the Patton translation of Polybius;

Oxford University Press for an extract from *Hannibal's March in History* by Dennis Proctor;

Penguin Books Ltd. for an extract from Juvenal: *The Sixteen Satires* translated by Peter Green (Penguin Classics, revised edition, 1974). Copyright © Peter Green 1967, 1974;

A. D. Peters & Co. Ltd. on behalf of Thomas Dorey and Donald Dudley for an extract from *Rome Against Carthage* published by Secker & Warburg Ltd.;

Thames & Hudson Ltd. for extracts from *Hannibal* and *Alps and Elephants* by G. de Beer;

University Tutorial Press Ltd. for an extract from *History of Rome* by Allcroft and Masom.

The author also wishes to acknowledge with grateful thanks the help of the staff of the London Library.

LIST OF MAPS

ITALY 218–216 BC
including Hannibal's principal
successes against Rome

INSUBRES
CENOMANI
Ticinus
Clastidium
Trebia
Cremona
Placentia
Po
Mutina
Bononia
(Bologna)
BOII
SENONES
Ariminum
Passo
Cottina)(
Pistoia
Faesolae
Arnus
Arretium
Cortona
Lake Trasimene
UMBRIA
PICENI
Perusia
Clanis
Spoletium
ILVA
(ELBA)
ADRIATIC SEA
CORSICA
Alba
Fucens
Tiber
Via Flaminia
Rome
Via Valeria
Via Latina
Via Appia
PELIGNI
FRENTANI
Larinum
Gerunium
Mons
Garganus
SAMNIUM
Aufidus
Teanum
Allifae
Luceria
A P U L I A
Cannae
Capua
Beneventum
Cumae
Nola
Venusia
Via Appia
Brundisium
Neapolis
CAMPANIA
HIRPINI
PICENTES
Nuceria Alfaterna
Metapontum
Paestum
(Poseidonia)
LUCANIA
Tarentum
SARDINIA
Uzentum
Thurii
Sybaris
TYRRHENIAN SEA
BRUTTIUM
Crotona
Messana
Rhegium
Lilybaeum
SICILY
Syracusa
Agrigentum
Carthage
MALTA

100 mis
0   100 kms

CEL

PYRENEES

ILERGETES

Tagus

CELTIBERIANS

Ebro

Tarraco

CARPETANIANS

SILVER MTS

Saguntum

BALEARES

Castulo

Calonae

PINE ISLAND

Ebusus

Betis

IBERIANS

New Carthage

Gades

Baelo

Malaca   Sexi   Urci

Tingis

Tamuda

Iol

Sala

MOORS

Siga

NUMIDIANS

ATLAS MOUNTAINS

THE WESTERN MEDITERRANEAN 218 BC
showing the different peoples recruited
into Hannibal's army for his march on Rome

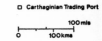

□ Carthaginian Trading Port

100 mls

0   100kms

CHRONOLOGY

208 Scipio defeats Hannibal's brother Hasdrubal in Spain. Hasdrubal crosses Pyrenees into Transalpine Gaul.

207 Hasdrubal crosses Alps into Cisalpine Gaul. Scipio defeats last Carthaginian army in Spain. Hasdrubal defeated and killed at Metaurus river.

206 Mago, Hannibal's youngest brother, evacuates Spain and sails to Balearics. War in Spain ends.

205 Mago lands in Liguria and captures Genoa and Savona.

204 Scipio invades North Africa.

203 Mago dies of wounds. Hannibal recalled to Carthage.

202 Hannibal defeated at Battle of Zama.
End of 2nd Punic War.

200 Hannibal becomes Chief Magistrate of Carthage. He reorganises the city's finances and holds supreme power for five years.

195 Hannibal forced to flee Carthage and offers services to Seleucid empire in the East.

183 Hannibal commits suicide in Bithynia.

In whichever way I might like to relate my life
to the rest of the world, my path takes me always across a great
battlefield; unless I enter upon it, no permanent happiness can be
mine.

Carl von Clausewitz

A man who exercises absolute authority is constrained to assume
a pose of invariable reserve.

Alfred de Vigny

PREFACE

DEATH IN EXILE

Hannibal was sixty-four when he committed suicide in Bithynia. An ageing, defeated war-leader, he had at long last reached the end of even his reserves and will to live. The year was 183 B.C. and the soldiers of his enemy Rome were taking up positions round his house with the intention of killing him or, preferably, taking him back to Italy to be the central figure in a Roman triumph. When that was over, he would be killed in any case.

An outcast from his own city of Carthage, to whose cause he had dedicated his whole life, Hannibal had come to this distant kingdom, bordered on the north by the Black Sea and on the west by the Sea of Marmora, as a guest of its ruler, King Prusias. It would be difficult to imagine a more obscure and tranquil setting than this country villa in Bithynia for the departure from this world of a man whose life had been a hurricane that had shaken the Mediterranean world from North Africa to Spain, France, Italy and Greece. Now, at the limits of the known world – the geographical heart of darkness – this Carthaginian nobleman, who has been described as 'the greatest soldier the world has ever seen', was about to take poison.

His implacable enemies, the Romans, had tracked him down to his remote retirement. They could never rest as long as he was alive. Hannibal had waged war against Rome for over sixteen years and had reduced their city and their state to the very edge of physical, economic and moral bankruptcy. He had bled their armies white, and in the course of one afternoon – at Cannae in Italy – had killed upon the field more men than in any single battle in recorded history. In the end he had been defeated, but he had always escaped his pursuers. His armies had long since been disbanded, but he had still survived in those countries of the eastern Mediterranean that had not yet yielded to Rome. He had warned all their rulers that unless they continued to fight against Rome they would all, one by one, lose their freedom.

Now, at the close of his life, he lived at the village of Libyssa on a quiet inlet from the sea leading towards the Bithynian capital, Nicomedia. Although Hannibal was the guest of Prusias, he had been careful to live outside the city, for he had no wish to call attention to himself. He knew that he had been declared throughout the known world an enemy of the Romans, and that no man, no king, no country was allowed to give him shelter. Prusias in far Bithynia had dared to do so, thinking that his country was so remote from Rome, or even from its ever-growing shadow, that Hannibal could remain unobserved. The king needed the advice of this famous soldier-statesman on the reorganisation of his kingdom.

Then Bithynia found itself engaged in a war with Pergamum, that prosperous city in Asia Minor which had become a client of the Roman state. The forces of Prusias were badly defeated, and he turned to Hannibal for advice. The latter would have been wise, however difficult it might have been, to avoid acting as counsellor to a king who was engaged against a client of the all-conquering Romans. But he had dedicated himself since the age of nine at an altar in distant Carthage 'never to be a friend of the Roman people'. Hannibal managed to change the course of the war and secure a victory for Bithynia at sea. It involved a stratagem so ingenious that the men of Pergamum when they encountered it were completely demoralised, broke off the action, and fled. It had occurred to Hannibal that in the semi-open vessels of that time, where the oarsmen were naked and even the marines were only lightly clad, nothing could be more fearsome than the explosion on board of 'bombs' of poisonous snakes. The countryside of Bithynia was scoured for them and they were then packed in slithery heaps inside pottery jars. When the two fleets engaged, and the jars bursting on the decks of the opposing ships released their venomous contents, there was widespread panic – and the Bithynians secured their victory.

Rome, like all imperial powers, depended upon the smaller states that fell within its orbit feeling secure, and Rome was not used to her allies and clients being defeated. Shortly after this incident the envoys of King Prusias were summoned to Rome to explain why they were at war with Pergamum in the first place. The king had kept Hannibal's presence in his country secret, but one of the envoys was not so discreet. The Roman Senate at once declared that this enemy of their people must be surrendered. Flamininus, a Roman general distinguished in affairs of the East, heard of Hannibal's whereabouts and determined that the Carthaginian should never escape again as he had so often in the past. 'Hannibal must be tracked down and captured or killed', in the words of Plutarch, 'like a bird that has grown too old to fly, and lost its tail feathers.'

Hannibal had long known what his fate would be if the Romans ever laid hands upon him. In a just cause, as he saw it, he had made war upon them for their infamous treatment of Carthage at the conclusion of an earlier war. He had taken an army right through Spain and into what is now France, crossed the river Rhône, traversed the Alps at a time of the year when no one believed it possible, and invaded Italy. For fifteen years he had used Italy as his battlefield and his home, destroying Roman armies with almost contemptuous ease. Hearing now from his servants that his house was surrounded by soldiers, he is said to have remarked: 'It is now time to end the anxiety of the Romans. Clearly they are no longer able to wait for the death of an old man who has caused them so much concern.'

His irony mocked his enemies to the last. When the Romans burst into the house they found their great adversary lying dead; even in his very end he had eluded them.

HANNIBAL

I

A DISPUTED WORLD

The dark giant lay sprawled on the sands of Tunis. Far to the north the new champion of the arena lifted his arms in triumph. The galleys passed upon the sea, the soldiers laid down their arms, cities were rebuilt and peace was everywhere welcomed. The supine giant was unconscious, but not dead. Slowly he began to raise himself upon his elbows.

Hannibal was born six years before the end of the first great war between Rome and Carthage. He was the son of Hamilcar Barca, Barca being one of the most distinguished families in Carthage. Their name meant 'Thunderbolt', and they could trace their descent back to Queen Elissa (Dido), the legendary founder of the great North African city. Hannibal's birth in 247 B.C. coincided with the appointment of his father to the supreme command of the city's forces by land and by sea. There is a legend that his birthplace was the small island of Malta, a Carthaginian colony, but it is almost certain that it was Carthage itself. Hamilcar's palace lay in that city of tall white buildings climbing the hill of Byrsa. It overlooked the deep Gulf of Tunis and the African Mediterranean flickering to the north.

Hannibal was only to know Carthage in the early years of his life, after which, throughout the formative years of young manhood and into middle age, he would be in Spain and Italy. He would see the city again only when, to all intents and purposes, his cause was lost and Carthage was ultimately doomed. Yet it was this city that inspired him to lead her armies against Rome, that fired him to lead them across the Alps and to carry into Italy a war that lasted for sixteen years and was described by the Roman historian Livy as 'the most memorable of all wars ever waged'.

Qart Hadasht, New Town, Carthage to the Romans, was traditionally said to have been founded in 814 B.C. by Phoenician traders who had discovered an ideal site for a trading settlement on a small peninsula well sheltered and deep in the Gulf of Tunis. The Phoenicians were not colonisers in the customary sense of the word: they were merchants backed by the greatest seagoing tradition in the ancient world. Carthage, at any rate to begin with, was no different from most of their other trading posts. They had already established these in Sicily and Sardinia, along the North African coast, and as far westward as Gades (Cadiz) where the Atlantic beats against Spain. Following the pattern of their great city of Tyre and other later foundations, they had chosen a place easily defendable against attacks from the hinterland, and one which provided a suitable anchorage for their trading vessels in the summer months, as well as a separate harbour for the lean war-galleys that protected their shipping. The Phoenicians were sailors, not soldiers. But instead of remaining no more than a trading post, Carthage rapidly developed into the greatest mercantile city in the Mediterranean. This in itself lends support to the story that it was founded by the exiled Queen Elissa and a group of nobles; for no ordinary Phoenicians would have been interested in expanding in such a manner – or have had the resources to do so.

The small bay, El Kram, protected by its headland, was almost certainly the site of the original trading post, and the long sand beaches in the area were ideal for drawing up their ships so that they would be safe from strong winds from the north. A little inland from the bay the colonists proceeded to construct an artificial harbour (Cothon) for their warships, where they could be safely moored all year round. This was circular, about a thousand feet in diameter, with an island in the middle for the naval headquarters. A similar but square-shaped merchant harbour lay to seaward of this, connected to the warship harbour, although the latter preserved its secrecy by being surrounded by a double wall. No one, not even from the mercantile harbour, could see what new construction or repair work was being carried out there. These two harbours, with their surrounding outbuildings, sheds and quays, were the heart of the city – its very *raison d'être*. Nearby was the sacred enclosure of Tanit, the Canaanite goddess of fertility, who had assumed a greater significance in Carthage than in her native Levant. Perhaps this was because she had absorbed a local nature goddess, perhaps also because the land by which Carthage itself was surrounded was so exuberantly fertile that even the Phoenicians, whose main concern had always been trade and manufacture, and the necessary dominance of the 'fish-infested' sea, now looked inland towards the rich earth of what is today called Tunisia. Eastwards the extent of their dominion ran along the coastal areas of Libya and Tripolitania. To the west, again extending along the limit of cultivatable earth, they gradually embraced Algeria and Morocco – lands which, like all the others, they farmed not themselves but with the enforced labour of the native population.

Out of this richness, coupled with their command of the western searoutes, their artisans' skill, and their inherited ability as the greatest entrepreneurs of the ancient world, the Carthaginians had gradually dissociated themselves from their ancestry. They had become a people in their own right and turned their port and trading depot into the greatest city of the day. Carthage ran back from the small headland and the artificial harbours towards the hill of Byrsa which formed the inner citadel. It was here that the temples of the other gods were sited, palaces of the nobles, and the tall many-storeyed buildings housing merchants and workmen and the skilled craftsmen of a nation which relied for its raw materials and sources of riches largely upon the mines and the materials of the lands that lay far away to the west. Principal among these was Spain – the peninsula which, as they had steadily retreated over many centuries before the advance of the Greeks, the Carthaginians had carefully preserved as their own and secret treasure-trove.

Carthage was cooled often in summer by the north wind, but it was also harassed by the easterly Levanter, and sometimes it sweltered under the simoon off that great desert to the south. The town itself, on its peninsula and its hill, was almost an island. In this respect it resembled in microcosm nearly all the North African coastal belt, where a combination of sea on the one hand and mountains and desert on the other produces a curious feeling of remoteness from the giant continent of Africa.

This was the home that Hannibal knew as a boy. It would have been impossible for him, even during that great war against Rome which was being waged across the sea to the north, to have been unaware that Carthage was a spider's web of trade and communications that spread eastward to Egypt and the Levant, and westward as far as scarcely imaginable places beyond Spain. Where the Mediterranean issued between the giant Pillars of Hercules (Gibraltar and Ceuta) into the misty Ocean that lapped the whole world round, the Carthaginians had planted trading posts. Their interests extended as far north as Britain and the Baltic, as well as to the Canary Islands, the Cameroons, and possibly even the Azores. In the Mediterranean, apart from western Sicily, the Maltese islands and the Lipari islands were Carthaginian ports of call, and Sardinia, Corsica and the Balearics were in their sphere of influence. The boy would have been early familiar with the multitudinous things that filled the warehouses of Carthage – gold from Africa, silver and tin from Spain, the skins of deer, lions and leopards, elephant tusks and hides, Greek pottery, faience from Egypt, perfumes from the East, Ionic columns for temples or the homes of the rich, marble from the Aegean islands, and dressed stone from the quarries of the Sacred Mountain (Cape Bon). Carthage was the great mart of the ancient world and the words of Ezekiel, in his prophetic lament for the fall of Tyre some centuries earlier, were even more apt for the colonial city that had far eclipsed its founder:

Thy borders are in the midst of the seas, thy builders have perfected thy beauty. . . . Fine linen with broidered work from Egypt was that which thou spreadest forth to be thy sail; blue and purple from the isles of Elisha was that which covered thee. The inhabitants of Zidon and Arvad were thy mariners: thy wise men, O Tyrus, that were in thee, were thy pilots. The ancients of Gebal and the wise men thereof were in thee thy calkers: all the ships of the sea with their mariners were in thee to occupy thy merchandise. . . . These were thy merchants in all sorts of things, in blue clothes, and broidered work, and in chests of rich apparel, bound with cords, and made of cedar, among thy merchandise. The ships of Tarshish did sing of thee in thy market: and thou wast replenished, and made very glorious in the midst of the seas. Thy rowers have brought thee into great waters. . . .

Young Hannibal grew up as the eldest son of one of the leading men of Carthage, and he inherited a fierce pride in his ancestry and the city, the Queen of the Mediterranean.

Nearly three hundred years before he was born Carthage had established her dominance over the central and western Mediterranean. In the eastern basin of the sea, like the Phoenicians before them, they had yielded before the pressure of the seafaring Greeks. As the struggle for land (largely on the Greek part) and trade (largely on the Carthaginian) had developed in the central Mediterranean there had been more or less incessant warfare between the Carthaginians and the Greeks. These battles on land and sea centred on and around the rich island of Sicily. The importance of this great island was clear enough to the ancients with their eyes fixed only upon this sea, but for the modern visitor, who observes its largely worked-out barrenness, it requires some imagination to realise that Sicily, to the land-hungry Greeks especially, had everything to commend it. There was good vine-growing country and ample regions for pasturage as well as for agriculture; there was all-important water, and there were harbours for a seafaring people, trees for fuel and boat-building, and craggy uplands for goats and even sheep. As well as the vine, the hardy olive flourished – that stone-fruit with its pulpy flesh which lies at the heart of all Mediterranean civilisation.

The result of centuries of warfare was that the Greeks controlled most of the eastern coast of Sicily, nearest to their homeland, while the Carthaginians had retreated largely to the west and north. They were not eager for the acquisition of land, having enough in the area around Carthage, but harbours, repair depots and trading posts were essential for maintaining their contacts with Sardinia and then – looking westwards – as staging-posts to the Balearic islands and, beyond them, their 'secret' and immeasurably rich territory in Spain.

The two marine contestants for the dominance of this sea and the harbours around it had almost, after much bloodshed, reached an unspoken truce when a newcomer upon the scene set the clock back by two or three hundred years – thus introducing a third party into a power-game that had almost been resolved into an agreed draw. This newcomer was Rome, the relatively little-known state to the north of Italy, which had been steadily consolidating its gains on the mainland while Carthage and the Greek states snapped and fought around the bone of Sicily and the sea-routes to the south. Neither the Greeks nor the Carthaginians had paid a great deal of attention to the Romans until this dour and tough land-based power arrived at the very gates of Sicily. Confronting both of them across the narrow Strait of Messina, Rome was now evidently interested in the rich island to the south. Such knowledge as the Greeks and Carthaginians had of this Latin power cannot have been comforting, but at the same time scarcely threatening. Carthage had concluded two treaties with Rome in the 6th and 4th centuries B.C., both designed to assure the Romans that they had no intentions against the mainland of Italy while the Romans, for their part, agreed to accept Carthaginian influence in Sicily. But as Roman interests expanded and the whole of southern Italy came under their sway, it became clear that they would not stop there.

It was the Carthaginians who were always prepared, whenever possible, to reach an accommodation with these powerful new neighbours who – so long as they had been content with the land – seemed no threat to them. It was Rome which was the military and expansionist power. The Carthaginians, as they had shown in previous centuries during their struggles with the Greeks, were often prepared to back down, provided that their vital concerns were not endangered. The wars which followed between Carthage and Rome, wars of exceptional scope covering the whole Mediterranean sea, were always triggered off by Rome. The Carthaginians had no territorial designs on Europe; they wished only to be left in peace in their North African territory, to conduct their manufacturing and trading. As a race they were few in number – with the result that, when they became involved in a large-scale war, the armies that they fielded had necessarily to be composed largely of mercenaries. Carthaginian-generalled, and with an élite of Carthaginian officers and troops, these armies comprised the many races that came within the sway of their sea-empire. (Some points of similarity can be found between the military systems of the British and Carthaginian empires.) Infantry came from Libya and all the other areas of North Africa while Numidian tribesmen provided what was later to become, under Hannibal, Carthage's greatest arm, the superb cavalry which astonished the world.

In the years following Hannibal's birth, his father Hamilcar had fought doggedly and with great skill to preserve the remnants of the Carthaginian garrisons in western Sicily. That he was finally unsuccessful was because the Romans had been quick to learn an all-important lesson – to succeed in the Mediterranean theatre it is essential to have command of the sea. In the early stages of this great war the Carthaginians, with centuries of experience behind them, had found little difficulty in trouncing the Romans in naval engagements and in harrying their coastline. But one of the Roman qualities which would greatly assist them to their successful imperial role was an ability to learn from mistakes. Taking as a model, so it is said, a Carthaginian warship that had run aground and been captured intact, the Romans built in a short space of time a fleet of a hundred and twenty ships. Before very long they had become so adept at handling them that they mastered their enemies at sea. The decisive battle took place off western Sicily – decisive because it rendered untenable the hold that Hamilcar Barca still had upon the last of the Carthaginian bases in the island.

II

LOOKING WESTWARD

For seven years Hamilcar had conducted a brilliant campaign out of his great mountain-fortress of Mount Eryx in western Sicily. The decisive defeat of the Carthaginian fleet finally induced the government to sue for peace. Weary of a war that had cost them so much money and lost them so many men, and which now left them defenceless at sea, they recalled their great general. The peace treaty between the two countries was concluded in 241 B.C. The Romans, fully conscious that Hamilcar was still in control of much of the Sicilian hinterland, and ready for peace themselves after a war that had lasted longer than any in recorded history, were even prepared to let the Carthaginian general and his army leave Sicily without a token submission.

Carthage, nevertheless, had to pay dearly for her defeat. All the islands between Sicily and Africa, including Malta with its magnificent harbours, had to be ceded to the victors. Sicily passed for ever from the Carthaginian sphere of influence and was reorganised as a Roman province. The Lipari islands to the north of Sicily, dominating the north-south trade routes of the Tyrrhenian Sea, were also ceded to Rome. At the same time the Carthaginians were compelled to pay a large indemnity to cover the cost of the war.

Hamilcar, foreseeing that the finances of Carthage might not be sufficient to meet all her debts at once, had been careful to return his mercenaries to the parent city in relatively small detachments so that their arrears of pay could be met in gradual instalments. The ruling party in Carthage, however, true to a cupidity that was understandable in trading but fatal in other affairs, attempted to haggle with the soldiers and delayed making payment until the whole army had returned from Sicily. The result of this was that the mercenaries revolted, to be followed by the slaves, and then by some of the tribesmen in nearby North Africa. In the vicious struggle that ensued – the 'inexpiable war' as the Romans called it – the Carthaginian general Hanno who had been appointed to quell the revolt was twice defeated. Finally, even those Carthaginians in power who were jealous of the Barca family were compelled to call upon Hamilcar. The same generalship that had kept the Romans at bay in Sicily was now turned against the mercenaries and their followers. In a savage campaign that lasted for three years (with no quarter on either side), Hamilcar finally brought the war to an end with the total destruction of the rebels. He had proved himself in his country's service, both overseas and at home, the greatest soldier of his time. His son, who had grown up with the rumour of war always in his ears, who had heard of his father's exploits in Sicily and then witnessed at first hand his part in suppressing the great rebellion, was marked as a soldier from his earliest years.

Even while Hamilcar was engaged in this war in Africa the garrisons which Carthage kept in Sardinia became infected by the revolt and made offers of the island to Rome. Italian traders supplied the mutineers with food and arms while the Roman Senate, taking advantage of the situation (and totally ignoring the treaty signed between the two states), demanded the withdrawal of the Carthaginian troops. Going even further, and using the cynical pretext that Corsica as well as Sardinia was a threat to the coast of Italy, Rome proceeded to annex both islands. Sardinia followed the pattern of Sicily: it became a Roman province, the second on the unfolding road of empire. When Carthage ventured to protest at this intolerable behaviour that was contrary to the peace treaty and all civilised behaviour, Rome once again declared war and then increased the amount of indemnity that Carthage was to pay in return for a humiliating peace. The loss of these two great islands, so important strategically to Carthage since they lay on the trade routes to the west, as well as being sources of timber and ore, was a further disaster when coupled with her expulsion from Sicily. For a long time the eastern Mediterranean had been largely barred to the Carthaginians by the Greeks, but now even the western basin of the sea – essential because of Carthage's interests in Spain – had become heavily threatened.

The 'peace at any price' party, concerned solely with seeing their mercantile fortunes revive, was even prepared to conspire against Hamilcar, his family and friends, with the Roman enemy. The Barca clan and their associates had their enemies, of course, among such influential families as that of Hanno (the discredited general), but there was a larger and more powerful group who saw quite clearly the fate of Carthage if she did no more than acquiesce in defeat. There can be little doubt that Hamilcar also had the backing of the people. He had not only emerged with great credit from the war in Sicily, but he had also saved the city of Carthage from the mercenaries and their followers when they had threatened its very existence.

Hamilcar, together with a number of members of other ruling families – including Hasdrubal, nicknamed the Handsome, who became not only Hamilcar's son-in-law but his right hand in the years to come – saw that the city, as things stood, was doomed. After the annexation of Sardinia it was clear to all but the most purblind in the immediate pursuit of self-interest that the word of Rome could never be trusted. With the central Mediterranean now firmly in their hands, together with command of the sea, it could only be a matter of time before the Romans made a successful landing in North Africa. There was no other direction for the Carthaginians to look but westwards. In Mediterranean Spain, and in Carthaginian settlements such as Gades on the Atlantic coast, where neither Greek nor Roman had yet penetrated, the Carthaginians could make good their losses. There in that broad peninsula, rich in mineral wealth, timber and men, the Carthaginians might yet build a second empire which, once tamed and unified, could challenge the ever-increasing power of Rome.

It is significant of the change in Carthaginian circumstances that when Hamilcar took his leave of Carthage in 237 B.C. with an army bound for the West on this unusual project – the establishment not of trading bases but of a land colony – he did not go with a large armada by sea, but marched along the North African coast. No doubt part of his aim was to recruit troops from the countryside through which he passed, but the almost total destruction of the Carthaginian navy in the recent war meant that the city could only spare some merchantmen to accompany him with stores and essential equipment. Hamilcar's wife, daughters, and two youngest sons, Hasdrubal and Mago, were left behind in the family palace in Carthage. His eldest son, Hannibal, although he was only nine years old, went with his father on the long march to this new country.

Many years later, an exile at the court of Antiochus the Great, ruler of Syria, Hannibal explained the circumstances which led to his accompanying his father at such an early age. 'When I was a boy of nine,' he said, 'my father Hamilcar took me with him to offer sacrifice at the altar of Melqart.' It was natural enough that before this great expedition his father, together with the other officers and nobles who were accompanying him, should take an oath to the 'God of the City', the principal god of Tyre and the god to whom Hamilcar had been dedicated. 'Taking me by one hand,' Hannibal continued, 'he led me up to the altar and placed my other hand upon the sacrificial offering. He asked me to swear that I would never be a friend to the Romans, and I did so.' Livy repeats much the same story – but with a difference. In his account Hannibal was boyishly urging his father to take him to Spain when his father took him by the hand 'and led him to the altar. He made him touch the offerings and bind himself with an oath that, as soon as he was able, he would be *the declared enemy of the Roman people* [my italics].' Livy then, accurately it would seem, gives the reason for Hamilcar's actions: 'The loss of Sicily and Sardinia was a continual torture to the proud spirit of Hamilcar. For he maintained that they had surrendered Sicily in premature despair, and that the Romans had wrongly appropriated Sardinia – and even imposed an indemnity on them besides – in the midst of their African disturbances.'

There is a distinction to be noted here between Livy's 'declared enemy of the Roman people' and Polybius' 'never [being] a friend to the Romans'.

The term 'a friend of Rome' was a definition, not a generalisation. It meant that the man or the state in question submitted to Rome and henceforth would not act independently but was unconditionally committed to Roman protection. Unlike an 'ally of Rome', who still retained some privileges and elements of freedom, a friend of Rome was more or less a vassal. What Hamilcar clearly had in mind was that his son, both as a private individual and (as he might later come to be) the representative of Carthage, would never accept the ignominy of being a humble dependent of the Roman state, whilst Livy cites Hamilcar's anger at the action of the Romans over Sardinia and their imposition of a further indemnity of twelve hundred talents as the primary cause of the next war that was to develop between Carthage and Rome.

In the spring of 236 B.C. Hamilcar and his forces crossed from North Africa into Europe. This was a momentous occasion: the invasion of the European continent by a Semitic and African army. Foreshadowing the great Arab invasions of many centuries later, it gave warning that the countries on the northern rim of the Mediterranean basin were no longer safe from any enemy to the south.

III

A NEW EMPIRE

Gades had been known to the Phoenicians for hundreds of years as a trading depot and major port in the tin trade. Operating out of what was at that time a small island, separated by a narrow arm of sea from the mainland (like Tyre itself), these seafarers had then begun to open up the west coast of Africa. It was from Gades that Hamilcar and his Carthaginians now set themselves a totally different objective – the colonisation of Spain. For nine years, conquering or winning over the native tribes, Hamilcar steadily expanded his grip upon the mainland. Carthaginian superiority in arms and their training in disciplined warfare were applied to bringing into being a colonial empire; hostages were taken for surety, and tribute was imposed upon the conquered tribes. Hamilcar was a great soldier but he was less of a statesman, and his rough-handed methods might have meant that Carthaginian Spain would have advanced slowly over the years. His death in battle in 230 B.C., however, left the command of the army to his son-in-law Hasdrubal 'the Handsome'.

The latter, as Livy puts it, 'relying more upon policy than upon arms, enlarged the Carthaginian power by establishing friendly relations with local princes and gaining the favour of new tribes through friendship rather than by war'. Gradually by this use of diplomacy the Carthaginian sphere of influence extended across southern Spain from Gades to the Mediterranean, spreading north towards the river Ebro, and finding a new base on the Mediterranean coastline at New Carthage (Cartagena). Here a superb natural harbour, reminiscent of those that they had lost in the central basin of the sea, would provide the base for both merchant and war ships, while the well-forested land, with its readily accessible minerals and other materials, made shipbuilding as natural a project as it had been in Sicily and Sardinia. New Carthage pointed eastwards like a dagger towards the coast of Italy.

The relationship between the Carthaginians and their Spanish subjects, or allied peoples, is an interesting one, setting a pattern that would become easily recognisable many centuries later when the European powers expanded throughout the world. First of all, the Carthaginians had a superiority in metal-working techniques (hence in weaponry) and, secondly, they came from an old and civilised race, enjoying the use of the alphabet (which their forebears had invented), and inheriting from centuries of warfare a knowledge of strategy, tactics, and discipline when in combat. The Iberians of southern Spain, partly of Berber stock from Africa, were brave enough, but incapable of withstanding either the horsemen or the organised infantrymen whom the Carthaginians brought against them. The latter themselves constituted an officer class, separated from their men by culture, education and background, but intelligently aware that they could not of themselves provide the manpower necessary for large scale warfare. (Again, one is reminded of the British in India.) In religion they inherited the Carthaginian pantheon of their Canaanite forebears, one where human sacrifice – although less and less as time went on – still played its part. On the other hand, the nobles like Hamilcar, his son Hannibal, and the other leaders had been largely influenced by Greek culture. Hannibal had been taught Greek by a Greek tutor, and later throughout his campaign was to take two Greek secretaries with him on his staff.

Under the leadership of Hasdrubal the Handsome the area subject to the Carthaginians was extended from Gades on the west to New Carthage on the east, and northwards as far as Castulo. This fortress-city dominated the Silver Mountains (the Sierra Morena) which now provided the conquerors – and therefore their home city far east in the Gulf of Tunis – with a rich source of the precious metal. It was on the basis of this area of conquest that Hasdrubal the Handsome proceeded to expand. Hannibal's father and now his brother-in-law were responsible for laying the foundation upon which their great successor was to build. Furthermore, there can be small doubt that the dream of using Spain as a base from which to attack the Romans was always present in Hamilcar's mind. The thought of vengeance – so often accredited solely to his son – must certainly have worked upon the father, who had known Carthage in its days of splendour and who had witnessed at first hand the perfidy of the Romans over Sardinia. (It is significant that throughout their later histories the Romans constantly refer to 'Punic faith', i.e. perfidious and untrustworthy behaviour. It is evidence of their uneasy conscience.)

If some members of the rich oligarchy that ruled Carthage had learned little from their first war against Rome – except a reluctant willingness to entrust the fate of their city and their empire to the hands of Hamilcar Barca – the Romans had learned a great deal. The first conclusion they had drawn, now that they had outstripped the long peninsula of Italy, was the importance of sea power. The aspirations of the northern hill-farmers, who had expanded into an agglomeration of small Italian states, had been completely transformed by their struggle against a mercantile and maritime power like Carthage. The taste of victory on a wider domain than the land had led to a change of attitude. If they were later, under Augustus, to accept the inspired rendering of their history by Virgil that they were descended from the Trojans, the seeds of this myth were certainly sown by the end of

32

the first war against Carthage. It was not too difficult by then for the Romans to believe that the leader of their ancestors had been Aeneas, a figure of Odysseus-like dimensions, who had triumphed (however meanly) over the Carthaginian Queen Dido.

Politically, the first Punic War had brought the Romans to a new maturity. Whereas the tribes or towns on the Italian mainland, which had earlier been conquered by the Romans, had become to one degree or another partners in the confederacy of Latin states, the towns and city-states of Sicily, with a few notable exceptions, became subjects. While the Latins on the mainland retained a certain amount of autonomy and paid no monetary tribute to Rome (supplying instead men and materials for the army), the Sicilians – and the Sardinians – paid tribute in money or in kind. Meanwhile, in the Italian peninsula itself the Romans had extended their northern frontier almost up to the Alps. In the year of Hamilcar's death they had also made their first major inroad into Greek territory. Disturbed by a constant threat to their eastern sea routes, posed by the pirates from the mountainous Illyrian coast of the Adriatic, they had despatched a powerful naval force to the area. In the course of operations, Corcyra (Corfu), that key to the Adriatic, fell into their hands. But for as long as Rome was concerned about the Carthaginians in the west, so long would Corcyra retain a technical independence – and the rest of Greece with it.

Throughout these years Rome was not unaware that far beyond Sardinia, across the long sweep of sea to the Balearics, and westward yet again, there in the Iberian peninsula – a land larger than Italy and almost totally unknown to them – her enemies were increasingly active. Merchants and sailors from the thriving Greek colony of Massilia (Marseilles) were well acquainted of most things that happened in the western Mediterranean. They knew that the Carthaginians were consolidating their hold on the land and they were concerned at, among other things, being denied the tin from southern Spain. The other main source was Cornwall, whence it was transported by sea to Brittany and then overland by a circuitous route which, in its closing stages, passed only a little north of the Pyrenees. Clearly, if a hostile power were allowed to dominate Spain north of the Ebro and extended up to the Pyrenees themselves, this all-important route might also be threatened.

For Massilia the economic threat was paramount, while for Rome the military threat could also be discerned on the horizon. In 226 B.C., anxious to effect some agreement before Carthaginian expansion might render it too late, the Romans sent a mission to Hasdrubal the Handsome to try to define the spheres of influence of the two powers. Hasdrubal, at that moment in the development of the new empire, did not want to become involved in any major disagreement with Rome. Aware that as his power grew steadily behind him he would – if he so chose – be able to break any treaty when it suited him, he agreed to the Roman suggestions. A treaty was signed between the two powers to the effect that the river Ebro should form the northern limit of the Carthaginian sphere of influence and the southern limit of the Roman. A specific clause, whose importance is shown by the fact that Polybius quotes it twice, stated that the Carthaginians would not cross the Ebro 'for the purpose of waging war'. Hasdrubal was clearly playing for time: the natural defence line of the Iberian peninsula was the Pyrenees, and to acknowledge Roman authority over so large an area of the country to the north was contrary to geographical and strategic sense. Hasdrubal was lacking in neither. There was, however, one small – but, as it proved, vital – point that was overlooked. Well south of the line of the Ebro, on the Mediterranean coast, there was a Greek colony called Zacynthus (Saguntum) which maintained close trading links with Massilia. The Massiliotes, for their part, who, as allies of Rome, must have had a hand in framing the treaty, certainly knew of its geographical relationship to the demarcation line. Possibly Hasdrubal discounted it as something that could be dealt with, amicably or not, at a later date. At the time that the treaty was signed Saguntum was no more than a Greek colony with close ties with Massilia, but not under the protection of the Romans. Yet Saguntum was in fact in alliance with Massilia (in turn, an ally of Rome), and this must have been well enough known to the Carthaginians.

During all these years in Spain – first under his father, and then under his brother-in-law – Hannibal had been familiar with the world of the soldier. He had lived in their camps ever since leaving Carthage and, though his education was no doubt well attended to by his Greek tutor, the daily canvas against which he grew up was a military one, set in the world of Spain. Spain, whose African face even in those days was marked enough in the southern regions, gradually changed the further north that the Carthaginians extended their sway by arms and by alliances. What memories Hannibal retained of Carthage, the palaces of the rich, the great temples of the ancient gods, or the towering tenements of the poor, is but conjecture, yet Spain must necessarily have become his homeland – and Spain was many countries. Ranging from the arid south to the eagle-haunted frozen mountains of the north, it differed also in its peoples. The Iberians and the Tartessians from the area of Tartessos (Tarshish) west of Gades were the first to be encountered by the Carthaginians. They were partly familiar, because of the centuries in which the Phoenicians had traded with them, and the closeness of their North African background meant that culturally and materially they had absorbed a great deal from the Semitic East. Further north, however, the colonisers encountered a racial mixture of Iberians with Gallic invaders (Celts), sometimes referred to as Celtiberians, while the northern third of the country was dominated by Gauls who had arrived later in successive waves across the Pyrenees. Over the centuries throughout the length and breadth of the country the original native inhabitants had retreated before these invaders and sought refuge in the mountains. It was with the Spanish inhabitants of Iberian and Celtic stock that the Carthaginians were to form the bulk of their army, the formation and training of which Hasdrubal had largely entrusted to his brother-in-law Hannibal in recent years.

So far Carthage had every reason to be happy about her trust in Hamilcar, and in the 'expansionist party' which had seen a new empire in Spain as the only solution to the city's difficulties. Exports from Spain more than made good the losses from Sicily and Sardinia and there was no sign of these exports declining – rather the reverse – under the leadership of Hasdrubal the Handsome. It was a blow, therefore, when the news was received in 221 B.C. that Hasdrubal had been murdered (traditionally by a local Gaul with some unspecified grievance). But there can never have been any great doubt as to his successor. Although Hamilcar Barca had acknowledged the formal jurisdiction of Carthage, he seems to have enjoyed these new lands almost as an independent kingdom of his own and had carefully laid the grounds of the succession. It was almost inevitable that, upon the death of Hasdrubal, Hannibal should succeed him.

IV

HANNIBAL IN COMMAND

Hannibal was twenty-six when he was unanimously chosen by the army as its new commander. The veteran soldiers seeing him daily over the years had long ago remarked his likeness to his father. 'They imagined', writes Livy, 'that Hamilcar was restored to them as he had been in his youth. They noticed the same lively expression and piercing eye, the same features and cast of countenance. It had not taken him long to show that his resemblance to his father was the least consideration in gaining him support. Never was there a genius more fitted for those two very different things – obedience and command. It was very difficult to decide whether he was dearer to the general or to the army. Whenever there was anything to be done requiring courage and resolution there was no one whom Hasdrubal liked better to entrust with it; nor did any other leader inspire his men with more confidence and daring.' These words, coming from the pen of the historian engaged in writing the definitive eulogistic history of Rome, carry more weight than if they had been written by the Greek secretaries whose accounts (alas, long lost) were compiled from day to day over the brilliant years of Hannibal's life.

He had been some sixteen years in Spain, and it is not difficult to see how they had trained him for his subsequent role. But it is also clear, from the evidence of his life and achievements, that upon him seemed to shine that special grace or talent which, in all ages and under all varieties of religious belief, has appeared to contemporary observers to have been God-given rather than acquired by circumstances, parentage or self-discipline. 'To reckless courage in incurring dangers he united the greatest judgement when in the midst of them,' wrote Livy. This is the difference between leadership and plain bravery. From the record of his life we know that he must have been well built, strong and agile, and with qualities of endurance that, even when pitted against the hardy Romans, seem to have been exceptional. Exceptional, too, was that strange power, possessed by other famous leaders but by few to so great an extent, of commanding the devotion of his armies. These were composed not of patriotic citizens fighting in defence of their country, nor of a whole people liberated from centuries of oppression and believing in their revolution as in a religion (the armies of Republican France wielded by Napoleon), but a mercenary mixture of Libyans, Numidians, and other North Africans, Iberians, Celtiberians, Gauls from

Spain and from France and, finally, Gauls from Italy. They were, it is true, Carthaginian-officered, but this officer class was only a handful in the multitude of men whom Hannibal led over the years. Nevertheless, there can be no doubt that this *corps d'élite* was of exceptional quality and it is unfortunate that so little is recorded of its individual members. A few names are known: Hannibal's brothers Hasdrubal and Mago, who joined his forces in Spain at some unspecified dates, Gisgo, another general, Maharbal an outstanding cavalry leader, and Synbalus, a distinguished physician from Alexandria. Aristotle describes how the Carthaginian officers were 'allowed to wear one bracelet for every campaign they had served'.

Livy's portrait of this great enemy of Rome continues: 'No toil could exhaust his body or overcome his spirit. He could endure heat and cold alike, and his consumption of food and drink was determined by natural want and not by pleasure. His times of sleeping and waking were not determined by night or day. Once his work was done he gave what time remained to rest, but he did not court this with a soft bed or by quiet. Many have often seen him lying on the ground wrapped only in a military coat amid the sentries and outposts of his soldiers. [This has such an authentic ring about it that one would like to know from what source contemporary with Hannibal – perhaps the missing diaries? – this vivid picture was drawn.] In his dress he was in no way superior to his equals, but he was conspicuous in his arms and his horse. He was always by far the first in the ranks of both cavalry and infantry and – foremost to enter the battle – he was the last to leave it once battle had begun.'

So far the Roman historian has painted a noble picture of the great adversary who had nearly prevented the emergence of that Roman empire which Livy celebrated. (It is, of course, necessary for the military historian to stress the qualities of his country's enemy, otherwise the victories of his own side would seem insipid.) Livy now turns to the other side of Hannibal's character, it being a natural assumption that no man can be of a piece but that, if he has good or admirable qualities, these must be somehow counterbalanced by the bad. Thus: 'These very great qualities of the man were equalled by monstrous vices: inhuman cruelty, a worse than Punic perfidy, having no regard for truth and none for sanctity; no fear of the gods, no reverence of an oath, and no religious scruples.' As will become clear, these major charges cannot be substantiated and there is no evidence – even in Livy's own account – of any of them. It is as if the historian, having acknowledged Hannibal's known virtues, suddenly became afraid of his own temerity and had to neutralise them with a recital of evil traits that would account for Rome's justifiable hatred of him and, in the eyes of the gods, her righteous triumph over such a monster.

It is even more curious that none of those later commentators on Hannibal

37

(including Livy) ever found anything scandalous to say about his private life. Julius Caesar, Octavian Augustus, Tiberius, and almost all other Roman rulers of distinction are commonly accused of drunkenness, adultery, fornication, sodomy, or sadism, and the unfortunate Tiberius of almost every aberration that can be found in the textbooks of sexual pathology. The writers of antiquity, in fact, who managed to find some more or less scandalous anecdotes about nearly all the great men in their history, found themselves baffled when it came to Hannibal. The second-century historian Justin says almost reluctantly that his behaviour towards his female captives was such that 'one would not think he was born in Africa' – an interesting example of early racial bias. The unreliable Appian, writing in the second century A.D., over three centuries after the events and basing his account on some unknown source, states that while wintering in Lucania in south-east Italy Hannibal indulged in luxurious living and 'the delights of love'. It would have been scarcely surprising if he had; certainly not unnatural in a soldier who by then had been years away from his home in Spain. He had married in Castulo the daughter of the local chieftain, called Imilce and possibly of Greek blood. There is no certain record of any children, although tradition has it that she bore him a son. It is unlikely that Hannibal ever saw her again after he left on his expedition to Italy. Certainly it would have been politic for him to have married into the ruling caste of that city, for Castulo commanded the Silver Mountains of the Olcades people and their friendship was therefore important to the Carthaginians. The poet Silius Italicus, in his epic, *Punica,* pictures Imilce pleading with her husband to be allowed to go with him across the Alps and being refused. Elsewhere he says that the love of Hannibal and Imilce was one of memories.

Just as no letters from Hannibal, whether to his wife or to anyone else, have been preserved (letters which might have told us more about the man than anything in the histories) so no bust or statue exists that can safely be identified with him. Of the coin portraits which may well depict him one of the most interesting was struck at Cartagena about 220 B.C., shortly after he had taken command. Since coins in the ancient world assumed for a mostly illiterate people an importance that it is difficult for the modern world to understand – being both pictures and pronouncements – it is very probable that Hannibal's succession to the leadership would have been marked by the striking of a number of silver coins. The Cartagena coin shows a handsome young man (the beardless head of Melqart, the Phoenician Hercules), with a profile unlike a Greek or Roman in that the straight nose ends in nostrils with a Semitic flare. The full mouth is slightly downturned and firmly delineated. The hair is curly and the eye large, prominent and thoughtful. It is interesting to note that this coin portrait is almost identical to a bronze bust of a young man found at Volubilis, Morocco, which on good authority has been claimed as being of Hannibal. Hair, eyes, nose, mouth and jawline are so similar to the coin as to make the attribution credible. This is not merely the head of a handsome young man, in the classic tradition, but of a thoughtful and powerful personality – quite different from the Antinous-like youths of which antiquity has yielded so many.

Hannibal, acclaimed universally by the army as Hasdrubal's successor, seems also to have been accepted by the Senate in Carthage without demur, and the personal nature of the Barcid rule in Spain seemed thus confirmed: first Hamilcar, then Hasdrubal the Handsome, and now Hannibal. This led to a somewhat natural misunderstanding of the real situation by the Romans – that the ultimate authority rested with the Carthaginian Senate, and not with Hannibal. When, within three years of taking command, he went to war with Rome he had consulted Carthage in advance. The fact that, when later challenged by Rome, Carthage did not surrender Hannibal as requested but accepted war reveals that there were more influential Carthaginians in favour of a war of revenge on Rome than there were against. The anti-war element, however, always remained strong in Carthage; it was composed not only of enemies of the Barca party but of others who saw a senseless diversion of their country's new wealth and strength into this expensive military expedition. Yet in the final analysis the judgement of Polybius remains true: 'Of all that befell both the Romans and the Carthaginians, the cause was one man, and one mind – Hannibal's.'

V

THE GREAT DESIGN

Hannibal's first task on taking command in Spain was to enlarge and consolidate the territorial gains that had been made by his brother-in-law Hasdrubal and his father. Not until he felt that Carthaginian influence was securely established in the area south of the Ebro could he embark upon that great plan which he had always had in mind (if not inherited). As yet, he was not ready for war with Rome. His involvement during the first year, taming the tribesmen in the area of the Tagus in order to secure the river-line behind him, may have served to allay Roman suspicions of his intentions, or to convince them that he had enough problems to cope with in Spain itself. In the following year, 220 B.C., he moved further north again and captured Salmantica (Salamanca).

A foretaste of Hannibal's brilliant usage of his cavalry was given to a massive combination of two tribes on the Tagus, where he showed how a brave and much larger enemy force can be confused by a night crossing. Hannibal was always to show that he had an appreciation as a cavalry commander that his enemies never had; at the same time he did not make the mistake of thinking that everything could be left to the horsemen. He knew that their dash and sudden violence must always be reinforced, and ultimately consolidated, by a hard core of disciplined infantry.

The cavalry that he used in Spain, and later in France and Italy, consisted of two basic units, still found centuries later – the heavy brigade and the light brigade. The heavy brigade was composed of Celtiberians, and later of Gauls, riding the powerful horses of the country, and having as weapons a short lance that could double as a javelin and a two-edged sword, slightly curved so as to make it suitable to cut as well as thrust. The light brigade was formed by the Numidian horsemen from North Africa. They were akin to those Arab horsemen who were to inflict such casualties upon the Crusaders many centuries later: mounted on wiry small horses, lightly armed, accustomed to mountains and desert alike, they were used to harass the enemy and then withdraw, creating among infantrymen a state of confusion which the heavy brigade could then exploit. Another arm which was to prove disconcerting to the Romans was provided by the famous Balearic slingers (whom Rome was later to incorporate into her own armies). These consisted of a corps of 'Davids', hurling round stones or lead bullets, who would open fire in the early stages of any conflict, withdrawing to join the light infantry before the major engagement took place.

The main body of the infantry, drawn from Carthage, Libya, and now Spain, were heavily armed in the Greek fashion with large shields, breastplates, helmets, greaves, cutting swords for close work and long spears for the first encounter. After a series of defeats had been inflicted on the Carthaginians during a Roman landing in North Africa in the First Punic War, their army had been completely reorganised by Xanthippus, a Spartan commander. He had introduced the disciplined order of the phalanx, which had triumphed over nearly all of the East in the campaigns of Alexander the Great. In the phalanx the men stood shoulder to shoulder, each man's right side being covered by his neighbour's shield, presenting a bristling wall of long spears to the enemy. While admirable for use in open country and against an ill-disciplined enemy, the phalanx had the disadvantage of being somewhat unwieldy. Hannibal was soon to learn from the Romans the use of more mobile tactical units, just as he was to adopt the use of Roman arms, especially the legionary's sword in place of the cutting swords of his Iberians and Gauls. The great Carthaginian weapon which was new to Europe, though long familiar in the East, was the elephant – so long a part of Hannibal's legend that it must be separately described in the account of his great invasion.

'From the day on which he was proclaimed commander-in-chief,' wrote Polybius, 'as though Italy had been assigned to him for his field of operations and he had been instructed to make war on Rome, Hannibal felt that no postponement was permissible, lest he too, like his father Hamilcar, and afterwards Hasdrubal, should be overtaken, while delaying, by some accident, and resolved upon attacking the people of Saguntum.' His hand was probably forced by evidence that the Romans were betraying a new interest in Spain; new in that recently their attention had been concentrated on northern Italy where the Cisalpine Gauls, who had settled on the Italian side of the Alps, had swept down south and even laid waste to Etruria. This brave but undisciplined enemy had gone on to defeat a Roman army – news of which must have encouraged Hannibal – and had threatened the city itself. Until Rome had mastered them and had established colonies in their area (laying the foundations of a new province, Cisalpine Gaul) they were too distracted to pay close attention to events in Spain. But in the first two years of Hannibal's command reports from Massilia, and no doubt from Saguntum, had renewed their concern about the Carthaginian threat from the west.

They had taken due note that Saguntum, lying about halfway between the Ebro and the new Carthaginian port and capital of Nova Cartago, might serve as a possible bridgehead in the event of any operations against the

Carthaginians. Its close ties with Massilia and the fact that the Romans had control of the sea in the western Mediterranean meant that they could maintain good communications with Saguntum. It was probably not long after their agreement with Hasdrubal the Handsome over relative spheres of influence that they entered into a diplomatic relationship with Saguntum, based on their alliance with Massilia. Their foot was now in the door, and about two years later they took advantage of a political dispute in Saguntum to set themselves up as arbitrators of the affair. The fact that they were interfering in political issues well south of the Ebro line does not seem to have troubled them. Their action followed the same pattern as their previous interference in Sicily, which had precipitated the First Punic War. This 'benevolent interference' was a technique that the Romans would often employ in the centuries to come: it is one which expansionist powers have always used to provoke a conflict or to extend their territory. The inevitable result of Roman intervention in the politics of Saguntum was that a party favourable to them seized power in the city.

Hannibal, after dispersing his troops at the end of the year 220, had spent the winter in Nova Cartago. There was much to attend to, for he could hardly ignore the fact that Saguntum was to all intents and purposes a Roman enclave in Carthaginian territory. Whatever the Romans might say about having concluded a treaty with the party in power in Saguntum, guaranteeing them Roman protection, the original treaty made with Hasdrubal had made no mention of Saguntum being a special case – and within the Roman sphere of influence. Hannibal had never had any cause to doubt the untrustworthiness of the Roman bond and he had no reason to do so now. He needed no justification for the steps that he was about to take.

Throughout that winter, in company with his brother Hasdrubal, who had now joined him (it is possible that his brother Mago, the youngest, had also left Carthage for the new family home), Hannibal laid his plans. 'The Lion's Brood', as the brothers were known throughout the army, were preparing for the most audacious military move in history – nothing less than an invasion of their enemy's homeland by way of the forbidding and hitherto untried route over the Alps. It is true that the Gauls had long used the Alpine passes to make their way into Italy, but theirs was the migration of clans or tribes. No one had ever conceived that a whole army could be moved from the west, through the passes, and down into Italy. Prior to the arrival of the Carthaginians in Europe, there had been no co-ordinating intelligence to see the possibility of such a move, nor indeed any reason for it.

It is clear that Hannibal had a ready-made intelligence service, both in Gaul to the north and Cisalpine Gaul in Italy, among these violent but freedom-loving people who resented the Roman yoke quite as much as Hamilcar had resented the treatment of Carthage, so that while the people of Massilia and Saguntum were keeping Rome posted as to Carthaginian activities in Spain, Hannibal was receiving military missions from the Gauls. He and his staff were collating all the reports reaching them as to their numbers and intentions, the relationships between one tribe and another, and their disposition towards Rome. He had plenty of evidence of their fighting abilities (fearless but undisciplined) but he needed also to know how deep was their hatred or resentment of Rome and of the threat to their liberty. The tribes who were in Italy had reason enough to fear Roman arms and to hate the Romans because of recent events. On the French side of the Alps the situation was more difficult to assess. Although some of the chieftains could appreciate the threat of Rome – troops being transported from Italy to Massilia and thence spreading out to annex all the countryside to the north – there were others who could not look ahead nor understand such a complex threat. As far as many Gauls living in the area of the Rhône valley were concerned, Rome was far away, but the neighbour with whom they were at variance was close at hand. Hannibal needed to know whether payment or the thought of plunder would induce them to join him against the Romans, and what supplies and what numbers of men were to be found in the areas through which he would pass. Some of the tribes from the western side of the Alps had joined the Boii and Insubres in Italy in their revolt a few years before, and Hannibal knew how their initial success had taken them as far south as Etruria – only to be defeated by Roman arms and discipline. The fact that wild tribesmen could achieve so much must have proved an encouragement to a man who was bent on attempting what to some seemed impossible. He was well informed, and he was lucky that the regular passage of Gauls between Italy and France could keep him up to date as to the exact state of things in the land of his enemies.

In 219 B.C. Hannibal took the first step to war and attacked Saguntum. The old city was strong, well defended, and enclosed by Cyclopean walls; its inhabitants were far from prepared to yield at the sight of the army encamped against them. In advance of Hannibal's move, preparations for which can hardly have gone undetected, two Roman envoys reached him with the message that the city came under Roman protection. This he knew, but he could also claim that the fact had not been mentioned in the treaty with Hasdrubal, and that the Romans had been meddling in affairs well south of the Ebro. The envoys, coldly dismissed, made their way to Carthage, where they hoped to convince the peace party that Hannibal had broken faith and that the senate in Rome was threatening war. Meanwhile the siege of Saguntum continued, the city holding out bravely for all of eight months, to fall with the inevitable rapine and massacre that marked the end of long-disputed sieges. A large portion of the spoil was set aside to be sent to Carthage as an earnest of the riches of further conquest. The news of Saguntum reached Rome at about the same time as the return of their envoys from Carthage, bearing the message that the Carthaginians had no regard for any treaty between Rome and Saguntum.

There followed a confused debate in Rome, some of the nobles declaring for war immediately and others favouring negotiations, while the assemblies of the people voted for peace. A compromise was finally reached and a delegation sent to North Africa to inquire whether Hannibal had been acting under his own initiative over Saguntum, or on the orders of the Carthaginians. If they disavowed Hannibal, then he must be handed over to Roman authority. Much argument followed, the Carthaginians denying that Hannibal had committed any offence against Rome and maintaining that, to their knowledge, there had never been any treaty of alliance between Rome and this city, which in any case was well within the sphere of Carthaginian influence. In conclusion they refused to surrender Hannibal and asked the Roman envoys what was now their intention. Fabius, the leader of the delegation, placed his hand in his toga with a melodramatic gesture and asked them to choose: 'Peace or war?' After some consultation with the senate, the elder of the two Carthaginian suffetes (the senior administrators and judges) told the Roman to make the decision himself. When Fabius said 'War', the Carthaginians replied, 'We accept!' The Second Punic War, the Hannibalic War as it came to be known, had been declared.

The news that Carthage was officially at war with Rome reached Hannibal when he was back at New Carthage. With a successful campaign behind him, and with his men well paid and snug in their winter quarters, it was pleasant to receive the reassurance that Carthage supported him. It was not difficult to arouse enthusiasm among the troops for a long and hazardous expedition (though it is doubtful if as yet he disclosed their real destination), for the news that the arrogant Romans had demanded the surrender of their general was enough to infuriate them and the thought of further plunder lured them on. The successful record of Hamilcar and Hasdrubal the Handsome and the infinite promise held out by this young Carthaginian lion made recruitment easy. The thought of a campaign beginning in the new year of 218 B.C. was as attractive as the thought of spring itself. The fact that the Romans had been unable to save Saguntum had so reduced their reputation that a Roman mission to northern Spain was sent back contemptuously to Gaul. Here they found little if any more friendliness. The Gauls were determined in any ensuing conflict between Rome and Carthage to remain neutral although, aware of the treatment of their kinsmen in Italy, their inclination was to take sides with the Carthaginians.

Hannibal knew all this, and knew also that the disconsolate Roman mission had returned to Rome with the news that Spain was hostile, the Gauls neutral but unfriendly, and only the people of Massilia firmly committed to their cause. When the two new consuls were chosen for the year the most active of them, Publius Cornelius Scipio, drew the lot which determined him to regard Spain as his 'province' – always the long-term Roman intention. Hannibal heard during the winter that Rome was fitting out a new fleet, and this, followed by Scipio's appointment, confirmed his judgement that the enemy had their eye on Spain. The siege and sack of Saguntum, which they claimed as an ally, was something that could not be tolerated if Roman prestige was not to be eclipsed among Gauls and Iberians alike. They had command of the sea – Hannibal having little more than a few warships for the immediate protection of shipping between Spain and North Africa – and a landing of the legions in Spain was now to be expected. Hasdrubal received instructions from his brother to take command in Spain should Hannibal be absent at any time during a Roman attack.

So far Hannibal's master-plan seemed to be bearing fruit. The enemy, conscious of their supremacy at sea, were clearly preparing to transport legions via Massilia for an invasion of the new Carthaginian territories south of the Ebro. But what the Romans could not have imagined was that Hannibal was not preparing to defend his new territories himself, nor even planning merely to cross the river to carry on his campaigns in the north. They themselves would never have envisaged traversing the wild Pyrenees, the unknown lands of savage Gauls, and then the fearsome Alps, in order to engage their enemy. Such a course would be nothing less than fifteen hundred miles of madness. . . . They had reckoned without the Carthaginian.

VI

OPENING MOVES

Hannibal now had his war – and on his own terms. He had most of Spain south of the Ebro united behind him, his brother in command in their strong new city-port, and all the men and more that he needed for his army. Owing to his political strategy the war had been declared by the Romans and it was they who could be seen as having broken the peace treaty with Carthage. This was not unimportant, for it could be quoted to hesitant Gallic tribes as an example of Rome's lack of faith – and a reminder to them not to take their word when treaties were in the offing. Outmanoeuvred by Hannibal as they were often to be in both political and military terms, it was hardly surprising that in years to come the Romans should coin the expression 'Punic faith' to signify untrustworthiness and lack of faith – something of which they were well aware that they had been guilty themselves. They knew they had been wrong over Sardinia and they either were, or had been made to seem, in the wrong over Saguntum.

Hannibal had made careful dispositions of his troops to safeguard Africa as well as Spain, and to ensure that his brother Hasdrubal was not confronted with any problems of loyalty while he was away. He adopted the wise policy of transferring Spanish troops to Africa and African troops to Spain. Polybius may be considered an accurate authority on the state of the military chessboard at the beginning of the campaign: 'The troops who crossed to Africa were supplied by the Thersitae, Mastiani, Iberian Oretes and Olcades, and numbered twelve hundred horse and thirteen thousand eight hundred and fifty foot, besides which there were eight hundred and seventy Balearians [Slingers]. . . . He stationed most of these troops at Metagonia in Libya and some in Carthage itself. From the so-called Metagonian towns he sent four thousand foot to Carthage to serve both as reinforcements and as hostages.' In Spain he left fifteen thousand men, twenty-one elephants, and a small fleet of about fifty warships. As evidence for his documentation of Hannibal's dispositions Polybius concludes: 'No one need be surprised at the accuracy of the information I give here about Hannibal's arrangement in Spain. . . . The fact is that I found on the Lacinian promontory [in southern Italy] a bronze tablet on which Hannibal himself had made out these lists during the time he was in Italy, and thinking this an absolutely first-rate authority, decided to follow the document.'

In the spring of 218 B.C., having left everything in order behind him,

Hannibal moved his own troops out of winter quarters. He set his face to the north and crossed the Ebro. At the beginning of the campaign his army numbered twelve thousand horsemen and ninety thousand foot. In Catalonia, between the Ebro and the Pyrenees, they encountered a number of tough mountain tribes who were not prepared to yield even before so large an army. Their way was fiercely contested and a number of townships had to be stormed before they came within reach of the Pyrenees, 'after many severe engagements and with great loss'. Perhaps Hannibal had not expected so severe a resistance. It is clear, however, that he had set out with a larger force than he wanted for his Italian campaign, since he left in charge of the new territory, and to keep guard over the passes between Spain and Gaul, one thousand horse and ten thousand foot under the command of his brother Hanno.

By-passing the Greek port Emporiae (Ampurias), Hannibal led the army towards the Pyrenees. Polybius, the most reliable guide to the events of Hannibal's great march, says at one point that he started at the beginning of summer – unfortunately not telling us whether by this he refers to the departure from Cartagena or to the crossing of the Ebro. Denis Proctor (*Hannibal's March in History*) comments: 'The first section of Hannibal's march, from Cartagena to the Ebro, a distance of about 480 kilometres through country under Carthaginian control, would have been accomplished in under four weeks, so that the whole of it could be described as being "at the beginning of summer"; and since there was clearly no longer delay after Hannibal had unfolded his plan of campaign to the troops than was needed to complete the final preparations for the march, there is no inconsistency in dating his address to the troops in the late spring and the march from Cartagena to the Ebro at the beginning of summer.'

Whatever one's conclusions about the time that Hannibal started out on the first leg of his campaign – across the Ebro to the Pyrenees – it is clear that there was some underestimation about the time needed to reach the Alps, which he reached later in the year than could have been intended. Hannibal had plenty of information about the Alps and their passes, and he can never have been in any doubt that the ideal time to traverse them was in summer. That he did not do so can be accountable to a late start (quite possible in view of the difficulty of ensuring that the troops came in from their home quarters at the required time), whilst the other likely cause of his being delayed is that he had underestimated the amount of resistance he would find among the tribesmen north of the Ebro.

Once the Pyrenees loomed ahead there can be little doubt that the ultimate destination of the army was revealed, however much it may previously have been a secret among the senior officers and corps commanders. The reaction of many of the troops was predictable: they had not found rich towns and easy loot in the land north of the Ebro; the Pyrenees looked fearsome enough; and now this appalling revelation that they were destined for the Alps. 'Influenced not so much by the war as by the long march and the impossibility of crossing the Alps', three thousand of Carpetanian foot turned back. Livy continues: 'To recall them or detain them forcibly would have been hazardous, for it might have aroused resentment in the savage hearts of the others. So Hannibal sent back to their homes above seven thousand more, whom he had observed were reluctant for the enterprise, at the same time pretending that he had also dismissed the Carpetani.'

His force was now greatly reduced from its original size. Polybius states that the army which went with him through the Pyrenees numbered only 'fifty thousand foot and nine thousand horse'. This meant that his infantry force, by desertion, by policy, and by losses in battle, had been almost halved and his horse reduced by a quarter. Polybius, who was a distinguished general before he became a military historian, comments with practical wisdom: 'He had now an army not so strong in number but serviceable and highly trained from the long series of wars in Spain.' Hannibal may well have reckoned that, in view of the arduous campaigns which lay ahead, he was better off with this diminished force of battle-honed veterans than with one twice the size, less experienced and lacking in determination.

The incongruous element in Hannibal's army, and the one which has inevitably attracted the attention of historians and non-historians over the ages, was the elephants. Thirty-seven of them, we gather, went with him from Spain, through the Pyrenees, across the Rhône, over the Alps, and into Italy. There is no account of any of them dying during the long march, but it is on record that when the great Carthaginian came down out of the snow and the Alpine peaks into Italy, his elephants were still with him. Why elephants when he had so many horsemen and, as they were to prove, horsemen superior to those that the Romans could field? Three hundred years after the events the satirist Juvenal (translated here by Peter Green) remembered Hannibal with the words:

> This is the man for whom Africa
> Was too small a continent, though it stretched from the surf-beaten
> Ocean shores of Morocco east to the steamy Nile,
> To Ethiopian tribesmen — and new elephants' habitats.

The use of elephants in warfare was almost as old as the history of war in the East, although the first historic mention occurs in the campaigns of Alexander the Great when, in 331 B.C., he defeated King Darius III of Persia, who had fifteen elephants in his army at the battle of Gaugamela. These beasts, trained for war, and mounting howdahs on their backs from which archers could shoot down at the foe, were of the Indian variety, about ten foot tall at the shoulder. Most of the elephants used by the Carthaginians in warfare, however, were African and not Indian elephants, but, as Sir Gavin de Beer has pointed out, they were not the African bush elephants, which are even larger than the Indian, but African forest elephants which stood a little under eight feet at the shoulder. Coins minted at Cartagena at about the time of the opening of the Hannibalic War depict this type of African elephant, as is proved by the relative size of the mounted driver to the animal, and the concave back, large ears, and ribbed trunk which distinguish the forest elephant from the other two varieties. 'The relative small size of the African forest elephant', Sir Gavin writes, 'means that they were not much bigger than horses, and their passage over mountains cannot have been attended with as much difficulty as the Indian variety would have encountered.'

Their drivers are always referred to as 'Indians' because the Egyptians, when they had first started importing elephants for work and warfare, had brought their trainers from India where – unlike Africa itself – elephants had long been used in the service of man. Elephants were mainly employed by Hannibal against cavalry whose horses, not having been trained to them, were terrified by the sight of them and their smell and trumpeting, while native tribesmen were also put to flight by their awesome size and appearance. (Centuries later, during Caesar's second campaign in Britain, an Indian elephant, mounting a howdah with archers aboard, struck terror into Cassivelaunus and his Britons, and facilitated the Roman crossing of the Thames.) It is probable that one of Hannibal's elephants was of the Indian variety; it was singled out for mention during the campaign in Italy and its name is given as Surus, 'the Syrian', and Syria was the area from which Indian elephants had long been obtained.

'While Hannibal was thus attempting to cross the Pyrenees, being greatly concerned about the Celts because of the natural strength of the passes,' writes Polybius, 'the Romans . . . on the news reaching them sooner than they had expected that Hannibal had crossed the Ebro with his army, determined to send the Consuls Publius Cornelius Scipio and Tiberius Sempronius Longus with their legions, the first to Spain and the second to Africa.' The Roman intention of striking directly at the heart of Carthage while at the same time attacking her new empire in the west was sound enough. What they could not have allowed for was that the Boii Gauls in northern Italy, elated by the news that Hannibal was on the march, revolted from Rome and, calling upon their old allies the Insubres to join them, overran the land which the Romans had been carefully colonising. The Gauls showed their usual dash and fire and, catching the Romans off guard, caused them to revise their previous plans. The legions destined for Spain could not be spared until the trouble in Cisalpine Gaul had been settled. The invasion of North Africa had to be postponed. The Gallic allies, upon whom Hannibal was relying when he himself would appear above the skyline of northern Italy, had already proved their worth. Rome, which had counted upon defeating the Carthaginians by attacking them at home and in Spain, now found her own territory threatened. Meanwhile the Carthaginian army, probably by the comparatively easy Col de Perthus route, was passing through the Pyrenees.

VII

ACROSS THE RHÔNE

Hannibal's first task was to come to friendly terms with the Gauls in their territory north of the Pyrenees. Sending ahead ambassadors to explain that his intentions were peaceful, he arranged to meet the local chieftains at Ruscino (Castel-Roussillon). Here he succeeded in convincing them that his war was with Rome, and that his army was marching against the enemies of their race and to aid their cousins in northern Italy. After some discussion they accepted his word – and his bribes – and allowed him to pass freely through their territory. Difficult terrain lay ahead : the vast, marshy expanse of the Rhône delta, scarcely tamed two thousand years later, and astonishingly primitive then. It was strange indeed to these Spanish and North African troops, accustomed to mountains, to long savannahs, or to the expanses of the desert, but not to a wild water-world.

The two consuls in Italy had been freed by midsummer from their attention to the uprising in the north and had returned to their original enterprises – Tiberius Sempronius making lavish preparations in Sicily for the invasion of North Africa and Publius Cornelius Scipio preparing to embark troops for the coastal voyage to Massilia. If Hannibal was behindhand with his march, so equally were the consuls. Scipio, having set out from Italy with sixty warships, reached Massilia five days after leaving Pisa and went into camp at the mouth of the Rhône near the city. Here information reached him that Hannibal was already crossing the Pyrenees but, confident that the difficulties of the terrain and the hostility of the Gauls would make for very slow progress, the Consul did not feel that there was any immediate urgency. His men and their horses needed a rest after the sea voyage and he could, as yet, only imagine that Hannibal was bent on stirring up trouble among the Gauls – with possibly Massilia as a target once he had gathered sufficient forces together. 'Hannibal, however, who had bribed some of the Celts and forced others to give him a passage, unexpectedly appeared with his army at the crossing of the Rhône. . . .'

Hannibal's speed of advance seems to have averaged about fourteen kilometres a day. According to Polybius, he now halted to make his Rhône crossing at a distance of about four days' march from the sea. Scarcely fifty miles of swampland and river estuary separated Scipio from Hannibal, but so poor were communications in the area that the Carthaginian moved his army of fifty thousand men together with cavalry and elephants up to a suitable crossing-place before any news reached the Consul in Massilia. Hannibal's forces now came into an area inhabited by a tribe called the Volcae, who seem to have been in command of both banks of the Rhône and clearly made a large part of their living out of transporting goods and people from one side to the other. The Volcae who were on the western bank, either unable or unwilling to leave their homes and their boat-building activities, were to provide the answer to Hannibal's transportation problems. But the majority of the tribe, seeing in the arrival of this large foreign army a threat to their liberties, had gathered on the eastern side and, using the Rhône as their moat, were preparing to give battle. Four days' march from the sea, as Polybius tells us, 'the stream is single'. At about sixty kilometres lies Fourques, where the river is indeed single, wide and smooth-flowing to this day (although the Rhône has changed considerably since the great dam was built at Donzères), and very probably, to judge from the lie of the land around, always with a gentle approach from the western banks.

It is possible that echoes of Sosilos (Hannibal's Greek tutor) who later wrote his life, or of another Greek, Silenos, who accompanied him on the march and whose account was translated into Latin, may be found in Polybius. Certainly there is an eye-witness feel about some of the passages describing the Rhône crossing:

Doing his best to make friends with the inhabitants of the bank, he bought up all their canoes and boats – a considerable number since many of the people on the banks of the Rhône engage in maritime traffic. He also got from them logs suitable for making canoes, so that in two days he had a very large number of ferry boats, every one doing his best to dispense with any assistance and relying on himself for his chance of getting across.

Meanwhile, a great number of Gauls had gathered on the opposite bank and it was clear that their army would never be able to land in face of such determined opposition. The problem of transporting fifty thousand infantrymen and nine thousand horses and their riders – let alone thirty-seven elephants – would have been daunting enough in itself, but to get them over in face of a hostile force would have been almost impossible. On the third night, having carefully weighed up the situation, Hannibal called for Hanno, a fellow nobleman and son of the suffete Bomilcar, and put him in command of part of the army. These troops were mostly Spaniards, the reason they were chosen being that the Spaniards were the best swimmers. Their task was to cross the Rhône at some suitable point to the north and remain concealed.

'Advancing up the bank of the river for two hundred stades [about thirty-five kilometres] they reached a place at which the stream divides, forming an island, and here they stopped.' They used timber ready to hand to make rafts and made the crossing safely. There was no opposition, for the Gauls, too preoccupied with the army that was facing them down the river, had omitted to post any scouts or lookouts beyond their camp. (As Hannibal had no doubt already discovered, the Gauls were brave in battle but unskilled in even the rudiments of warfare's disciplines.) Polybius continues: 'Occupying a post of some natural strength, they remained there for that day to rest after their exertions and at the same time to prepare for the movement which they had been ordered to execute.'

Hannibal had calculated that on the morning of the sixth day the army would be ready at the crossing-point. The fifth night, therefore, was devoted to getting all the boats into place for the assault. His attention to detail in this amphibious landing is shown by the fact that, although the transport had been swiftly assembled, much of it made on the spot, and under the view of the enemy, there was no question of the crossing being carried out in a haphazard manner: 'He had filled the boats with his light horse and the canoes with his lightest infantry. The large boats were placed highest up stream and the lighter ferry-boats farther down, so that the heavier vessels receiving the chief force of the current the canoes should be less exposed to risk in crossing.' The horses were to be towed swimming astern of the boats, with a man on each side of the stern holding the reins of three or four horses so that a considerable number of them could be got across at the same time. Others were saddled and bridled and put on board the larger ferries so that their riders would be ready for instant action when they reached the far side. The elephants presented a very different problem but, as will be seen, one that would be dealt with efficiently when the time came. On the fifth night, while the main body was making ready for the morning, the troops under Hanno began to move southward. As soon as they were in position to the rear of the Gauls, they made a smoke signal as pre-arranged with Hannibal.

On the morning of the sixth day, seeing the smoke lift in the sky to the east, Hannibal gave the order for the crossing to begin. Boats large and small, ferries, dugout canoes, and individuals paddling their own logs now launched themselves on the silky sweep of the great river. All the Gauls at once left their encampment and joined the throng on the bank shouting war cries, clashing their shields, and brandishing their spears. On the other bank, the Carthaginians who had not embarked shouted encouragement as their vanguard swept across; some managing to stem the current, while others were swept down to make a landing south of the enemy. The heavier craft carrying the horses and their riders were on the point of touching down when the troops under Hanno struck in the rear of the Gauls. At once there was a great outcry as the Gauls saw their tents and their encampment going up in flames. Caught between two fires, they ran wildly back and forth —

their willingness to fight no compensation for their disorder. Hannibal took the measure of these people quickly enough, and it is significant that in his campaigns he used Gallic manpower quite cynically, exploiting their bravery but never putting them in a position where they were not flanked by trained troops, nor without a rearguard that would hold them if they tried to break and run.

As the full weight of the Carthaginian landing began to make itself felt the Gauls took to their heels. Hannibal had established his beachhead on the eastern bank of the Rhône, and the other troops were swift to follow as a regular ferry-service was established. By sunset that night they were fully encamped on the eastern bank. The following morning grave news reached them: a Roman army had disembarked and was assembled near the eastern mouth of the Rhône. If Scipio was astonished to hear that Hannibal was across the Pyrenees, Hannibal was hardly less surprised to hear of the Romans at so short a distance from him. Five hundred of the Numidian horse were immediately sent off to observe the whereabouts of the enemy and to take stock of their numbers. Hannibal had no wish to fight in Gaul – however successful the outcome might be – for his aim was to get his army into Italy. Owing to the delay in Spain, he was already far behind in his timetable, and the crossing of the Rhône, which should have been in mid-summer, or earlier, almost certainly took place towards the end of September. If he delayed any longer the mountain passes of the Alps would be irrevocably closed.

Meanwhile large piers had been built out into the river with rafts attached to them at the far end, for the transport of the elephants. To these in their turn were fastened towing-lines for the boats that were to pull them across. 'After this they piled up a quantity of earth on all the line of the rafts, until the whole was on the same level and of the same appearance as the path on shore leading to the crossing.' One senses again in Polybius' account the long-lost manuscript of that Greek eye-witness.

The animals were always accustomed to obey their mahouts up to the water, but would never enter it on any account, and they now drove them along over the earth with two females in front, whom they obediently followed. As soon as they set foot on the last rafts the ropes which held these fast to the others were cut, and the boats pulling taut, the towing lines rapidly tugged away from the pile of earth the elephants and the rafts on which they stood. Hereupon the animals becoming very alarmed at first turned round and ran about in all directions, but as they were shut in on all sides by the stream they finally grew afraid and were compelled to keep quiet. In this manner, by continuing to attach two rafts to the end of the structure, they managed to get most of them over on these, but some were so frightened that they threw themselves into the river when halfway across. The mahouts of these were all drowned, but the elephants were saved, for owing to the power and length of their trunks they kept them above the water and breathed through them, at the same time spouting out any water that got into their mouths and so held out, most of them passing through the water on their feet.

While the last of the arrangements were being made and the crossing of the elephants engineered, Hannibal had been joined by a number of chieftains from the plains of Po, men who had fought against the Romans and who now urged him not to delay his passage into Italy. Hannibal was aware that many of his troops were concerned about the journey that lay ahead. They had had to fight hard after leaving the Ebro: they had tasted the Pyrenees – but under good conditions – and they had crossed this formidable river after several days in delta land that was strange and alarming to them. Now they were confronted by these mysterious and frightening Alps. It was hardly surprising that an army of so many races – let alone tribes – should feel divided and uncertain. Hannibal used the presence of these Boii and in particular one chieftain, Magol, who was perhaps their senior, to point out that the Alps were far from insurmountable: these men had just come from Italy through the passes. They need not fear the Romans either, for men like these had often defeated them. (He must have hoped that the point was taken: 'You have just defeated a large number of Gauls so, if Gauls can defeat Romans, who should you fear?')

Both Polybius and Livy (and, of course, all subsequent historians) have pictured Hannibal, on this and other occasions, addressing the assembled army in the rhetoric so dear to the classical heart. But, one must ask, in what language or dialect was he speaking? Hannibal was from childhood acquainted with the Semitic Punic (some words of which may still be found in the Lebanon and the Maltese islands), his second language was Greek, his third almost certainly the tongue spoken by the Spanish tribes south of the Ebro, and the fourth was Latin. He had a quick and agile mind and undoubtedly mastered some basic Gallic (different dialects again). One must imagine that on this and other similar occasions he used a number of interpreters in order to get his message over to the assembled troops. At the same time he, the general, speaking in person to them all, was a very necessary element in his maintaining a grasp upon his multi-racial force – Hannibal, the brother in-law of Hasdrubal, the son of the great Hamilcar, the victor of Saguntum, their leader. . . . Since his senior officers were Carthaginians, and since the heart of the army itself was composed of Carthaginians and Libyans (the latter of necessity had to learn their rulers' language) it is most probable that he spoke in Punic. It may have sounded a little like the Arabic still to be heard in Libya and Tunisia.

'[He] began by reminding them of their achievements in the past: though, he said, they had undertaken many hazardous enterprises and fought many a battle they had never met with ill success when they followed his plans and counsels. Next he bade them be of good heart considering that the hardest part of their task was now accomplished, since they had forced the passage of the river and had the testimony of their own ears and eyes to the friendly sentiments and readiness to help of their allies. . . .' It was up to him – and they knew his worth – to attend to the details. What was required of them was to obey orders and show themselves brave men. There was to be no delay. They would strike camp in the morning and begin the great march.

The return of the Numidian horse would have been sufficient to confirm Hannibal in his haste. On their reconnaissance sortie they had run into a force of three hundred of Scipio's cavalry, sent out on a similar mission. After a savage encounter, in which the Numidians had come off badly, they had retreated with the Romans in hot pursuit. It is worth noting that this is the only time in the long campaign that the Numidians seem to have been worsted, and one can only assume that they had come up against heavy cavalry – an arm against which they were not designed to operate. Hannibal and his great cavalry commander Maharbal were always careful to use them in the future for harassment, keeping their own heavy brigade to deal with the Roman equivalent. On this occasion the Roman cavalry was able to sweep within sight of the Carthaginian camp, calculate the number of men in it, and report back to Scipio.

The latter, not unnaturally, thought that the presence of Hannibal's army on the east bank of the Rhône could only mean that the Carthaginian was preparing to give battle. It could be assumed that he had known of the Roman troop movements in Italy – such things could hardly be kept secret and the doors of the temple of Janus had stood open (indicating a state'of war) ever since Saguntum. Hannibal must have known that a strike against Carthage was being prepared in Sicily while he, Scipio, was on his way by sea to attack the Carthaginian empire in Spain. What would be the response of Hannibal to such a threat? To march north, cross the Ebro, bring the tribes in the area between the river and the Pyrenees under his control, and then to invade southern France so as to secure Spain against attack from the north. Scipio's duty was clear: he must attack as soon as possible, before Hannibal was able to seduce many of the Rome-hating Gauls to his army. He set out to cover the sixty miles from his base camp with two legions (4,500 to 6,000 men apiece), some fourteen thousand allied infantry and sixteen hundred horse. After only three days' march (no mean feat since he was covering roughly the same distance that had taken Hannibal four days) he reached the point on the Rhône where the Carthaginians had been encamped.

It was deserted. His cavalry had not misled him, for here were all the traces of the camp, as well as local Gauls to confirm that the strange men from the south had been there only three days before. They had gone north following the banks of the great river. . . . There could only be one conclusion, for nothing lay to the north except further unmapped lands inhabited by savage Gauls. Hannibal must be attempting the unthinkable – to march as far as one of the Rhône's tributary rivers that came down from the Alps, and then follow a route given him by the Gauls that would lead into Italy.

Scipio turned his legions about and made haste back to Massilia. It is a great tribute to his coolness and foresight that he did not embark at once with all his men and return to Italy. But he had been given Spain as his sphere of operations and he realised that, whatever happened, Spain still remained the key to the whole war. With Hannibal and his army away from his home base, Roman arms might well achieve victory there and destroy the heart of Carthaginian wealth and power. For himself, it was clear that he must return to Italy to take charge of the troops in the north. He sent his fleet and army on to Spain under the command of his brother Cnaeus and embarked for Italy. If, and it seemed unlikely at this season of the year, Hannibal's troops managed to cross the Alps, they would find him waiting.

VIII

ISLAND, RIVER AND ALPS

With the elephants, and a rearguard of cavalry, following the main body of the troops, Hannibal's invading army moved up on the Rhône. They would have been marching as fast as possible in order to lose the Romans, and they were clearly successful for there were no further reports to Scipio of the enemy being sighted. It is doubtful, in view of the restrictions such as the elephants and their impedimenta, if they can have made any more speed than they had in the early part of their march to the north, so one may assume that fourteen kilometres a day represents their average progress. From Polybius we learn that 'Hannibal, marching steadily from the crossing-place for four days, reached a place called the "Island", a populous district producing abundance of corn and deriving its name from its situation; for the Rhône and the Skaras running along each side of it meet at its point. It is similar in size and shape to the Egyptian Delta; only in that case the sea forms the base line uniting the two branches of the Nile, while here the base line is formed by a range of mountains difficult to climb or penetrate, and, one may say, almost inaccessible.'

Much scholarly controversy has arisen over the location of this area known as the 'Island', controversy which may never cease, although Sir Gavin de Beer, by combining scholarship with geography, would seem to have produced an answer which is more watertight than most of the theories previously expounded. The argument arose through the variant spellings in the manuscripts of Polybius and Livy of the name of the river forming the third side of the triangle. It need hardly have happened if scholars had been prepared to accept the text of Polybius, who gives the river's name as Skaras. Polybius was not only writing a great deal earlier than Livy (the latter leaned heavily upon the Greek historian for his account of the Hannibalic War) but, unlike Livy, he had himself carefully covered the ground and followed in the footsteps of Hannibal on his great march. Polybius, furthermore, was a soldier as well as an historian and – unlike the study-bound Livy – it is most improbable that he would have made a gross geographical error.

Polybius states clearly that Hannibal marched a further four days up the Rhône after leaving the crossing-place. This makes his distance from the sea, after eight days' march at fourteen kilometres a day, 112 kilometres – and at exactly this point there flows into the Rhône a large tributary, the Aygues. Not only does the Aygues lie at the appropriate distance from the sea but it forms, together with the Rhône and a mountain range called the Baronnies, a large fertile delta. It is well cultivated and populated today, as doubtless it was two thousand years ago since it has all the requirements for valley farming. Only in one respect does this triangular piece of land fail to match up to Polybius' description and that is in its size, for it is nowhere near as large as the Nile Delta, but, to quote Sir Gavin de Beer: 'As there is no piece of land whatever on the eastern side of the Rhône, enclosed between it and any river, approaching anything like the size of the Delta of the Nile, this must be an error somehow introduced in the texts.' Over the centuries since the river was recorded in Latin as *Aqua Iquarum* (the *s* has become an *i* as is not uncommon in Romance philology), *Iquarum* subsequently fell away, leaving only *Aqua* which, as in many other place names, became *aigue* or *aygue* ('water' in Provençal). The river's name today is the Aygues. Its position alone, relative to the Rhône and the Baronnies, and at exactly the right distance from Hannibal's crossing-place and the sea, seems to confirm that this is Polybius' Skaras.

On arrival at the 'Island', Hannibal found a great gathering of Gauls, divided into two parties and clearly on the point of taking arms against each other. Two brothers were in dispute as to the leadership of the tribe, and the elder (rather like a native chieftain appealing to some British general in a remote part of the world in the nineteenth century) came to Hannibal and asked him to resolve the issue. Having listened to the arguments, and carefully considered the rights and wrongs of the case, Hannibal pronounced in favour of the elder brother. Since it was clear that the weight of Hannibal's army would be thrown on this side, the younger claimant was driven from the territory. The newly-confirmed chief now showed his gratitude to this dark-skinned leader of the strange foreign army by supplying him with corn and other provisions and, in particular, winter clothing and footwear which would be badly needed if they were set on crossing the Alps. Even more important, he provided Hannibal with a rearguard to protect the Carthaginians on their passage through the land ahead against attacks from the Allobroges, another tribe into whose territory they would be venturing as they made their way towards the foothills of the distant mountains.

After three or four days in the 'Island', Hannibal continued to march 'along the river' for ten days. Although the accounts of Polybius and Livy regarding the approach to the Alps vary somewhat, Livy being far more explicit in naming details of tribes and places, the two historians agree on the basic route. Where Polybius says that they marched 'along the river', Livy says that Hannibal was now ready for the Alps but, instead of marching directly towards them, 'he turned to the left. . . .'

Standing on the eastern bank of the Rhône and facing the Alps, the river descends from the north – that is to say, from the spectator's left. There is no confusion here, although some commentators have found one. Livy detailed information about the tribes through whose lands he passed provides further clues. First, he came to 'the country of the Tricastini, an thence proceeded through the outer territories of the Vocontii to th Tricorii. . . .' These tribal areas, as a distinguished French scholar, August Longnon, has shown, corresponded very closely to the dioceses of the earl Christian church, which in their turn have changed little down to the presen day. The Tricastini occupied the area north of the 'Island' along the Rhôn bank, while the Vocontii were to the north-east in the area of the rive Drôme, a tributary flowing into the Rhône from the Alps. It was almos certainly at the point where the Drôme enters the Rhône – where far in the blue distance the Alpes du Dauphine bar the horizon – that Hannibal turnec east. The army still had its flank on the river, but this was now the clear swift-flowing, mountain-born Drôme.

After ten days, about 140 kilometres since leaving the 'Island', the army began to leave the rich valley and the ascent of the Alps began. So long as they were in relatively open land, where the cavalry could deploy, the Allobroges, against whom they had been warned, had left them strictly alone. When the friendly Gauls who had been acting as their guides and escort turned back for home, the Allobroges began to collect more men and to post lookouts on the heights towards which the army was advancing. They waited for the moment when their mountaineer skills could be deployed against this sluggishly approaching giant.

> . . . The Allobrogian chieftains got together a considerable force and occupied advantageous positions on the road by which the Carthaginians would be obliged to ascend. Had they only kept their project secret, they would have utterly annihilated the Carthaginian army. But their scheme was discovered, and, though they inflicted considerable damage on Hannibal, they did more injury to themselves; for the Carthaginian general having learnt that the barbarians had seized on these critical positions, encamped himself at the foot of the pass and remaining there sent on some of his Gallic guides, to reconnoitre and report on the enemy's plan and the whole situation.

Intelligence work was always one of Hannibal's strong points. His Gauls came back with the news that the enemy stayed strictly on guard throughout the day but that at night they retired to a township nearby, being of the opinion that night warfare was an impossibility. Hannibal was to show them how wrong they were (something that he was also to show the Romans later in Italy). Having approached openly in daylight to the entrance to the narrow pass the army encamped and, as dusk came down, lit their camp fires and pitched tents and waited, passively – so it appeared – for the dawn. Hannibal, meanwhile, selected a task force, possibly Spaniards from mountain areas, and as soon as it was dark moved up to occupy the vantage points where they had seen the Gauls at their posts. They found that their information had been correct and the positions on the heights dominating the pass below were completely deserted. Here again, as is known from his earlier exploits in Spain, it is noticeable that Hannibal did not delegate the task of leading this commando force to any of the members of his staff. Personal leadership was all, and without it Hannibal would never have inspired his mercenary army the way he did – not only over these weeks on the march, and the months of his first campaign, but throughout year upon year of waging war in a hostile country.

There is one cliff-bound corridor on Hannibal's probable route during the early stages of his advance towards the Alps which has been credibly identified with the place where the Carthaginians first came into conflict with the mountain Gauls. This is the Gorge de Gas – a passage so narrow in places that only about six men in column abreast could pass through it. The gorge was a potential death trap, and if it was by this route that the army came one can only assume that Hannibal had made no reconnaissance and was misled by his guides or that he took a chance. Neither of these suppositions seems likely, but the geography of Hannibal's route has generated so many books and theses, none to be finally verified unless one day some archaeological evidence is found to prove that 'the Carthaginians once passed this way', that at best one can only say 'It might have been'.

At daylight the army, confident that the commanding positions were held by Hannibal and his advance force, began to form up for the passage through the gorge. By this time the Allobroges had discovered that their vantage points had been occupied over night. 'At first they desisted from their project,' writes Polybius, 'but afterwards on seeing the long string of sumpter-animals and horsemen slowly and with difficulty winding up the narrow path, they were tempted to molest their march.'

The Gauls, although aware that Hannibal commanded the heights above them, could not resist the sight of such plunder and stormed down the lower slopes to fall upon the advancing column. The Carthaginians were hard pressed to defend themselves; horses and mules plunged down the side of a steep escarpment, the wounded horses screaming and turning back caused chaos in the column, and within minutes the orderly advance turned into a panic-stricken mêlée. At this point, seeing that the destruction of the baggage train would mean the death of the army through starvation, Hannibal led the men with him down in a wild charge to come to the assistance of the head of the column. He fell upon the Gauls like an eagle from the heights, cutting them to pieces and, in the savage hand to hand battle that developed, proving that his men from the south were more than a match for these wild northerners. The Gauls scattered and fled with the Carthaginians in hot pursuit. While the baggage train was being sorted out and the army carried on through the pass Hannibal followed the Gauls.

Determined to allow the army plenty of time to reorganise and, with restored morale, to continue the march, Hannibal and the troops with him pressed on until they reached 'the town from which the enemy had issued to make their onslaught'. He found it abandoned and, as well as recovering a number of men, pack animals and horses that had been captured, he found enough cattle and wheat to feed the army for two or three days. He gave them all twenty-four hours in which to recover and take their ease (morale must have been shaken by this first attack at the beginning of their approach to the haunted Alps). Ahead lay the first major pass through the mountain chain, probably the Col de Grimone which leads into the upper valley of the river Durance (*Druentia*, in Livy). After leaving this Gallic settlement the army had the pleasure of marching for three days through clear, open country with no enemy in sight and no geographical hazards. They needed their respite, for they were not finished with the Gauls and there was an infinity of mountains ahead.

Hannibal was now about half way on his march, on that crossing of the Alps which no one had ever thought before could be made by a large army – by nomad Gauls, yes, but not by a sophisticated army with all its weaponry, the need for provisions, and with thousands of horses, let alone ponderous elephants. Hannibal was coming down from the north-west, from the Col de Grimone, and was in the area occupied by the Tricorii tribe, whose headquarters was the town of Gap. He now had to cross the Durance in the river's middle reaches. Livy, who incorrectly has Hannibal crossing the Durance near its mouth – rather than high up, somewhere before it is joined by the Guil tributary – nevertheless gives a description that must reflect something of the conditions that the army now encountered: '. . . by far the most difficult of all the rivers of Gaul to cross; for, though it brings down a vast volume of water, it does not admit of navigation, since, not being confined within any banks, but flowing at once in several channels, not always the same, it is ever forming new shallows and new pools – a fact that makes it dangerous for foot-passengers as well – besides which it rolls down jagged stones and affords no sure or stable footing to one who enters it. . . .' The sight and sound of that army, with elephants, horses, and thousands of foot soldiers, all at the command of the one indomitable Carthaginian, crossing the Durance in spate (as Livy tells us), against the crisp background of the mountains, provides one of the most durable images of antiquity.

If the soldiers now felt that they had put behind them the hostile Gauls and were entering an area where few men dwelt, and where they might pass in peace, they were to be disillusioned. On the fourth day of their march since leaving the township of the Allobroges, they were met by a group of natives who came towards them holding out olive branches as a sign of friendship. (It is worth noting that the olive, that symbol of fertility and peace, is to be found in the upper valley of the Durance.) Hannibal had no reason to believe in them, even though they brought him gifts of cattle and provided hostages as a pledge of their good faith, yet he was wise enough not to antagonise them by showing his distrust. They told him that they knew of his capture of the township and the rout of his attackers, and that they came to him as friends willing to help him through the mountains. Since they were prepared to provide guides, Hannibal, although always keeping a wary eye on these unlikely friends, thought the risk worth taking. It is clear that the Gauls who were already with him were as ignorant of the mountains and passes that lay ahead as were the Carthaginians themselves. If he kept a close watch on these supposedly 'friendly' natives it was possible that they would see him through – even at the risk of some attempted treachery.

In order not to leave a dangerously indefensible train of pack animals and baggage in the rear, Hannibal carefully positioned them immediately behind the main body of the cavalry, in the van; next came the bulk of the army; and then the cream of the heavy infantry as rearguard. If he had not made these wise dispositions it is almost certain that he would have lost the whole of his army. After two days' further march, the Gauls, who had been quietly gathering in the mountains around, prepared to strike. The army was passing through a narrow gorge, the track they were following running alongside a fast-running small river (possibly the Guil) which fed into the Durance that they had left behind them. It was October and in that late season of the year the Carthaginians can have had little sense of basic direction – let alone of the specific lie of the land. Hannibal knew that Italy lay somewhere to the south-east, but even such elementary co-ordinates as the rising and the setting of the sun were masked by mountains. The guides, as he had all along suspected, proved treacherous.

Riding at the head along with the cavalry, Hannibal heard the great thunder in the rear, the cries of men and of wounded animals, and the wild shouts that echoed back and forth off the barren crags. 'The rear-guard bore the brunt of the attack,' wrote Livy, 'and as the infantry faced about to meet it, it was very evident that if the column had not been strengthened at that point, it must have suffered a great disaster in this pass. . . .' Great boulders came roaring down the cliff-sides, tearing their way through the lines of men and beasts while, hot on their heels, following the tumbling path of these rocky battering-rams, the Gauls came charging down on the stricken troops. The river roared below and gaps appeared in the long column as men and animals were swept away by the thundering boulders.

The Gauls had been counting largely on the element of surprise, but this, fortunately for the Carthaginian army, was lacking – Hannibal's foresight in his new disposition of his forces having put the hard core of his best infantry in the tail, where the enemy had expected to find the 'soft' baggage-train. Despite this, a great many men, pack-animals and horses were lost, and the enemy managed to throw 'the Carthaginians into such extreme peril and confusion that Hannibal was compelled to pass the night with half his force at a certain place defended by a bare rock and separated from his horses and pack-train, whose advance he waited to cover, until after a whole night's labour they managed to extricate themselves from the defile.' On the morning of the eighth day of his passage through the Alps, the army was reunited and, despite their losses, advanced with good heart towards the highest passes. (It is possible that the 'bare' or 'white' rock where Hannibal and his half of the army encamped for that night was the vast isolated rock from which the Château Queyras now keeps watch over the Queyras valley.) Throughout this day, although there was no co-ordinated attack made by the enemy, the labouring columns were subjected to sporadic raids, and the steady toll of men and animals continued relentlessly. The army with which he crossed the Rhône, its hardened veterans full of confidence, its horses, elephants and pack-animals strong and well fed, was gradually being whittled away with every day that passed. Disease and accident, as well as enemy action, must by now have considerably thinned its ranks.

The following day, advancing steadily through the pass, above the tree line as they were, the army moved almost unmolested: the mountain-men disappearing since it was now clear that these strangers were no threat to their territory. Hannibal also discovered that they were terrified of the elephants, and never dared to approach that part of the column in which these animals were. So at long last, 'after an ascent of nine days, Hannibal reached the summit. . . .' On his right loomed the giant bulk of Monte Viso and ahead, as in the vee-sight of a rifle, the sky was visible, unencumbered by further mountains – a promise of hope after days of seeming despair. The horsemen at the head of the column reached the place where the great barrier of mountains, lying like a protective wall to the north of Italy, suddenly burst open. Far below was revealed the dark green of Italy – their land of promise. For this many had died, and only the impossibility of return and the fierce inspiration of their leader had kept this multi-racial, polyglot army moving through the hazardous immensity of the Alps. Surely a cheer started from the ice-dry throats of the leaders, to be taken up uncomprehendingly by rank after toiling rank until it died far away among those for whom the cause was unknown and unrelated to their present sufferings.

IX

LIKE A THUNDERBOLT

Hannibal waited for two days at the point where the track climbed no higher. Those barren heights provided no welcome resting-place, but it was essential for the army to remain there while stragglers, both men and beasts, moved up to join them, as Livy describes:

> The soldiers, worn with toil and fighting, were permitted to rest; a number of baggage animals, which had fallen among the rocks, made their way to the camp by following the tracks of the army. Exhausted and discouraged as the soldiers were by many hardships, a snowstorm – for the constellation of the Pleiades was now setting – threw them into a great fear. The ground was everywhere covered deep with snow when at dawn [on the 12th day since the ascent of the Alps] they began to march, and as the column moved slowly on, dejection and despair were to be read on every countenance. Then Hannibal, who had gone on before the standards, made the army halt on a certain promontory which commanded an extensive prospect, and pointing out Italy to them, and just under the Alps the plains about the Po, he told them that they were now scaling the ramparts not only of Italy, but of Rome itself; the rest of the way would be level or downhill; and after one, or at the most two battles, they would have in their hands and in their power the citadel and capital of Italy.

Polybius puts the address to the assembled army on the day *before* they began their descent, but he too mentions that the season was 'close on the setting of the Pleiades'. This double reference provides an all-important clue to the time that Hannibal breasted the Alps before descending upon Italy. The setting of the Pleiades refers to the time when the constellation is visible declining out of sight in the west at the same moment that the sun is rising in the east. It was a very important date in ancient times, for it was the signal to begin the ploughing and sowing for the next year's harvest. Some northern commentators have been led sadly astray by forgetting that in Mediterranean latitudes such activity in late autumn is still the case – as distinct, say, from England or Germany where winter has the land in its grip.

Hannibal seems to have set out from Cartagena about mid-June in 218 B.C. and to have been five months between Cartagena and the plains of the Po. It was, therefore, mid-October at the earliest when he halted at the watershed above Italy and gazed southward. Undoubtedly he had not intended to cross the Alps so late, having hoped, perhaps, to make a start in May. He had been delayed, as has been suggested, by the late arrival of many of his troops from their winter quarters, and delayed again, as we know, by unexpected heavy fighting throughout northern Spain. It would seem, in fact, that his arrival at this point was even later than October, for the setting of the Pleiades would have been visible in the latitude in which he stood during the first fortnight in November in the year 218 B.C.

Contrary to the optimism expressed in Hannibal's speech, the descent from the watershed was even worse than had been the long climb towards it. The enemy was no longer the mountain Gaul but the wintry conditions – the snow falling on earlier snows of that year, beneath which at those heights lay the hard, impacted snow of the year before. 'The descending path was very narrow and steep, and as both men and beasts could not tell on what they were treading owing to the snow, all that stepped wide of the path or stumbled were dashed down the precipice.' Livy takes up from Polybius with the account of their perilous descent, both historians depicting similar scenes and events which they may well have drawn from a common source : 'They then came to a much narrower cliff, and with rocks so perpendicular that it was difficult for an unencumbered soldier to manage the descent, though he felt his way and clung with his hands to the bushes and roots that projected here and there. The place had been precipitous before, and a recent landslip had carried it away to the depth of a good thousand feet.'

The cavalry came to a halt – it seemed that they had at last reached the end of the road and the final inextricable position – and word was sent back to Hannibal that the route was impassable. It was not only this landslip that had checked the army but also the nature of the snowdrifts. The fresh snow concealing the old hardened layers meant that when the animals broke through the surface, their feet went on down to the lower layer while the soft snow above closed around them, holding them in an icy grasp. The men were little better off, for when they tried to raise themselves on hands and knees they could get no purchase on the old, deeply-frozen snow, and slipped further downwards on the steep slopes. Hannibal realised that there was no way of making any detour but that the narrow mountain pass must be built up and the whole track levelled off. It says a great deal for the expertise of his engineers and for the sheer courage of his men (he appears to have used Numidians for this road-building task) that a passage sufficient to allow the horses and baggage animals to proceed had been constructed within three days.

Livy adds another famous detail to the story of the army's descent into Italy – the cracking of the rock-fall that barred their path by the application of liquid and heat. It was fortunate that the fall had taken place at a point below the tree-line, for if it had taken place where there was no wood available their situation might indeed have been hopeless: 'Since they had to cut through the rock, they felled some huge trees that grew near at hand, and lopping off their branches, made an enormous pile of logs. This they set on fire, as soon as the wind blew fresh enough to make it burn, and pouring vinegar over the glowing rocks, caused them to crumble.' The rock-fall was clearly more than half way down the pass, where 'the slopes are grassy and wooded'. The reference to vinegar has produced much ridicule over the ages, but accords with an ancient belief that vinegar helped to make stones friable (Hannibal's 'vinegar' would undoubtedly have been sour wine, but he would hardly have had enough left at this stage of the journey to make much impact). The fact is that, on certain kinds of stone, a douche of water would have been quite sufficient, when they were red hot, to help split them and make them disintegrate under the pickaxes of the pioneers.

Despite the delay caused by this avalanche the head of the army was down in the plain three days after it had left the high pass, but it must be assumed that it was several days more before the tail-end of stragglers and worn-out beasts had completed their descent. Polybius, who is followed by Livy, says that the crossing of the Alps had taken fifteen days in all, a figure that is at variance with the number of days enumerated in his own narrative. The length of time between the beginning of their climb to the Alps and their assembly on the plains of the Po, as he gives it, adds up to eighteen days. This may be accounted for in two ways: the figure of fifteen days applies to the actual crossing of the Alps and not to the beginning of the ascent towards them, which probably took a further three days; or the difference may be made good between the arrival of the head of the army at their camp in Italy and the final assembly of all the troops and animals. One thing is certain: in spite of the lack of fodder in the higher reaches of the mountains, and the terrible conditions through which they had come, there is no mention of any of the elephants having been lost, while the losses of horses, pack-animals and men are recorded.

The exact pass through which Hannibal led his army down into the plains of the Po has excited much controversy over the centuries and has occasioned several volumes, quite apart from many monographs. Some passes, such as the Great St Bernard and the Little St Bernard, are comparatively easy to dismiss since they do not lead into the country inhabited by the Taurini – the tribe into whose territory Hannibal's forces emerged on their descent from the Alps. What is quite clear from the accounts of Hannibal's crossing of the Alps is that the pass he used was one of the high, dangerous ones, and that it led down steeply into Italy. The four best claimants after all the data, let alone the theories, have been digested, remain the Mont Cenis (made famous by Charlemagne and Napoleon), the Col du Clapier, the

Montgenèvre, and the Traversette. The Mont Cenis pass and the Col du Clapier both afford places close to the summit where the army could have encamped, but the Col du Clapier has preference, being a high and awkward pass. It also has a projecting spur early in its descent into Italy, from which there is a dramatic view of the plain beneath. The Montgenèvre, which has had many supporters over the years, offers a good camping ground but it is the lowest of all the passes and does not accord with the portrait of the hazardous route taken by Hannibal. The highest pass of the four, the Col de la Traversette, fulfils nearly all the requirements of the narratives but lacks a suitable camping ground. Strong cases can, and have been, made for each of these four approach routes. The final choice seems to lie between the Clapier and Traversette passes, with the odds slightly in favour of the Col du Clapier.

Writing in the first century A.D. Juvenal shows here, and in several other references in his *Satires*, that even three hundred years after Hannibal's death the memory of the great Carthaginian remained deep-etched in the Roman consciousness:

> Now Spain swells his empire, now he surmounts
> The Pyrenees. Nature throws in his path
> High Alpine passes, blizzards of snow; but he splits
> The very rocks asunder, moves mountains with vinegar.
> Now Italy is his, yet still he forces on:
> 'We have accomplished nothing,' he cries, 'till we have stormed
> The gates of Rome, till our Carthaginian standard
> Is set in the City's heart.'

Juvenal also confirms that his astonishing exploit of crossing the Alps was a subject set for schoolboys' essays and verses. Indeed, the cry 'Hannibal ad portas!' ('Hannibal is at the gates!') was used to frighten mischievous Roman children just as, centuries later in Britain, 'Boney will have you!' evoked the shadow of Napoleon and produced the silence of fear in British nurseries. The Roman historian Florus, writing even later than Juvenal, compares Hannibal's descent into Italy with a thunderbolt launched from the skies above the horrendous Alps upon the fair land of Italy. For there can be no doubt that when the news first reached Rome that the impossible had happened – that Hannibal and his Carthaginian army had swooped like an eagle from the passes of the Alps – there was panic in the city. It was a bedraggled and emaciated eagle, however, that now preened its wings in the pale winter sunlight of northern Italy and tried to make good the damage from that horrific march.

Assembled together once more in a land that provided grazing and grain, and beasts for slaughter, the troops, who 'resembled in appearance and condition animals rather than men', were able for the first time in many months to take their ease – though not for long – and regain their strength. Hannibal could now take careful count and see just what his unbelievably hazardous venture had cost him. For the advantage of surprise, and for securing the attachment to his cause of the Gauls in Italy, he had paid so dearly that most generals would have considered the campaign already lost. According to Polybius, our best authority, he had crossed the Rhône with about 50,000 foot and 9,000 horse and, since there is no record of any losses after that or during the Rhône crossing, one must assume that it was with something approaching this number – allowing for natural wastage from accident and disease – that he had begun his ascent towards the Alps. Livy gives conflicting figures as to the number of men who started out and the number lost in the crossing. Some of these are so exaggerated that they were clearly part of later Roman propaganda, designed to inflate the Roman ego as to the size of the army that their forefathers had faced. For instance, one of the Latin sources which he quotes has Hannibal arriving in Italy with 100,000 foot and 20,000 horse – far more than he started out with. Polybius is more trustworthy since, as he tells us, he had seen the inscription at Lacinium in which Hannibal himself had set down the facts and figures of his campaigns. His account reveals Hannibal reaching Italian soil at the foot of the Alps with 12,000 African and 8,000 Iberian foot, and not more than 6,000 horse. Between the Pyrenees and Italy, therefore, he had lost – mostly in the Alps – some 30,000 foot and 3,000 horse. This more or less confirms one statement of Livy's, that a Roman who had been a captive of Hannibal left it on record that Hannibal had told him that 'after crossing the Rhône he lost thirty-six thousand men and a vast number of horses and other animals'.

Quintus Fabius Pictor, earliest of Latin historians and known as the Father of Roman History, fought against Hannibal in the war which was about to begin and reckoned that at this period the Romans and their allied states could field 750,000 men. Hannibal knew from previous communications with the Gauls in Italy that many thousands of them would rise, hailing him as liberator, and would join his forces in the war against Rome. He knew their bravery (as well as their lack of discipline), but what he cannot have known, as he contemplated his bedraggled army recuperating at the foot of the Alps, was exactly how many of them would join his standard. He had subdued the tribes of northern Spain, and as much of the Iberian peninsula as they could ever need was now a Carthaginian colony; he had crossed the Pyrenees and the Rhône; and he could look back towards the lucent Alpine peaks, which he had conquered with so severe a loss, as the last great natural hazard between him and his goal. But now he must face the tough and disciplined armies of Rome – and at that moment he had no more than 20,000 half-starved soldiers, 6,000 cavalrymen on bony horses, and 37 emaciated elephants. It was little enough with which to try conclusions with the greatest power in the Mediterranean world.

X

FIRST BLOOD IN ITALY

Publius Cornelius Scipio, the consul who had failed to arrest Hannibal's advance at the Rhône and who had returned to Italy after sending his army under his brother into Spain, was appalled to learn that the army of Carthage was now encamped at the foot of the Alps. When Hannibal had evaded him by marching north along the bank of the Rhône he had scarcely found it credible that he would attempt the passes of the Alps so late in the year — let alone that he would succeed. His fellow consul, Tiberius Sempronius Longus, was still in Sicily with the army which had been readied for the attack on Carthage. He had taken the Lipari islands as well as the Carthaginian trading post of Malta when the news reached him that the enemy was in Italy, and he was to return with all possible speed to join Scipio. The latter, having taken command of the legions in the north, had marched to the plain of the Po where he encamped, ready to give battle the moment that Hannibal moved southward. His troops had suffered a severe mauling during the Gallic revolt at the hands of the Boii, and their morale was consequently very low. Scipio did his best to put spirit into them by reminding them that the Romans had defeated the Carthaginians before; that Hannibal's army must be in a sorry condition after the crossing of the Alps; and that it was with them alone that there rested the ultimate defence of their city and their land.

The Republican army was destined within three centuries (from 350 B.C.) to conquer first Italy and then the known world. 'This army broke in succession the stout native soldiers of Italy and the mountaineers of Spain and overthrew the trained Macedonian phalanx,' wrote F. J. Haverfield. 'Once only did it fail — against Hannibal. But not even Hannibal could oust it from its entrenchments, and not even his victories could permanently break its morale.' And it was upon her legions — the principal unit of her army — that Rome depended most. The legion usually consisted of a division of 4,500 men — 3,000 heavy infantry, 1,200 lighter-armed, and 300 horse — although sometimes it might include as many as 6,000 men. The backbone of the legion was the heavily-armed infantrymen, equipped with a large shield, metal helmet, leather cuirass, and a short sword for cutting or thrusting. Levied from the whole body of Romans who possessed some private means (maybe no more than a small farm plot), they were above all a citizen army. In many respects they resembled the Puritan army of Cromwell — of excellent character, rigidly disciplined, and highly trained. When drawn up for battle they formed into three lines: first the *hastati*, 120 young men armed with swords and two short throwing-spears; secondly, the *principes*, slightly older men, similarly armed, and also 120 in number; thirdly, the *triarii*, 60 veterans, armed with swords and a long spear or pike. These sub-divisions of the legion, known as maniples, were arranged in chess-board fashion (*quincunx*) so that the first row could retire through the second without disorganising it, while the second in its turn advanced; the *triarii* formed a reserve. This formation gave the legion considerable flexibility and was an improvement upon the solid phalanx with which the Greeks since Alexander had dominated the ancient world, and which the Carthaginians had adopted. Hannibal was not slow to perceive the advantages of such tactical units and to modify his own dispositions accordingly.

Apart from the legions, the Roman army contained contingents drawn from the Italian 'allies', subjects of Rome, who were armed and drilled like legionaries and often appear to have equalled the latter in number. In these days the cavalry attached to each legion seems to have been of little account – a fact of which Hannibal and his well-organised Numidians and Iberians took great advantage – and it was not until Scipio Africanus, the son of the Scipio who now advanced to meet Hannibal, learned from his enemy how to handle cavalry that the balance was redressed. The centurions were the backbone of the legions, professional long-service soldiers who took the name of Rome from India to Scotland – the finest N.C.O.s in history. Above them there were six tribunes to a legion, either veteran officers or young noblemen at the beginning of their careers.

The normal practice was that when a consul took the field he had with him an army of two legions, together with an appropriate number of 'allies'. When two consuls took the field together they had, accordingly, four legions, allied infantry, legionary cavalry, and allied cavalry. According to Polybius, in the first major engagement between the Carthaginians and Romans in 218 B.C. at the river Trebia the two consuls with their combined forces had an army of 16,000 legionaries and 20,000 allied infantry. The great disadvantage under which the Romans laboured – at any rate in the early phases of the war – was that the consuls were changed every year and, when the two were together, they commanded the combined force in rotation. Such a 'democratic' Republican procedure was almost certain to come to grief when matched against the military intelligence, command and will-power of one man – particularly when that man was a genius of warfare.

Roman tactics in battle were comparatively simple and, since they had proved so successful in previous wars, were used against the Carthaginians until the latter demonstrated, by a flexibility designed to match each new occasion, that what had triumphed over Latins and Greeks and Gallic tribes needed adaptation. First of all, the Roman front line would open fire with their throwing spears, following this up with a charge with their swords – somewhat akin to the musket volley and bayonet charge of later wars. If this failed to break the enemy front, the second line, passing through the first on their chess-board principle, would repeat the procedure. The veterans held as reserve could then be used if necessary, while all the time the lightly-armed infantry were skirmishing on the flanks of the enemy, aided by the cavalry. These tactics had served the Romans well in the past – and were to do so in the future – but proved inadequate to deal with a general who modified his own tactics to suit each new battlefield, and who used elements of surprise and carefully laid traps, into which the Romans more often than not were prone to blunder. Some of the accusations of Punic perfidy and bad faith which were made against Hannibal by later Roman writers undoubtedly stemmed from the fact that he did not make war according to the established rules. He was unconventional. It was with somewhat similar unconventional genius that Napoleon was to destroy the eighteenth century armies of Europe, who marched in careful order to the chosen battlefield, and were dismayed to find that their enemy was not 'playing the game' according to the well-known rules, but was fighting to win by any available means.

The revolt of the Boii against the Romans which, no doubt, Hannibal had hoped would more or less coincide with his own arrival in northern Italy had been premature. (Possibly it provides further evidence that Hannibal was some two months late in his campaign?) What it meant in effect, even though it had seriously damaged Roman morale, was that there were Roman legions in the north at a time of the year when, under normal circumstances, the only troops would have been limited garrisons in places such as Cremona, Placentia (Piacenza) and Ariminum (Rimini). Scipio was thus able to find an army ready in the field which, though it needed his presence and exhortation, was already disposed not far from the chosen battleground.

Hannibal's first task, when his army and the animals were sufficiently recuperated to be fit for action, was to ensure that the Gauls of northern Italy recognised the Carthaginians as their deliverers from the Roman oppressor. Unfortunately, the very tribe in whose area he had arrived, the Taurini, were unwilling to accept his offer of friendship and were at war with the Insubres, another Gallic tribe – but one which was prepared to accept the Carthaginian as their leader. Hannibal had learned long ago from his experiences in dealing with the tribes in Spain that nothing succeeded with them so well as swift and determined action. He moved rapidly against the Taurini and attacked their main town – later to be known as Augusta Taurinorum

(Turin). In three days he had taken it and put to the sword all who still opposed him, while welcoming those who joined his standard. This simple success had the desired effect, and from now on all the Gauls in the surrounding area hastened to join his ranks against the common enemy. Scipio, however, had moved equally fast and had crossed the Po – at this time of the year a cold, fast-flowing torrent – and had brought his troops up to the river Ticinus (Ticino). By doing so, he had isolated many of the Gauls in the area of the Po and though their sympathies were with Hannibal, the Roman presence prevented them from joining him.

The ensuing actions of the two leaders – at this crucial moment before the clash of arms resounded throughout Italy – may seem strange to the modern reader, but must be viewed in the light of a time when individual communication between a general and his troops assumed an immense importance. When there were no printed 'Daily Orders' there was no other form of exhortation possible than for the commander to stand up and address as many of his men as could be gathered in one place to hear him. The formal speech before battle (so often heavily embroidered by ancient historians, but true to the spirit of the time) could have an immense effect upon the morale of soldiers, most of whom were illiterate, and many of whom were ignorant even of the events that had led to their being called upon to give battle. Publius Cornelius Scipio, for instance, seems to have been concerned to stress that it was a just war that they were fighting, because the Carthaginians had treacherously attacked Saguntum – thus breaking the peace that had been agreed between Rome and Carthage after the First Punic War. He pointed out that, as they had shown in this previous war, the Romans were superior on the field to the Carthaginians in their prime, while all that they now had to face were the half-starved remnants of Hannibal's army, not yet recovered from their crossing of the Alps. Furthermore, he reminded them, there were no more Alps to protect their land or Rome itself – and no other army save their own.

Hannibal's approach to his men was slightly different, and it is easy to see why. He had to communicate to an army composed of several races and, no doubt, speaking many dialects. He chose, therefore, to keep words to the minimum, but to provide his audience with a visual and easily comprehensible image of their present situation and of how, if they fought well, they might yet turn it to good account. The army was formed into a large circle into which were introduced a number of prisoners taken from the Gauls who had attacked them during their march. These were given the option of remaining prisoners and slaves or, if they were willing to fight in single combat with one another, the victor would gain his freedom, arms, armour, and a horse. As for the vanquished, death at least would spare him from his present sufferings. With one accord, all the Gallic prisoners voted for combat. After these gladiatorial fights were over, and the dead had been dragged away and the prisoners who had not been lucky enough to be selected by lot to take part had been led off in their chains, there was scarcely any need for words. There, said Hannibal, was the true picture of his men's situation : if they fought well and triumphed, Rome and all the riches of this country were theirs; if they died in battle they were spared further suffering; but if they fought and lost, then nothing but the misery of slavery awaited them.

The first meeting between the Romans and Carthaginians hardly deserves to be termed a battle : it was more of a cavalry skirmish in which, and not for the last time in the war, the superiority of Hannibal's cavalry over the Roman was soon established. The Romans at this time still rode without bridles (as had the Greek cavalry before them). So did Hannibal's light brigade, the Numidians, but it is noteworthy that Polybius points out that on this occasion Hannibal put 'all his bridled and heavier cavalry in front of the army'. This was the Spanish heavy brigade, and no doubt he was remembering his experience when the Numidians had been worsted by the Romans during their previous encounter near the Rhône. Scipio, advancing to meet his enemy, had bridged the Ticinus, a tributary of the Po. He had got his troops across and was marching northwards while Hannibal was coming down to meet him. The flat land in that area was ideal for cavalry, even though the hard weather of northern Italy in winter must have made the going unpleasant for both armies – in particular the Iberian and North African foot soldiers, who could scarcely have recovered from the hardships in the Alps.

As the armies neared one another and encamped, both generals took command of their cavalry and set out to reconnoitre. Clearly the heavy winter rains had not yet turned those plains into their customary fields of mud, for both Polybius and Livy comment on the fact that each side had advance warning of the other's approach by the thick clouds of dust kicked up by the horses. Hannibal, putting his heavy cavalry in the centre, led them to the attack himself, while distributing the Numidians on his wings to outflank the enemy if possible. Scipio, for his part, advanced with his light horse in the centre and kept his heavier Roman and Gallic cavalry in the rear. Meeting head on, the light-armed Roman horse were compelled to withdraw, after an ineffectual discharge of their javelins, before the weight of the Carthaginian centre. Many riders on both sides either were unhorsed or dismounted deliberately, so that the clash now became almost as much an infantry as a cavalry engagement. While confusion reigned in the centre, the Numidians on both of Hannibal's wings rode round and outflanked the Romans. The latter turned in flight and, to add to the confusion, the consul, Publius Cornelius Scipio, was severely wounded. (Tradition has it that he was only saved from capture by the action of his son, later to become known as the famous Scipio Africanus – ultimate victor over Hannibal – who led a charge into the mêlée around his father and brought him safe from the field.) The Romans now withdrew at speed and in good order, but the wounded consul, having noted the superiority of the enemy cavalry and being concerned for the safety of his army, ordered a total withdrawal to the line of the Po. The action was inconclusive enough, but it had given both sides a chance to assess their enemy. Furthermore, the wounding of Scipio had disheartened the Romans, as well as depriving them of his leadership in the battle that was later to follow.

While Scipio crossed the Po and assembled his men at Placentia on the east of the river Trebia, which at this point flows into the Po from its birth-place in the Apennines, Hannibal followed hard on his heels. He reached the place where the Romans had bridged the Ticinus and captured 600 men from the force that had been set to guard it. He then marched up the Po for two days until he found a place where it was comparatively easy to cross. Here, Polybius tells us, 'he halted and constructing a bridge of boats, ordered Hasdrubal, his senior commander, to see to the passage of the army while he himself, crossing at once, gave a hearing to the envoys who had arrived from the districts around.' His capture of the headquarters of the Taurini, followed by this early success against the Romans, had confirmed the Gauls in their promised allegiance to the Carthaginian and they came flocking in from the countryside around.

Some days later, having marched down the south bank of the Po and drawn up his army in full view of the Roman camp – daring them to come out and engage him – Hannibal's self-assurance again paid dividends. Some two thousand Gallic auxiliaries, together with two hundred horsemen, revolted against their Roman masters in Placentia and came over to him. At the same time the chieftains of the Boii made their way to the Carthaginian camp and promised all their assistance in the forthcoming war. Despite the heavy losses which he had suffered in his passage of the Alps Hannibal was now able to field an army large enough to meet any that the Romans could – as yet – muster against him. The physical strength and the innate bravery of the Gauls would have to be used in the ensuing conflict to wear down the Romans, while his own hardened and trained professionals would always have to be kept in reserve for the kill. It was upon this general strategy that he based his tactics in the assault on Rome.

XI

BATTLE AT THE TREBIA

Ill from his wound and disturbed by the defection of the Gauls, Scipio was determined not to be drawn into battle against the Carthaginian until he had been joined by his fellow consul, Sempronius. The latter, having put his legionaries under oath to make their way to Ariminum at their best speed (an astounding march from the heel of Italy to Ariminum on the north-east coast in some forty days), was now in a position to take his two legions across to Placentia. Scipio, however, rather than stay at the garrison-town, decided, according to Polybius, 'to break up his camp and march towards the river Trebia'. He hoped that in the hills surrounding the river he would find a more secure position in which to encamp and hold the Carthaginians until he was reinforced.

Hannibal could hardly fail to notice this troop movement and, as soon as Scipio began to withdraw, sent out his Numidians to harass the Romans on their march. This was the moment when Scipio might indeed have been brought to battle and utterly destroyed. The Numidians, however, unable to resist the temptation to plunder and loot, turned aside from the pursuit and, having ransacked the remains of the Roman camp, set fire to it. Although some of his rearguard were killed or captured, Scipio was able to establish himself in a strongly fortified camp along the small hills above the river. Hannibal was not to be drawn after him. When battle came, he wanted it on his own terms, and he had no intention of taking his troops across the Trebia to be met on the far side by an already entrenched Roman army. At about this time a piece of good fortune came his way: the neighbouring township of Clastidium, used as a store depot by the Romans, was betrayed by its commandant (for a large bribe, says Livy), and its granary served the Carthaginians well as the cold winter of northern Italy set in. Rain, sleet, icy winds and the flat land around growing steadily more muddy – these were the conditions which both sides faced as the year drew to a close.

Sempronius now moved across from Ariminum and joined Scipio. Although his army had marched from Sicily and had then traversed almost the length of Italy – as fine a proof as there could be of Roman endurance and discipline – it was still comparatively fresh. Unlike Scipio's troops, who had been mauled during the Gallic uprising, and who had now experienced the first blows of the Carthaginians, Sempronius and his men, geared as they had been for the attack on Carthage, were eager to make contact with the enemy. This was especially true of Sempronius himself, an ambitious man and one who was particularly eager to give battle before his consular term expired. The fact that Scipio seems to have been almost completely disabled by his wound meant that, in practice, the command fell into the hands of Sempronius, although the weakness in the system – the divided command – undoubtedly affected the whole Roman reaction to Hannibal's presence in the area. Scipio was in favour of delay, of waiting through the winter, holding Hannibal at bay, but not committing themselves to a major engagement until the better weather in the new year – by which time they would also have been reinforced from Rome. Sempronius judged that with their two consular armies united, and with the forces of their Latin and Gallic allies, they had more than enough men to engage the Carthaginian forces without much risk. The weather was worse for the enemy than it was for them – accustomed as they were to such winters – and even though Hannibal's troops had been reinforced by Gauls, they were hardly likely to be in good condition so soon after their descent from the Alps.

At this juncture, immediately before the battle of the Trebia, the consular forces numbered about 16,000 Romans, together with 20,000 allies and 4,000 horse. The army under Hannibal was smaller – consisting of 20,000 infantry composed of Africans, Spaniards and Celts, while his cavalry, including Celtic allies, amounted to some 10,000. Hannibal, therefore, was superior in cavalry but inferior in infantry, and the majority of his men were unlikely to be in the best physical condition. It is almost certain that each side had a fairly accurate estimation of its enemy's strength, for the Gauls who were passing between the lines – some pro-Roman and others pro-Carthaginian – must have carried their assessments to the officers of the opposing armies. Nonetheless, it is likely that Hannibal's information system was better since more Gauls were inclined towards the Carthaginians. He had also, from the early days when he was still planning the campaign, maintained a very efficient espionage system in Italy. It is unlikely that he did not know of the differences between the two consuls, and that he had not taken stock of the fact that Sempronius was in effective command – particularly when the armies were committed to battle – as Scipio would be unable to take the field. It was upon the known ambition and desire for a quick victory on the part of Sempronius that he had to base his overall strategy.

Looking for a pretext for action, Sempronius was not slow to find one. Hannibal was concerned that a number of the Gauls in the area between the Trebia and the Po were negotiating with the Romans as well as with the Carthaginians – endeavouring to hedge their bets in the impending conflict.

He despatched 2,000 infantry and 1,000 horse to raid their land, hoping to frighten them into the Carthaginian camp and also to provoke a Roman response. This was not slow in coming, for when the Gauls approached the Romans and asked for help, Sempronius at once sent out most of his cavalry and a thousand foot soldiers. Once he had crossed the Trebia and engaged Hannibal's raiding party, there ensued a confused minor engagement in which the Romans gained the upper hand. This had the desired effect and, as Polybius tells the story, 'Tiberius [Sempronius], elated and overjoyed by his success, was all eagerness to bring on a decisive battle as soon as possible.' Scipio's counsel that they would do better to wait, improve the quality of their legions by a winter's drilling, and count upon the fact that the unreliable Celts would soon desert Hannibal was ignored. Sempronius 'was eager to deliver the decisive blow himself and did not wish Publius [Scipio] to be present at the battle, or that the consuls designate should enter upon office before all was over – it being now nearly the time for this.'

Everything was playing into Hannibal's hands, and his view of the situation was similar to Scipio's. The Romans would, indeed, be better to wait but, as for him, he wanted action swiftly – while Sempronius was in effective command, while his own Gauls were still eager for battle, and before the Romans had had more time to train up their raw levies, as yet untested in battle. Of the morale of Hannibal's own men, Polybius sagely comments that, 'when a general has brought his army into a foreign country and is engaged in such a risky enterprise, his only hope of safety lies in constantly keeping alive the hopes of his allies.'

Like all great generals Hannibal was a man who knew how to make the land work for him. Trained since a boy in camp, and since a youth in war, he had assimilated that knowledge of space, of density, and of the configuration of the earth around, which distinguishes his rare kind from other military men. He had noticed, during his inspection of the territory between his own camp on the western side of the Trebia and the river itself, a small watercourse with steep banks that were dense with scrub and thicket. At first glance it would pass unremarked, especially in the grey light and rain of winter. It lay to the south of his camp, south of the plain across which any army would have to pass to attack him. If Hannibal could only lure the Romans across the Trebia, drawing up his own troops to the north of this place 'well adapted for an ambuscade', then he could conceal troops in the area who had but to wait until the enemy was past before attacking in their rear. Polybius with his military expertise comments : 'Any water-course with a slight bank and reeds or bracken . . . can be made use of to conceal not only infantry, but even the dismounted horsemen at times, if a little care be taken to lay shields, with conspicuous devices inside, uppermost of the ground and hide the helmets under them.'

Hannibal now held a council of war. He knew that Sempronius, especially since his small success over the Carthaginian raiding party, was ready and eager to engage. He only needed a little encouragement – a further raid, perhaps, but this time on his own camp? In his mood of aggressive confidence the Roman consul would never be able to tolerate an impudent gesture like an attack on the Roman camp itself. All depended on the success of the ambush. Hannibal selected his younger brother Mago – eager to win his spurs – and put him in command of a picked force of 1,000 foot and 1,000 horse. Mago's orders were to leave the camp after dark and take up his position in the scrub around the small gulley and to lie there concealed until he judged the moment ripe. Hannibal now explained exactly what his plan was for the major action itself.

At dawn the next day all the light-armed Numidian horsemen would cross the Trebia and then, in the grey early light, make an attack on the Roman camp. Their part in the day's work was all-important, and Hannibal promised them suitable rewards if they achieved the result he expected. As soon as the Romans roused themselves and began to react to the darts and javelins of the marauding horsemen they were to withdraw, but not so fast that they did not give the enemy time to mount their own horses and follow in pursuit. The aim was to lure not only the Roman cavalry but the whole army across the Trebia and into the flat land where Hannibal's troops would be drawn up for battle.

Sempronius, as the Numidians came thundering down towards his camp, immediately sent out his own cavalry to engage them. The whole matter might possibly have ended in no more than a skirmish, with the Numidians withdrawing as the heavy cavalry began to drive them back, but the consul had risen to the bait. Determined to give the Carthaginians a severe mauling – if no more – he sent out 6,000 infantry armed with javelins, and then began to move the whole army. It was, as Livy tells us, 'a day of terrible weather . . . the time of the year when the days are shortest, and it was snowing in the area between the Alps and the Apennines, and the proximity of rivers and marshes intensified the bitter cold.' By sending in his Numidians at first light Hannibal had ensured that the Romans, caught without having had a morning meal, were compelled to hasten out unprepared and still half-asleep. His own army, however, forewarned and well advised, had breakfasted at leisure and had then settled down in front of roaring fires to warm themselves and to oil their bodies against the cold, wind and sleet. The horses had been fed and watered, groomed and readied; the elephants were similarly looked after, for they would be used in advance of the cavalry on each wing of the army to give protection to their own horsemen. For Hannibal it was to be a setpiece battle, a model of care and preparation over which he would reminisce in the years to come.

The Romans, with their characteristic dour bravery, formed up and made their way towards the river. It was here that Hannibal made the forces of nature work for him: 'At first their enthusiasm and eagerness sustained them, but when they had to cross the Trebia, swollen as it was owing to the rain that had fallen during the night higher up the valley . . . the infantry had great difficulty in crossing, as the water was breast-high.' Polybius continues: 'The consequence was that the whole force suffered much from cold and also from hunger, as the day was now advancing.'

Hannibal waited, making no attempt to attack until the Romans were across the river, and then sent forward about 8,ooo pikemen and slingers to harass the enemy as they were reforming. The Balearic slingers, with their deadly accuracy, were able to pick off soldiers like sitting birds as, streaming with water, they staggered into line; the lightly-clad pikemen darted in and selected individual targets, skewering them to the ground while themselves remaining outside the cut and thrust of the Roman *gladius*. (This fine short sword had its merits when used by soldiers in a disciplined line, but was at a disadvantage in single combat.)

Moving at ease while the advance forces disrupted the Romans as they formed rank, Hannibal's troops had time to draw themselves up almost as if for a ceremonial parade. For the operation this day, Hannibal favoured a long line for the infantry; the heavily-armed Africans and Spaniards reinforcing the Gauls; the cavalry on each wing, with the elephants and their drivers looming ahead of the horse – ominous in the cold and heavy overcast skies of winter. Sempronius, we read, 'advanced on the enemy in imposing style marching in order at slow step'. The light-armed troops began the battle, but even here the Carthaginians were at an advantage, for the Romans had spent most of their missiles against the first wild Numidian attack. As the light forces withdrew between the gaps left in the lines for them, the first clash of the heavy infantry occurred. When the centres were engaged the Carthaginian cavalry pressed home their attacks on both flanks of the enemy, coming fresh to the assault and having superiority in numbers. The Roman wings began to yield and, as they did so, the Numidian light horse and the Carthaginian pikemen, following up their own heavy cavalry, took advantage of the weakness left on each flank of the Roman infantry.

While both centres held in hand-to-hand combat, the Roman cavalry fell back and their infantry on each flank began to collapse. Hannibal's trap was sprung. Rising from their hiding-place in the rain-enshrouded gulley to the rear of the Romans, Mago and his special force charged out with a great cry to take the enemy's centre from the rear. Trumpeting through the driving sleet the elephants helped to roll up the wing which, tormented by the Numidians and other light troops, began to fall back upon the rushing cold river behind them.

The Roman legionaries in the van, each flank exposed and their rear attacked, fought their way courageously ahead and broke through the thin Carthaginian line. Ten thousand of them managed to maintain a disciplined formation and to retire upon Placentia. Theirs must have been a notably organised withdrawal, with an efficient rearguard fighting off the pursuing Carthaginians, for they still had to cross the Trebia again to reach the garrison-town (something that Livy fails to observe). The rest of the Roman army, cavalry and infantry alike, were scattered into ragged groups by the Carthaginian advance and by the sudden onslaught of Mago and his men in their rear. Most of those who did not die in the field were hacked down as they made to cross the swollen river; those who did escape joined the general retreat towards Placentia. The Carthaginians were wise and – no doubt on Hannibal's orders – did not attempt to pursue the enemy beyond the river-line.

The day was a triumph of strategy and of tactical planning. The Romans had been outgeneralled, and their armies cut to pieces or dispersed in flight. Thousands of Romans and their allies had been killed and thousands taken prisoner. The path south through the Apennines lay open to the invader. Something in the way in which the battle had evolved – the failure of his own centre before the heavy Roman thrust – may have suggested to Hannibal a stratagem that he would employ one day in the future on the distant field of Cannae. Most of his own casualties had occurred among the Gauls, possibly because of their wild and undisciplined charges, possibly because they were not so well protected by body armour as the Carthaginians. (This was something that Hannibal would rectify by carefully training his new troops and by the distribution among them of captured Roman shields, helmets and armour.) Heavy losses had been incurred by the elephants – Polybius says that all but one were killed. and Livy says 'nearly all' – but this did little save demonstrate their unsuitability for the terrain and climate of Italy.

An attempt was made by the Romans, and particularly by Sempronius, to disguise the nature of their defeat, and it was put about that they had only been deprived of a victory by the violence of the weather. The true state of affairs could not long be concealed, for the Carthaginians were still encamped as before; the Gauls who had been hesitating as to their future allegiance came over to Hannibal without any further reservation; and the remnants of the two consular armies had withdrawn into Placentia and

Cremona. The news that Hannibal was across the Alps had sounded the alarm in Rome; the cavalry encounter at the Ticinus had been the first peremptory tap on an ominous drum; but the rout of two consular armies on the Trebia was no murmur of thunder in the distant hills. It was the deep rumble of an advancing avalanche that would shake Rome to its foundations.

XII

TRASIMENE

Eager to press home his advantage, Hannibal would have liked to attempt the passage of the Apennines immediately, but the increasing severity of the weather and the poor health of his own troops were against him. Furthermore, he now had to contend with the Gallic temperament – and the Gauls did not reckon that a victory was followed by further action, but by plunder and enjoyment. It was a factor that Hannibal would have to bear in mind for the future. For the moment he gave them, as well as his own troops, free rein to ransack the lands around, and 'the Romans were given no peace even in their winter quarters'. Livy tells us that the garrison towns of Placentia and Cremona, housing the survivors of the legions, were completely cut off from local supplies and could only be maintained by ferrying all their requirements up the Po in barges. In Rome itself, now that the real situation was evident, there was 'such consternation that people looked for the immediate appearance of the hostile army before their very City, and knew not which way to turn for any hope or help in defending their gates and walls against its onset.'

The arrival in Rome of Sempronius, who had made his way back with great hazard through a countryside that was dominated by Hannibal's cavalry, facilitated the election of the new consuls for the year 217 B.C. Gaius Flaminius and Gnaeus Servilius were the consuls chosen, the former for the second time. He was a man who had won great popularity with the people for his hostile attitude towards the senate and the aristocratic party; he had also a high opinion of his military prowess from a previous campaign against the Gauls. While Servilius was to command the legions which would be based on Ariminum, to Flaminius fell the welcome task of taking over the troops at Arretium (Arezzo), where he would be seen to be barring the passage of the invader towards Rome. Since both existing consular armies had been decimated at Trebia, four new legions were immediately levied – an early sign that the manpower of Italy would prove its greatest asset.

Before all the operations for that year ceased, Hannibal, despite a wound incurred in a cavalry action, had captured the large trading post of Victumulae. Here he had been met by a hostile Gallic population who had tried to oppose his attack on their township. They were routed and then exterminated for their faithfulness to Rome. It was vital, in this early stage in the war, that the Gauls of northern Italy should realise from the start that fortune and freedom lay in joining the Carthaginian, but that he was more merciless than the Romans if opposed.

Hannibal's personal relations with the Gauls who joined his army, now and later in his campaigns, were all-important for his success in Italy. What he promised them, as he did his own men who had followed him from Spain, was complete freedom and the right, by conquest, to the lands that they made theirs. Since the lives of Gallic warriors at that time revolved around warfare, usually against their fellow Gauls, and they had hardly attained the settled ways of the Italians, who were agriculturalists first and foremost, the appeal of battle and plunder was irresistible. They asked for nothing more, believing that to die in battle was the proper thing for a man – and that their spirits would, in any case, survive. Their outlook on life was in a sense Homeric, and in almost all respects they resembled the Norsemen of later centuries. Feasting and drinking wine, boasting of their exploits, listening to tales of heroism from their bards, they were brave and simple children. Gold torques and heavy wrist- and arm-bands of gold showed their wealth; their unarmoured bodies displayed their contempt for the enemy (until trained into Carthaginian and Roman usage of corselets); and they went trousered through the world – unlike the men of the Mediterranean, who saw in the long leggings of the North the mark of the savage. The historian Diodorus writes of them that they would happily engage in single combat with one another over trivial incidents at their drinking parties and that they were fond of songs about the great deeds of their ancestors. 'They enlarge the bronze helmets that they wear with horns, to give an appearance of great size. They carry shields as long as their bodies, embossed with the bronze head of some beast. They speak in riddles, hinting darkly at their meaning, while always extolling themselves. Terrible in aspect, they appear threatening; yet they have sharp wits and are often clever in learning.'

These were the men who were to form the bulk of Hannibal's army for many years, and these were the men whom he had above all to impress – not only with his superior intelligence and cunning, not only with a bravery that would equal theirs on the battlefield, but with some quality that seemed to set him apart from other human beings. As a cultured man and as a Carthaginian noble, sprung from generations of rich and noble men, he was accustomed to the ways in which the simple may be impressed and overawed. (Among his personal staff was a Carthaginian priest and soothsayer, and Hannibal must have been conversant with the skills with which the priesthood worked upon the superstitions of the ignorant.) Polybius, almost certainly quoting some earlier and contemporary authority, tells us that it was 'during this winter that he also adopted a truly Punic artifice. Fearing the fickleness of the Celts and possible attempts on his life, owing to his establishment of friendly relations with them being so very recent, he had a number of wigs made, dyed to suit the appearance of persons differing widely in age, and kept constantly changing them, at the same time also dressing in a style that suited the wig, so that not only those who had seen him but for a moment, but even his familiars found difficulty in recognising him.'

Hannibal had, indeed, good reason to fear an attempt upon his life, for during his few months in Italy he had already been responsible for the death of many Gauls – among the Taurini, prior to the battle of Trebia, and recently at Victumulae – and he knew how the code of the blood-feud operated among them. He remembered the fate of his brother-in-law Hasdrubal, assassinated in Spain for some unspecified grudge. His recent wound may well have served to remind him that it was upon him, and him alone, that the success of the war against Rome depended. Not only Hasdrubal but also his father Hamilcar, killed in battle, had died before they could work out the great oath that they had taken upon the altar – to wreak vengeance upon Rome for her perfidious treatment of Carthage. Many thousands had already fallen in pursuance of that oath, and it was clear to Hannibal that by his hand upon the sacrificial offering not only had he committed himself, but also, without him, the Carthaginian cause was doomed.

The news from Spain was bad. Under the attack of the Roman legions, commanded by the brother of the consul Scipio, the Carthaginian forces in northern Spain had been defeated. Most of the region between the Pyrenees and the Ebro was now in Roman hands with the result that, contrary to his hopes and expectations, he could no longer be reinforced overland by the way that he had come. Furthermore, the Romans, putting to good use their command of the sea, had thwarted a Carthaginian attempt to land reinforcements near Pisa. Hannibal's communications were efficiently strangled and, although his first onslaught on Italy had proved successful, the long-term Roman strategy of reducing the Carthaginian source of power – Spain – and of denying him assistance by sea was already bearing fruit. 'Rome', wrote William O'Connor Morris, 'was a great nation, Carthage an ill-governed state', and the truth of those words would become increasingly apparent as the years went by. Hannibal had no other sure source of reserves but the Gauls of Italy : he was dependent upon them, and the whole success of the expedition was dependent upon him staying alive. His hopes at this time must also have been geared to the possibility of seducing away from Rome the Latin allies, who in many respects formed the bulk of her armies. If he could shatter the confederation that held these states together he could deprive Rome of a principal source of manpower and isolate her. For this reason, both now and in the future, he was careful to make a distinction among the prisoners that he took : Romans were reduced to slave status, but the allies were treated kindly and, whenever possible, sent back to their homes with the message that the Carthaginian had no enmity against them. His war was against Rome.

Early in the spring, well aware that the Gauls were restive and that they were eager to leave their own territory and live off the land of their enemy, Hannibal gave the order for the army to move south into Etruria. Knowing that the eastern route by Ariminum on the Adriatic coast would be guarded by two consular legions, and having no doubt found out that the other main force awaited him on the western flank of the Apennines at Arretium, he decided to take a route which the Romans would not have anticipated. The way that he chose was more direct, but its disadvantages would become apparent only too soon. It seems likely that, having marched as far as Bologna he then turned west, crossing the Apennines by the Passo Collina to come out near Pistoia. He emerged into the valley of the lower Arno, an area at that time undrained and marshy in the extreme. The order of the army on the march, as given by Polybius, is interesting since it shows what reliance he placed upon the various national units. In the van went the Africans and the Spaniards and all the more disciplined troops, the baggage train being interspersed among them; behind, forming the main body, came his thousands of Gauls; and in the rear came the cavalry, both heavy and light, ready for action if any attempts were made to harass the army and forming also a formidable warning to any Gauls who might think of deserting if the going got difficult.

The crossing of the marshes of the lower Arno was almost as hard upon the troops, in its quite different way, as had been the latter stages of the Alps. 'All the army', says Polybius, 'suffered much, chiefly from lack of sleep, as they had to march through water for three continuous days and nights. The Celts were much more worn out and lost more men than the rest. Most of the pack-animals fell and perished in the mud, the only service they rendered being that when they fell the men piled their packs on their bodies and lay upon them, being thus out of the water and enabled to snatch a little sleep during the night. Many of the horses also lost their hooves through the continuous march in the mud.' Only one elephant now survived out of the thirty-seven with which he had crossed the Alps: this was ridden by Hannibal himelf in the passage through the marshes. This was possibly the one Indian elephant in the troop since the elder Cato referred to the survivor as Surus ('the Syrian') and Indian elephants used in ancient warfare came via Syria.

Livy paints an even harsher picture of the plight of the invading army than Polybius, but both confirm that it was here that Hannibal suffered a severe misfortune. 'Hannibal himself, whose eyes were suffering in the first place from the trying spring weather, alternating between hot and cold, rode upon the sole surviving elephant, that he might be higher above the water. But lack of sleep, damp nights, and the air of the marshes affected his head, and since he had neither place nor time for employing remedies, he lost the sight of one of his eyes.' Juvenal later refers to him as 'the one-eyed commander, perched on his monstrous beast.'

Whatever he and his men had suffered in these days through the marshes of the Arno valley was redeemed by the immense tactical advantage that he had stolen over the enemy. Far to the east of them Servilius and his troops watched the roads and passes on the Adriatic side of Italy, while to the south Flaminius waited at Arretium to bar the road to Rome. Hannibal had no intention of meeting the enemy on a field of the latter's choosing and not of his own. He intended to by-pass Flaminius and carry straight on towards the central plains of Italy. His troops had asked for rapine and plunder and to live off the land of their enemy and he was leading them directly into the rich plains of Tuscany – the desired treasure-land of many armies in the centuries to come. Rich in grain and cattle, the smiling land of ancient Etruria yielded up its villages, its animals and its crops to this furious horde that, locust-like, moved easily through it in the warm days of spring. Hannibal was well aware that Flaminius, left high and dry at Arretium, would be tortured at the reports reaching him of these depredations. Flaminius had set himself on the road to Rome like the champion of the city – and had been ignored. He must also have been aware of the political danger to Rome arising from Hannibal's apparently uncontested march of success. The Etruscans, former masters of the land, had always resented the dominance of the city which they had fought so long and so hard, and they might consider this Phoenician descendant as nearer to them in blood and culture than the Romans.

Hannibal dragged the lure in front of his opponent, and Flaminius rose to the bait. Although a number of his officers strongly advised him not to attack until he had been joined by his fellow consul and his forces, Flaminius broke up his camp and set off in pursuit of Hannibal, 'utterly regardless of time or place, but bent only on falling in with the enemy. . . .' Like Sempronius before him, he wished to be seen as sole champion and defender of Rome and, even if this side of his nature had not played its part, he – as the consul nearest the invader – could hardly allow this public humiliation of Roman arms to continue any longer. Hannibal must soon have heard the news that the Roman army was on the march, and permitted himself the luxury of a smile. Calmly and confidently he trailed his forces past the ancient city of Cortona to his left and moved towards Lake Trasimene on his right.

Like many other sites of ancient battles the area around Lake Trasimene has changed considerably over the centuries. A small flat plain to the north of the lake, surrounding the river Macerone, is largely the result of alluvial deposit (as well as a deliberate lowering of the level of the lake in the fifteenth century) and did not exist in Hannibal's time. The way by which Hannibal approached the lake was by the defile of Borghetto, 'Malpasso' as it is appropriately called, with the great misty surface of Trasimene and its two islets, Isola Minore and Isola Maggiore, lying mirrored in the waters on his right hand. To the left of him as the army came into what was then a small basin, the valley of the river, the hills bulked up all round in the shape of a U. Barren or scrub- and cistus-tangled today, the hills most certainly held thicker coverage at that time. Once through the narrow entrance by Malpasso, a bottleneck with the water on one side and slopes the other, Hannibal could see ahead the long conspicuous ridge where the valley of Tuoro lies. Here, readily and immediately visible to the Romans as they entered through Malpasso, he would station a prominent part of the army.

At Trebia he had had to use some ingenuity to make the land work for him, but at Trasimene nature had prepared a trap designed for slaughter. Like the last chamber into which the great tunny fish are driven, the *camera della morte*, the lake shore provided the bottom and the hills to west, north and east the enclosing sides. East, then, on the long ridge Hannibal sited his best troops, the Africans and Spaniards. Drawn up formally with standards and banners, they would at once proclaim to the consul, as he came through the defile, that Hannibal had arranged his army for a setpiece battle, taking advantage of the fact that the legions would have to advance up a slope to attack. The Romans would not shirk that – and Flaminius with his eagerness to get at the enemy would not let the unfavourable approach deter him. On the western slopes, which ran down towards the lake and which would be on the left flank of the Romans once they had entered the basin of the Macerone, Hannibal stationed the Gauls and the Carthaginian heavy cavalry; and on the east, in an extended line, on flat ground below the hills he stationed his light troops, the slingers and pikemen. All was set. All that remained was for the long body of the Roman army to insinuate itself through Malpasso and then Hannibal, after waiting until they were all in place, would close the door. The Gauls and cavalry would drop down the slopes on their left and seal off the road behind them.

That night, Flaminius and the head of the Roman column reached the lake and encamped to the west, outside Malpasso. They had been following close on Hannibal's heels and they knew that he must be quartered not far away – somewhere ahead, perhaps on the far side of this neck of the great lake. They waited for the dawn.

It was a very misty morning – not so rare in spring – the damp air rising off and hiding the lake, and lying thick over the river valley. Eager to get to grips with the Carthaginian before he could move on further towards Rome,

Flaminius gave the order for the advance. Hannibal waited until the first of the consul's troops were in contact with his own men, stationed below the main body of his army, then the trumpets blared out, brazen and ominous through the mist. From the western slopes near Malpasso, north as far as the village of Sanguineto, the Gauls and the heavy cavalry came thundering down, taking the legions on their left flank and closing the passage behind them. To quote Livy: '. . . their onset was all the more sudden and unforeseen inasmuch as the mist from the lake lay less thickly on the heights than on the plain, and the attacking columns had been clearly visible to one another from the various hills and had therefore delivered their charge at nearly the same instant.'

Held in the front, and taken from flank and rear, the consular army had not even time to take up battle order when the waves of attackers hit them. The lake on their right, gradually emerging luminous and still as the sun rose, gave the legions no promise of hope. Through the wavering mists the wild Gauls, the heavy cavalry, and the gadfly Numidians came charging in again and again. The Romans were killed where they stood, or forced back, step by reluctant step, towards the shallow margins of the lake. All order – that disciplined order upon which the yeoman soldiery of Rome relied for their strength – was lost, or never even asserted, so sudden had been the attack. While the advance ranks, true to that stubborn courage which distinguished the Romans, fought their way steadily up the slopes towards the Carthaginian camp, the main body of the army and the rear were cut down in swathes. 'It was no ordered battle,' writes Livy, 'with the troops marshalled in triple line, nor did the vanguard fight before the standards and the rest of the army behind them, neither did each soldier keep to his proper legion cohort and maniple: it was chance that grouped them, and every man's own valour assigned him his post in van or rear; and such was the frenzy of their eagerness and so absorbed were they in fighting, that an earthquake, violent enough to overthrow large portions of many of the towns of Italy, turn swift streams from their courses, carry the sea up rivers, and bring down mountains with great landslides, was not even felt by any of the combatants.'

For three hours the battle raged in that small U-shaped stretch of land to the north of Lake Trasimene. Polybius, with memories no doubt of ancient Greece in his mind (the Spartans at Thermopylae, perhaps), records with fitting words the destruction of the Roman army: 'So there fell in the valley about fifteen thousand of the Romans, unable either to yield to circumstances, or to achieve anything, but deeming it, as they had been brought up to do, their supreme duty not to fly or quit the ranks.' The consul himself was killed by an Insubrian Gaul who recognised him from his armour and, remembering Flaminius' campaign against his fellows, took his revenge upon the man who had devastated his homeland.

The remnants of the decimated army, driven inexorably back before the onrush of Africans, Spaniards and Gauls, were massacred at the edge, or in the very waters, of the lake. Some 6,000 men who had been in the vanguard fought their way out of the trap and made their way to high ground, where they were able to see, as the mist lifted, the utter devastation of Roman arms. (The following day they were rounded up and captured by the Numidian horse under their leader Maharbal.) Hannibal, courteous as always in the rituals of war, ordered a search to be made for the body of Flaminius in order to give it decent burial, but, doubtless already stripped of his distinguishing armour, the consul was never found. Fifteen thousand Romans and their allies died in the battle of Lake Trasimene, and a similar number were taken prisoner. The Carthaginians lost 1,500 – one tenth of the enemy – mostly Gauls. True to his political aim of upsetting the allegiance of the allies with Rome, Hannibal sent the former to their homes with the message that his war was not against them, but only against the Romans. The latter were distributed among the army as prisoners and slaves.

The battle of Lake Trasimene was the greatest reversal of Roman arms that had yet occurred. So absolute was it, and coming so soon after their defeat at the river Trebia, that when the news of the disaster reached Rome, it could in no way be concealed. As the first rumours spread throughout the city, the people swarmed, like ants whose nest has been callously disturbed, around the main public buildings. The praetor, the senior Roman magistrate, a dignified figure respected above all partisan politics, consulted with the senate and summoned a meeting of the commons. 'There has been a great battle,' he said. 'We have been defeated.'

XIII

A PAUSE FOR THOUGHT

The spring of 217 B.C., which had begun for Hannibal with what seemed near-disaster in the swampy marshland around the Arno, had turned into a triumph. It was one that was engineered by his willingness to take the risk of approaching Etruria by an unexpected route, and then by his military genius at Lake Trasimene. This new victory was to be followed up by a further blow to Rome, when an advance force of 4,000 horse sent ahead by the other consul, Servilius, was met by Maharbal and the Carthaginian cavalry. The Romans had just crossed the Apennines and emerged into Umbria when they were sighted by Maharbal who was scouting ahead of the main body of Hannibal's army. In the ensuing battle all the Romans were either killed or captured, thus depriving Servilius of his scouting force as well as an essential part of his army. Since Servilius could no longer safely move his legions, Rome was to all intents and purposes deprived of both her consular armies and left defenceless.

No longer able to communicate with the surviving consul, for no one knew where the army or the cavalry of Hannibal was from one day to the next, the news of this further disaster reduced Rome to a state of deepest shock. Yet it is interesting to note that, even at this moment, despair did not enter into the Roman consciousness. Defeat was so little known to them, and for so long had they been masters of their chosen battlefields, that, as the historians confirm, they do not seem to have realised the full danger of their position. Other states at that period of history only needed one major defeat on the battlefield to abandon hope and sue for peace. The Romans, however, did realise that the situation called for a drastic change in the constitution. 'They did what had never been done until that day,' writes Livy, 'and created a dictator by popular election. Their choice fell on Quintus Fabius Maximus, and Marcus Minucius Rufus they made master of the horse. To them the senate entrusted the task of strengthening the walls and towers of the City, of disposing its defences as seemed good to them, and of breaking down the bridges over the rivers [the Anio and the Tiber]: they would have to fight for their City and their homes, since they had not been able to save Italy.'

Hannibal was now the undisputed master of the land, free to ravage and roam wherever the inclination took him. But his army, reconstituted though it was, remained an army of conquest, with no capacity for conducting siege warfare. He had no siege train – with its storming towers, its battering rams and its catapults, nor indeed any technicians for this kind of work – all of which were essential in order to reduce cities and garrisons and hold down a countryside. Already, at what seemed a point of triumph, the essential weakness of Hannibal's position was made clear: he could conquer but not consolidate.

But the greatest weakness of the Carthaginian lay in his lack of a political aim of any consequence. His immediate political aim was to seduce from Rome the allies within her confederacy, restoring to them their freedom. But freedom for what? They had known the advantage of living under Roman rule and law, and they were hardly likely to put these aside in order to return to the condition of something like the old Greek city-states. Hannibal was not proposing that Carthage should take over the dominant role now held by Rome and substitute Carthaginian laws, manners and financial control. His ultimate aim, it would seem, was no more than a return to the *status quo* before the First Punic War. If Rome and her allies and dependencies were content to stay within the sphere of Italy, even conceding Sicily to them, then all would be well. Carthage would continue trading throughout the Mediterranean and elsewhere, and the Mediterranean would carry on snugly divided into Carthaginian and Roman spheres of influence.

One may sympathise with Hannibal, but the lesson of history – if there is one – is that 'one cannot go back'. The world before the First Punic War, the world that his father Hamilcar had remembered and had pledged him to make new again, was far lost and gone. The collapse of Greece in the East, and the decadence of the Greek states that had come under the control of Alexander's generals and their successors, had left a power vacuum that must one day be filled. The very lack of territorial ambition on the part of Carthage – her lack of manpower in itself – meant that the energetic and expanding power of Rome would ultimately fill it.

The man who was chosen to act as dictator and rally Rome and the Latin allies at this hour of need was a Roman of the old type – one of those whose clean-shaven tough faces stare out from many a bust depicting the men of the Republic. Quintus Fabius Maximus, to be nicknamed from his caution 'cunctator', 'the delayer', was to prove the right man at the right time. Unlike the consuls, he was tied to no term of office and he had no 'name to make'. The family of Fabius was so well established in the history of Rome that it would have been difficult for an individual to have added to its lustre. Descended from Fabius Vibulanus, who had on three occasions been made consul in the fifth century B.C. – despite the fact that he had opposed the patricians – the Fabius who was elected to the supreme office to oppose Hannibal was a man who could command the support of the old aristocratic families as well as of the populace. Conservative by nature, Fabius was the first to appreciate that the Romans had been neglecting a number of religious ceremonies, and that others had been incorrectly performed. He made sure that in all respects the divine element was not neglected, thereby to a great extent restoring the morale of the citizens, while his practical efforts to ensure the defence of the city reassured both the religious and the pragmatic.

Fabius expected Hannibal to march on Rome, and concentrated his efforts on preparing the city and its citizens for such an event, but he may have been aware that the Carthaginian did not yet have a siege train with which to invest the capital. The non-appearance of his enemy may have suggested that the latter was away preparing his troops and making the mechanical and technical preparations necessary for the siege. Fabius had time, meanwhile, to consider his approach to this Carthaginian general who had invaded Italy – something no one had thought possible – and who had already displayed an aptitude for warfare that had shown up harshly the deficiencies of the Republican system. Fabius, as defender of the land, had time on his hands and he also had manpower. He took over the two legions of the consul Gnaeus Servilius and added a further two legions to the army that now lay at his disposal. At the same time he gave orders for all the people who lay ahead of Hannibal's line of march to abandon their farms, burn the buildings, and destroy the crops. (Centuries later his basic strategy was to be adopted by the Russian general Kutusov against Napoleon.) The people of Italy should withdraw into their land, leaving as little behind them as possible, and he himself – as commander of the only organised army – should avoid a pitched battle at any costs. Guerrilla tactics, harassing the flanks of the enemy, cutting off his foraging parties and gradually bleeding the invader to death, were the methods that Fabius was to employ against the general whom, very wisely, he was unwilling to meet on normal terms.

The one thing that Fabius had to do, he realised, was avoid defeat. The victory that he must aim for was not the traditional one upon the battle-field – something that the genius of his opponent rendered unlikely – but success achieved over a very long period of time, if need be. The presence of his troops must be used to reassure the allies and their cities that Rome was watching over them. Time and the extent of the land itself must be made to work for him. The Carthaginian's army must be reduced slowly, its morale snapped, and its opportunities for engaging him in a straightforward battle reduced to the minimum.

Hannibal had decided against an attempt on Rome itself and had moved his troops through Umbria and Picenum to the eastern coast of Italy. His army laden with booty and driving cattle before them reached the Adriatic and settled down to enjoy the fruits of their success, while Hannibal waited for the climate and the good living to restore the health of men who had endured a hard winter, had then been taxed to the utmost through the swamps of the Arno, and had finally gone on to win a great and decisive victory. Among their spoils were arms and armour captured at Trasimene and he began to re-equip his own men and the Gauls, training the latter in the use of the new arms and trying to instil into them some of the discipline of the professional soldier. The scorbutic disorders of the troops were relieved by fresh fruit and oil, while the horses which had been suffering from mange were restored by good fodder and by alcohol (wine) rubs. While the horses grew glossy and the tired men strong and healthy, he sent messengers by sea, possibly using vessels captured on the coast, to report on the state of affairs to Carthage. At no time did he make the mistake of thinking that his own campaigns alone could bring his city a conclusive victory. He would need support by sea or overland by the Alps, and it was all-important that the security of the empire in Spain should be preserved.

When Hannibal moved south Fabius followed him, keeping his men in the foothills of the Apennines whence he could send out raiding parties to cut off foragers and to harass the enemy's flanks. He made it clear from the start he would avoid any pitched battle and, whenever Hannibal seemed to offer him the opportunity, he carefully ignored it. The Carthaginian now recrossed the Apennines and made for the plain of Capua, 'the most celebrated in all Italy, both for its fertility and beauty'. But this was not the only reason, as Polybius observes, why Hannibal had decided to transfer his attentions from the east coast to the south-west: it was because 'it is served by those seaports at which voyagers to Italy from nearly all parts of the world disembark'. Hannibal hoped not only to terrorise some of the major cities into deserting the Roman alliance but also to open sea communications with Carthage. It is very likely that at this moment the only man in the Carthaginian army who felt any tremor of concern was Hannibal himself. Although he had been careful to point out to his troops that the Romans avoided battle because they were afraid, and that their spirit was broken, he was too intelligent to be deceived. Hannibal had taken the measure of his opponent and, as Livy tells us, 'in the silence of his heart he was troubled by the thought that he had a general to deal with by no means like Flaminius or Sempronius.'

The plain of Capua into which he had led his army was not only rich and fertile but also difficult of access. On the west lay the Tyrrhenian Sea and on the other sides lay lofty mountain ranges through which there were only three main passes, one from the territory of Samnium, the second to the north from Latium, and the third to the south, from the country of the Hirpini. Hannibal hoped that by threatening Capua, the richest city in Italy after Rome, he might draw Fabius down into the plain and engage him in a setpiece battle. He knew that there was in ancient Capua a party hostile to Rome and seeking independence from the Latin confederation. He felt confident that, if only he could destroy the Roman army, not only would Capua secede but also the rich seaports around the gulf of Naples. The peoples of these coastal areas were largely of Greek stock and he may well have hoped that they would prefer independence in the form of city-states to their present position as allies of Rome. In this he was to be disappointed, for he was to find that the mercantile citizens preferred the security that Rome afforded, while at the same time the Greeks had never forgotten their hatred of their Semitic competitors, the Phoenicians, and their descendants, the Carthaginians.

Hannibal now encamped on the northern bank of the Vulturnus (Volturno) and gave every impression that he intended to stay there, enjoying the richness of the land which his Numidian cavalry were sent off to harry with fire and the sword. The indignation which had been steadily growing in the Roman camp as they saw district after district of summer Italy going up in flames began to reach explosion point. In all their campaigns the Roman practice had always been to seek out the enemy, to march to meet him, and then by the combined skills of their arms and discipline to bring him to his knees. Yet here, in the very land of Italy itself, they found themselves – four legions of them – compelled by the orders of Fabius to trail slowly behind this Punic invader. Minucius, the Master of the Horse, a somewhat typical cavalry officer of the impetuous, fire-eating style, was leader of the dissidents. No doubt, having heard how badly the Roman cavalry had fared against the Carthaginians in previous actions, he was eager to prove himself and his men, and re-establish the proud supremacy of the 'cavalry type' over that of the low-born, pack-carrying infantryman. (Such distinctions had been common enough in Greece and were naturally not unknown among the Romans – nor among other European armies in the centuries to come.) Not only had Fabius to contend with the opposition in his own camp but he also had his detractors in Rome, and it was even rumoured that the dictator had been bought off by Hannibal (who had been canny enough to leave alone some property and land belonging to Fabius, while harrying the area around it so as to implant this suspicion). Nevertheless he could not be moved from his wise policy and did no more than follow Hannibal to Campania, encamping in the foothills of Mons Massicus where he could guard the pass through which the Carthaginians had come, and yet avoid any pitched battle with the enemy. An unsuccessful cavalry engagement, led by a young officer who belonged to the 'action at any cost' school, was turned into a rout by the Numidians. This proved the wisdom of Fabius' tactics, even if the lesson was not fully absorbed by all under his command.

Fabius had in fact acted with extreme discretion and great common sense in his approach towards Hannibal, and for once it looked as if the latter had fallen into just such a trap as he loved to set for others. Fabius had garrisoned the town of Casilinum behind the Carthaginian army, blocked the Via Latina by strengthening the troops already there, and held the Via Appia. The pass by which Hannibal had entered the plain was now guarded by four thousand men and was also overlooked by the greater part of Fabius' own troops from their camp on a hill in front of it. It was late summer and Fabius knew that Hannibal would soon have to move, for the land around, although rich and fertile, provided no suitable place for winter quarters. It was reasonable to conjecture that Hannibal would retire towards the east coast. The Carthaginian army, furthermore, was encumbered with slaves and prisoners, bag and baggage, loot and provisions, and thousands of cattle. When Hannibal approached and made his camp under the hill where the Romans watched and waited, Fabius felt confident that at last he had his enemy in a position from which there was no escape. He refused the pitched battle which he was clearly being offered and, as Polybius recounts it, 'thought that at least he would be able to carry away their booty without their disputing it and possibly even to put an end to the whole campaign owing to the great advantage his position gave him.'

Fabius, for the first time in his long pursuit of the Carthaginian, was allowing himself a little optimism and, to quote again from Polybius, 'He was in fact entirely occupied in considering at what point and how he should avail himself of local conditions, and with what troops he should attack, and from which direction.' His offer of battle having been ignored, Hannibal was not the man to waste any time, nor allow the Roman a chance to complete his dispositions and attack according to a careful plan of action. He summoned his commander Hasdrubal and ordered him to get together as many faggots and made-up firebrands as possible and drive some two thousand head of cattle to the front of the army. Before the night came down he pointed out to Hasdrubal a rise in the ground, above the pass through which he intended to lead the army, and told him to detail off sufficient army servants to manage a carefully co-ordinated cattle-drive. The wooden torches were bound to the horns of the cattle and then after dark, they were driven up the ridge which lay above the pass on the far side from the bulk of the Roman army. Hannibal sent some of his invaluable pikemen to accompany this strange task force and then, having ensured that his forces had all eaten and were ready for a night march, waited for the execution of his orders. As soon as the cattle were up on the higher ground he took the lead at the head of his heavily-armed troops, putting the cavalry behind, then the captured cattle, and placing the Celts in the rearguard together with his reliable Spanish troops. Suddenly the slope began to twinkle with lights and the silence was broken by the cries of men as they shepherded the beasts up and along the ridge. With firebrands burning on their horns the cattle ran wildly through the night in front of their herdsmen. Hannibal gave the order for his army to move forward and begin their march.

The Roman troops guarding the head of the pass saw the lights advancing over the ridge above them and naturally thought they were being outflanked. Despite the orders of Fabius that no one should on any account attempt to make a move against the Carthaginians, they set out to meet the threat.

> ... As soon as they saw the lights advancing up the slope, thinking that Hannibal was passing on rapidly in that direction, they left the narrow part of the pass and advanced to the hill to meet the enemy. But when they got near the oxen they were entirely puzzled by the lights, fancying that they were about to encounter something much more formidable than the reality.

The moving army that the Romans expected turned out to be no more than cattle – their drovers escaping into the night in the confusion. As they blundered about along the scrub-covered hill, seeking for a real enemy, the pikemen rose up amongst them. Out of the dark, out of the rough and boulders, the formidable Carthaginians, wielding the pikes that (as had already been shown) outmatched the legionary's sword in individual combat, moved in to kill.

Fabius and his staff, roused by the noise and the moving lights on the slope, were uncertain what to make of the whole issue. But of one thing Fabius was sure: he would not be drawn into any form of action until daylight, when he could see for himself exactly what was required. He, too, who had seemed to have eclipsed his predecessors by avoiding the traps set by the wily Carthaginian, had in his turn been tricked and deluded. He had set a snare for Hannibal and had been taken in by an aspect of it that he had never envisaged. Hannibal had taken the measure of his cautious and wily opponent and rightly presumed that the Roman dictator would never make a move during the night. He had also accurately conjectured that the troops who were guarding the head of the pass would never allow themselves to be outflanked by what they would reckon to be the passage of the Carthaginian army. Whereas before he had allowed the impetuous natures of Sempronius and Flaminius to lead them into situations from which there was no escape, he had calculated on Fabius' caution and arranged for it to work against him. While the main body of the Romans stayed in their camp, the army of Hannibal marched out in silence through the darkness.

With the light of day the Romans looked down and saw how they had been deceived: no Carthaginian army lay encamped at their feet. Before they could fully appreciate what had happened, Hannibal sent back some of his Spaniards to give assistance to the troops who had been engaged in the night operation. A sharp clash developed on the slopes where those weapons of deception, the long-horned cattle, were now grazing. The Spaniards and the lightly-armed pikemen were more than a match for the heavy legionaries on the awkward terrain and, after killing about a thousand Romans, made their escape and joined up with Hannibal's rearguard. The invading army, with its swollen baggage-train, its cattle and its prisoners, passed on in confidence.

XIV

THE DIVIDED COMMAND

Hannibal's successful evasion of the trap set for him by Fabius had solved his immediate problems, but had not affected the long term issue: the Roman army still remained intact and undefeated. This was clear enough to the Carthaginian and clear enough also to Fabius – if not to his men and his officers. To most of the army, and to most Romans remote from the battle area, Hannibal's escape was yet another example of the failure of the dictator's policy.

Hannibal now proceeded in a leisurely manner up the valley of the Vulturnus as far as Venafrum whence he appeared to threaten the eastern approaches to Rome. He hoped, no doubt, to induce Fabius to make some explicit move. When nothing was forthcoming he moved into Samnium, across the Apennines to Sulmo, plundering the land as he went, and finally storming Geronium, a rich grain depot, where he established a fortified camp. Yet, in a year which so far had been one of unequivocal success, Hannibal had not achieved what he had set out to do. Despite the fact that, in military terms, he had clearly demonstrated to the Romans and their allies that Italy was open to him to ruin and ravage as he would, and despite his proven superiority in arms and generalship over the Romans, not a single town had come over to the Carthaginian cause. The Roman confederacy remained as solid as a rock.

Fabius, true to his principles, had done no more than follow Hannibal across the Apennines into Apulia, and had camped not far away from the Carthaginian base at Geronium. His strategy remained the same: to cut off stragglers, harass the enemy's foraging parties, but to avoid action on the battlefield. In the autumn of that year he was recalled to Rome, officially to attend to some religious duties incumbent on him as dictator, but probably also to face the critics of his military policy. Before he left he is said to have enjoined Minucius and the other senior officers on no account to enter into any major action.

Marcus Minucius Rufus, the Master of the Horse, although as eager to get to grips with the enemy as some of his predecessors, was an able soldier and well capable of seeing the advantages of Fabius' methods. He decided, however, to improve upon them and, having noticed that Hannibal and his men had grown casual through contempt of the Romans, took advantage of their relaxed foraging methods. Observing that something like two-thirds of Hannibal's forces were scattered throughout the countryside and only one-third left behind in their base at Geronium, he sent out his cavalry and light troops to attack the foraging parties. A great many of the plunderers were killed and Minucius was sufficiently emboldened to make a direct attack on the Carthaginian camp itself. For the first time since he had entered Italy Hannibal found himself in an embarrassing and disadvantageous position, from which he was only extricated by the return of a large party led by his commander Hasdrubal. If Hannibal had learned a lesson – more caution and less confidence – Minucius could rightly feel that he had given the Carthaginian a taste of his own medicine. The news of this victory, for such it seemed to be, was rapidly relayed to Rome where it had the desired effect. It was the first success that the Romans and their allies had had since the beginning of the war, and it appeared to show that an aggressive policy, when conducted with intelligence such as shown by Minucius, would pay dividends where the shaming, hesitant tactics of Fabius allowed the land to be devastated.

Romans of all classes seem to have felt that they had endured as much contempt from these invaders as could be tolerated and the news of Minucius' 'victory' inspired them with fresh hope. By an unprecedented decision it was agreed, at a meeting of the People, that Minucius should have equal powers with Fabius. This division of the dictatorship completely nullified its whole concept, and in effect – as least when it came to the direction of the army – reduced Fabius and Minucius to the same situation as if they had been two consuls. However, since the dictatorship was divided, this meant that there was an option open for each man to take two legions under his sole command, or to act as if they had been consuls with each man in command of all four legions on alternate days. The latter was refused by Minucius, with the result that when Fabius returned from Rome in the autumn of 217 B.C., there arose the absurd position of two 'dictators' in command of two divided Roman armies – and both men were of different persuasions as to the conduct of the war. It cannot have taken long for Hannibal to have found out what had happened, if only from the fact that the two halves of the Roman army were now in separate camps. Such a situation was made for him to exploit, and he did not waste time in deciding on a course of action.

His experience throughout the summer had taught him that Fabius was not to be drawn, while his recent encounter with Minucius had shown him that the latter, even if able enough, was capable of being lured into attack. He proceeded, then, to lay an ambush very similar in style to that which had been so successful at the Trebia and, using once again his assessment of his opponent's character, to make this factor work for him, as well as the lie of the land itself. Polybius tells the story:

There was an eminence between his own camp and that of Minucius capable of being used against either of them, and this he decided to occupy. . . . The ground round the hill was treeless but had many irregularities and hollows of every description in it, and he sent out at night to the most suitable position for ambuscade five hundred horses and about five thousand light-armed and other infantry. In order that they should not be observed in the early morning by the Romans who were going out to forage, he occupied the hill with his light-armed troops as soon as it was daybreak. Minucius, seeing this and thinking it a favourable chance, sent out at once his light infantry with orders to engage the enemy and dispute the position.

Eager to drive what he imagined to be Hannibal's advance guard from the hill and deny it to him, Minucius sent forward his cavalry, then himself advanced with his two legions. All the attention of the Romans was entirely fixed upon the hill where the preliminary battle was taking place. In order to convince the Romans that this was the main object of his interest, Hannibal kept sending forward reinforcements to assist his men who were holding the position against the Roman attack. The Roman light forces were gradually driven back by the weight of the Carthaginians and, as they retreated, fell foul of the legions advancing to support them and threw them into confusion. Now was the moment – and the signal was given. Hannibal's concealed troops rose up from all directions, and fell upon the legions in the rear. The whole of Minucius' army was now in a perilous position . . . another Trebia was imminent. They were saved only by the action of Fabius. For once 'the delayer' delayed no longer, and brought his own two legions to the rescue. Hannibal, seeing the fresh legions advancing, wisely abandoned the pursuit of Minucius' panic-stricken army and withdrew his own men. The Romans had lost many of their light troops and even more of their best legionaries.

It was a lesson that Minucius took to heart. He not only apologised to Fabius, while thanking him for his rescue, but also admitted that the whole idea of two dictators and the division of the army was wrong. He handed over his part of the command to Fabius and willingly relegated himself to his former position of Master of the Horse. The two separate Roman camps were broken up and the army once more composed itself into a single strong unit with one base: everyone acknowledging that Fabius was rightfully the sole leader and that his strategy had all along been correct. Hannibal was not slow to realise that this deliberate choice by the Romans of a new unity boded ill for his campaign. The willingness of the defeated troops and their commander to accept the leadership of Fabius, whom he had learned to respect over those summer months, showed a new spirit. 'Then for the first time,' comments Livy, 'they realised that they were fighting with Romans and in Italy.' During the campaign of the past year, and ever since the engagement at the Ticinus the year before, they had grown to despise both the Roman soldiers and their generals, but already there was evidence of change. 'And Hannibal is said to have remarked, as he was returning from the field, that at last the cloud which had long been hanging about the mountain-tops had broken in a storm of rain.'

Hannibal now had a stockade erected around the hill and linking this position up by trenches with his camp at Geronium settled down for the winter. Until the spring of 216 B.C. the two armies lay opposite one another, and the months went by without any further real action. Fabius' term of office as dictator came to an end and until the election of new consuls in the following year, Servilius, who had commanded the legions at Ariminum, and Marcus Atilius Regulus, who had succeeded Flaminius on his death at Trasimene, held the command. Hannibal had much to think about. The year which had begun so well for him, and during which he had nothing but success over the Romans, was not entirely happy for the Carthaginians. Things had not gone well in Spain. There had been a revolt among the Celtiberians, the Romans were consolidating their hold over the northern part of the country, and his brother Hasdrubal had withdrawn south of the Ebro for the winter. Everywhere at sea the power of the Roman fleet had shown that the control of the Mediterranean still remained firmly in their hands. He had not been able to take advantage of his victory at Trasimene by attacking the Roman capital; and not a single ally had come over to him. No reinforcements had reached him from Carthage and, as Carthaginian spies within the city must have sent word, seaports like Neapolis had declared their allegiance to Rome to be unshaken.

O'Connor Morris, in *Hannibal: Soldier, Statesman, Patriot*, has summed up the position at the end of the year:

And if Rome had been defeated by a great captain, her resources for war were still enormous. She had already summoned eight double legions to the field, the numbers of men in the ranks being largely increased, for the campaign of the coming year; she was about to oppose 90,000 men to Hannibal, who had not more than 50,000, three-fourths of them being, perhaps, Gauls; she had prepared an army to march into northern Italy, to prevent the Gauls from assisting their terrible enemy. Her stern national spirit, too, was as bold as ever; she sent threats to the court of Macedon, and to the Illyrian tribes, warning them that they had better remain quiescent; and with admirable wisdom, she refused gifts of money offered by Hiero, her vassal king in Sicily, and by several of the allied Italian states, accepting, however, their aid for the war.

The only news that may have inspired Hannibal with confidence was that the Romans did not intend to re-elect a dictator: they were reverting to the consular system. The names and the histories of the two new consuls may also have given him cause to feel that his enemies were repeating their old mistake. One was a partisan of the aristocracy and the other was a known demagogue. The former was Lucius Aemilius Paulus, member of a celebrated patrician family, who had held the office of consul in 219 B.C. and who had a good military record. He was known to be a staunch adherent of the aristocracy and had been voted into office by them for this second time in order to counterbalance the influence of his fellow consul, Gaius Terentius Varro. Two men more dissimilar could not have been chosen. Varro was a plebeian of ultra-democratic opinions who had managed to get voted into office by the people for his defamatory attacks on Fabius the dictator. His arguments, and those of his supporters, will be familiar to those who have observed the pattern of similar politicians in later centuries: the nobles had been seeking war for many years, and it was they who had brought Hannibal into Italy. It was their machinations, too, that were spinning out the war, when it might be brought to a victorious con-clusion; the consuls had employed the arts of Fabius to prolong the war, when they could have ended it. The nobles had all made a compact to this effect; nor would the people see an end to the war until they had elected a true plebeian, a new man, to the consulship. . . .

Hannibal would have been familiar with the nature of the two consuls, for he had his informants in Rome (Livy mentions one Carthaginian spy who was caught and had his hands cut off). He could only hope for some almost inevitable division of opinion between the patrician and the plebeian, something of which he could take advantage in order to force upon the Romans the battle that Fabius the dictator had denied him. Despite his triumphant record in Italy over the past two campaigning seasons, Hannibal badly needed a victory. He needed a victory so decisive that the allies of Rome would at last begin to break away from her.

THE BATTLE OF CANNAE 216 BC
Phase 1

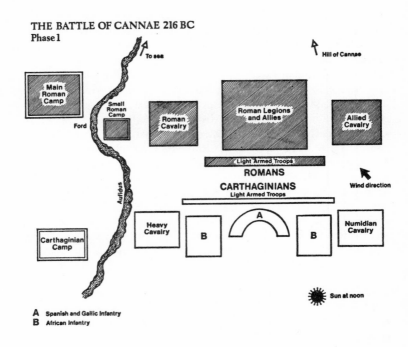

A Spanish and Gallic Infantry
B African Infantry

Phase 2

Phase 3

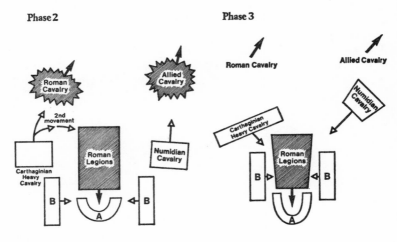

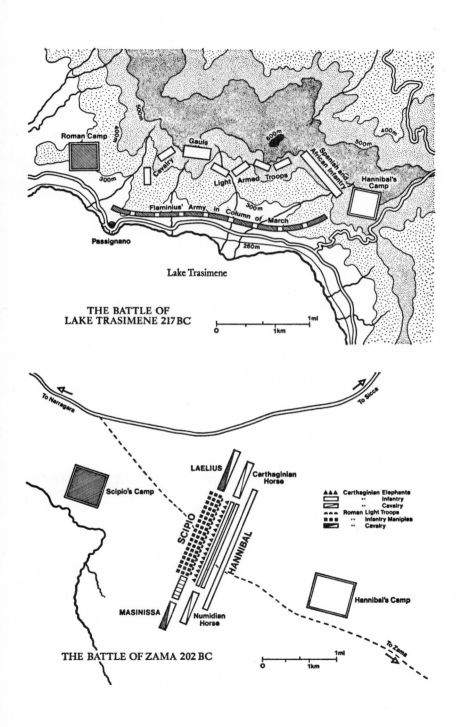

**THE BATTLE OF
LAKE TRASIMENE 217 BC**

Roman Camp

Gauls

Cavalry

Light Armed Troops

Spanish and African Infantry

Hannibal's Camp

500m
400m
600m
500m
400m
300m

Flaminius' Army in Column of March

300m

Passignano

260m

Lake Trasimene

1ml

0   1km

To Narragara

To Sicca

LAELIUS

Carthaginian Horse

Scipio's Camp

▲▲▲ Carthaginian Elephants
     ·· Infantry
        Cavalry
■■■ ·· Infantry Maniples
     ·· Cavalry

SCIPIO

HANNIBAL

Hannibal's Camp

MASINISSA

Numidian Horse

To Zama

THE BATTLE OF ZAMA 202 BC

1ml

0   1km

XV

CANNAE

In the spring of 216 B.C. Hannibal began to move. The grain of Geronium was almost exhausted and there was nothing further to be taken from the surrounding land. While the Romans maintained a steady supply system to their army in the field, Hannibal was always compelled to capture a rich depot or to live off the country, a disadvantage that he was to suffer throughout his campaigns. He marched southwards, and crossing the river Aufidus (Ofante), descended upon the town of Cannae. It was a place of no importance in itself, but it was one of the original Roman grain depots, and one from which they had been supplying their army. The town was sited on a hill that stood up abruptly out of an undistinguished plain through which the Aufidus flowed in serpentine fashion down to the Adriatic some six miles away. By seizing Cannae, Hannibal deprived the Roman army of a main source of supply, as well as securing more than adequate food for his own army. Furthermore, the early corn of Apulia was ripening and he was thus in a position to cut off the Romans from these future crops.

Servilius and Atilius, the consuls of the previous year who were still with the army, were in a dilemma. Until they had been officially relieved by the two new consuls, Paulus and Varro, they were technically in command. They certainly had no wish to give battle against the formidable Carthaginian, particularly since they knew that the army that was due to join them provided about the only hope that the Romans had of defeating their enemy. Apart from giving battle, their only real options were of following Hannibal at a safe distance and drawing their supplies from depots far away, or withdrawing the army altogether until they were joined by the new legions.

The senate were determined that year on battle. They had the support not only of the people but also of the equites, the aristocratic knightly caste. All sections of the population, although there was great division among them – division that had been fostered by men like Varro – were determined to avenge the defeats that Rome had suffered in the campaigns of the previous two years, and to expunge the slight that had been cast upon the Roman name by the presence of this Carthaginian general and his makeshift army in the land of Italy. Not only their honour and their traditions called them out to offer their services; it also seems that plebeians and aristocrats alike realised that Rome, not just the city but the whole concept of *Roma eterna,* had reached a crisis point. Although Rome was still a Republic, it was a fact that Imperial Rome had already begun to come into being – and no empire can survive which cannot deal with an invasion of its homeland. It was essential, to maintain the respect of the countries that were already under its sway, or were about to become so, that the invader should be annihilated. Determined, then, on a decisive battle on a grand scale the Senate gave orders for the proconsuls to remain with the existing army and make no move until they were joined by Paulus and Varro – and the new army of 216. So, to quote Livy: 'The will of the majority prevailed, and they proceeded, under the malign influence of Fate, to make famous the name of Cannae for the disaster that there befell the Romans.'

The legions under Servilius and the new ones under Paulus and Varro, according to Polybius, numbered eight in all – a figure which he himself describes as unprecedented. Certainly no Roman up to that time had had any experience of handling such numbers of men and, although arguments have been advanced to suggest that not more than four reinforced legions took the field, the disaster of Cannae – the total confusion in the latter stages – does suggest that things had got completely beyond the control of the consuls, something unlikely to have happened if they had been handling an army of familiar size. Livy is unsure of the constitution of the army and gives a number of variants, but the very minimum would be 45,000 men, exclusive of cavalry, and more probably 60,000. Polybius points out that each legion consisted of about five thousand men 'apart from the allies' and, if there were eight legions (40,000 men) and each legion was as usual accompanied by an equal number of allies, it is not difficult to accept the traditional figures of some eighty thousand men in the army that went to meet Hannibal at Cannae. Their great weakness lay in cavalry, of which they seemed to have had no more than 6,000. Against them Hannibal opposed 40,000 infantry and 10,000 cavalry.

Part of the argument which has arisen over the exact number of the Romans engaged at Cannae seems to have stemmed from the fact that commentators have been unwilling to accept that there could have existed such a disproportion between the size of the two armies: at the most the Romans being double the number of their enemy, and at the very least about a quarter greater. But enough examples exist throughout the ages of small forces triumphing over large ones, and at Cannae there were many advantages on Hannibal's side that far outweighed any numerical superiority enjoyed by the Romans. First of all, he was not only a genius of warfare but he was also in sole and undivided command. Secondly, his other commanders were exceptionally brilliant, had worked and fought together on many a battlefield, and knew and respected the quality of their leader. (Like

Nelson's 'band of brothers' they did not need any orders once action had commenced, for they completely understood one another.) Thirdly, the Carthaginian army, composite though it was, consisted entirely of experienced soldiers (soldiers who enjoyed the advantage that previous success had given them – complete confidence), whilst the majority of the Romans and their allies, on the other hand, were untried new levies. Last, and by no means least, the Carthaginians, by being first upon the scene, were refreshed and had had time to explore the whole area around Cannae and the Aufidus river, whereas the Romans were arriving after a long march at an unfamiliar place, and with commanders who were at variance with one another. Despite the disproportion in numbers, therefore, the real odds were in favour of the Carthaginian and it is extremely unlikely that Hannibal suffered much more concern than any general who is about to commit his army to battle.

Hannibal had at first encamped slightly to the south of the hill of Cannae. On hearing of the Romans' approach, he moved his troops across the Aufidus and set up a new camp on the west bank. Since the land on that side was even flatter and more suitable for cavalry, he hoped to be able to engage them where the superiority of his horsemen could more easily make itself felt. On the day that the two armies first came in sight of one another Aemilius Paulus was in command and, recognising that the land ahead clearly favoured a cavalry action, he cautioned Terentius Varro that the legions would enjoy more advantage if they moved up to hillier ground. Varro did not agree and on the next day, having the command, he decided to take the legions down to the Aufidus and face Hannibal across the plain. Although Polybius puts the speech to the troops into the mouth of Paulus, there can be no doubt that the following words reflected Varro's opinion:

> ... It would be a strange or rather indeed impossible thing, that after meeting your enemies on equal terms in so many separate skirmishes and in most cases being victorious, now when you confront them with your united forces and outnumber them by more than two to one you should be beaten.

Varro was well aware that this new army had been sent out to gain a great victory and to rid Rome of the Carthaginian once and for all. He had no use for any tactics that savoured of Fabius 'the Delayer', and talk about moving to hilly ground only made him the more determined to come down into the plain.

So the whole Roman army moved to the west bank of the Aufidus where they established their main camp, facing Hannibal's troops and about two miles away from them to the north. At the same time part of the army was sent across a ford to establish a smaller secondary camp on the eastern bank of the river. While the Romans were in column of route they were attacked by some of Hannibal's Numidian light horsemen and suffered a few casualties. This encounter was of no great consequence and the Numidians withdrew when they found themselves up against the heavy Roman cavalry reinforced by the legions. If anything, the Romans had the advantage in this first clash and a certain optimism must have been engendered by it, 'the Carthaginians not having had the success that they had hoped'. On the following day Aemilius Paulus resumed the command and 'seeing that the Carthaginians would soon have to shift their camp in order to obtain supplies, kept quiet, after securing his two camps by covering forces'. In this he was quite correct, for by moving across the river Hannibal was now on the far side from Cannae and his supplies. He again sent out the Numidians, with orders to harass the Roman watering parties who were busy working out of the smaller camp on the east bank of the river. Roman tempers became frayed as they saw this far camp besieged by flying squads of horsemen and their water supplies denied them.

It was June. The hot summer had set in, water was all important, and the plain around the Aufidus river was beginning to shake with heat. During that night, or early on the following day, the wind shifted into the south and a sirocco (known locally as a Volturnus) began to blow. Puffing up lazily along the Adriatic, and reaching the two encamped armies over mile upon mile of Italy, from the Ionian Sea and the distant Gulf of Taranto, the humid air brought up the dust of the land with it. A debilitating wind, the sirocco lays a film of dust and moisture on even the unencumbered traveller; the new legions, scarcely used to living with arms and armour, unlike Hannibal's veterans, sweated as the sun came up. Already it was the pitiless 'lion sun' of summer and men would have to contend not only with their enemy but with the greatest enemy of all in southern lands, the noonday heat. On that day, the fourth since the armies had come in sight of one another, it was Terentius Varro's turn to take the command, 'and just after sunrise he began to move his forces out of both camps'.

He crossed the river with the main part of the army and joined the smaller camp on the east bank. His reasons for doing so were not investigated by early historians, and yet this movement, which determined the site of the battlefield, is surely important. First of all, the second camp had been primarily established to provide a watering place from a convenient ford, and water would be crucial on a summer day. Secondly, by moving over to the side on which rose the hill of Cannae and its granary buildings, Varro was threatening Hannibal's food supplies. Thirdly, by being the first to move and to have his forces drawn up in line before the heat of the day began, he may have hoped to surprise Hannibal and, anticipating that the latter's forces would naturally move to meet the Romans, to catch the Carthaginian army while still in disarray after their river crossing. Fourthly, the land on the eastern bank of the Aufidus, though flat enough, possessed a number of undulations and irregularities which would make it more difficult for the cavalry. Varro did not act with precipitate stupidity. (Some historians have placed the battle of Cannae on the west bank of the river, but a careful study shows that this was not so. In any case, if it had taken place on the western bank it would undoubtedly have been called after the river Aufidus. It was the ship-like hill of Cannae that dominated the scene and gave the battle its name.)

As soon as he saw the Romans beginning to move on that steamy day, Hannibal sent his light-armed troops – the slingers and pikemen – across the river. He knew who was in command of the Roman army and he knew, even before the main body of the opposing troops began to debouch towards the river, that at long last he had brought the main body of Roman arms to battle. Ever since Lake Trasimene he had waited for this moment, and the year of waiting – foiled always by the temperate intelligence of Fabius – could now perhaps be brought to the necessary and dynamic conclusion.

The Romans were drawing up in battle formation as Hannibal and the body of his army crossed the Aufidus in two separate places and went into the tactical pattern that he had designated for them. If he had been fighting on the west bank of the Aufidus he would have put his light Numidian horse on his left flank where their mobility could be put to the best use, and his heavy cavalry on his right nearest the river where it would not matter so much that their charge would be restricted. As it was, drawing up his army in the land below the hill of Cannae, he put the Numidians on his right flank where they could again make use of the open country, and the heavy brigade, consisting of Spaniards and Gauls, on his left next to the winding river. They would be facing the cavalry of the Roman right wing and it was his hope that their greater skill and numerical superiority would enable him to crush the Romans on the river side. Next to them he stationed half of his African veterans, heavy infantry armed largely with equipment taken from the Romans at Trasimene. In the centre, where he himself commanded, he placed the bulk of his troops, the Spaniards and Gauls, with the other half of his Africans on their right, and beyond them the Numidian horse. Polybius comments that the Africans 'were armed in the Roman fashion. The shields of the Spaniards and the Celts were very similar, but their swords were entirely different, those of the Spaniards thrusting with a deadly effect as they cut, but the Gaulish being only able to slash and requiring a long sweep to do so. As they were drawn up in alternate companies, the Gauls naked and the Spaniards in short tunics bordered with purple, their national dress, they presented a strange and impressive appearance.'

Hannibal's brother Mago was with him in command of the centre,

Hasdrubal, Hannibal's staff officer, commanded the Carthaginian left, and Hanno the right, with the great cavalry commander Maharbal leading the Numidian horse. Meanwhile the largest army that Rome had yet fielded was drawn up against him in conventional manner with cavalry on each wing, the allied horse on the left facing the Numidians and the Romans on the right, next to the river, facing Hannibal's heavy horse. In the centre were the legions, line upon line of them : 'the maniples closer together than was formerly the usage and making the depth of each many times exceed its front.' It was hoped that, as on many another battlefield, the armoured weight of the disciplined legionaries would punch a hole clean through Hannibal's centre. Aemilius Paulus, capable but reluctant for this action which he considered ill-advised, commanded the Roman cavalry while Terentius Varro led the allied cavalry. Geminus Servilius, the consul of the previous year, commanded the Roman centre composed of the legions.

At that moment, as both armies faced one another and the sheer weight and numerical superiority of the Romans was plain to every eye, there must have been a moment of trepidation among the Carthaginians, and among the small group of staff officers surrounding Hannibal. Plutarch relates how one of them named Gisgo voiced the thought that lay uppermost in his mind :

'It is astonishing to see so great a number of men.'
Hannibal sensed his anxiety and decided to turn it in his own way : 'Yes, Gisgo, you are right, but there is one thing you have not noticed.'
'What is that, sir?' asked the puzzled officer.
'In all that great number of men opposite us there is not a single one named Gisgo!'

The small group burst into laughter, the tension broke, and the ranks of men behind them felt their confidence restored by the laughter of their leaders on the summer air.

By the time that the armies had drawn up in battle array – the light-armed troops, slingers, skirmishers and pikemen, advancing to initiate the opening stages – the sun was high in the sky. As it swung round to the south the Romans had it in their eyes, the Carthaginians at their backs. The sirocco began to blow more strongly as the day advanced, 'a wind', as Livy says, 'that blows clouds of dust over the drought-parched plains'. It lifted over the land behind the Carthaginian lines and blew steadily in the face of the Romans and their allies. When the trampling of thousands of men and horses, the clatter of armour and swords, the neighing of the horses, and the ordered shouts of officers and centurions had subsided, the two armies faced each other in the uneasy half-silence that precedes a storm. To the brazen sound of trumpets the light troops advanced through the dense air to make those first exploratory jabs at one another, like boxers searching for an opening.

As the armies began to move it was noticeable that the Carthaginian centre was drawn forward in a curious crescent-shaped formation, the cusp of this crescent projecting towards the enemy, 'the line of the flanking companies growing thinner as it was prolonged'. Hannibal was going to open the battle proper with his Spaniards and Gauls, leaving the heavy-armed Africans as reserves on either wing. They formed, as it were, strong rectangles flanking the projecting crescent. Dour and dark, equipped with their Roman arms, the African troops were like shadows on either side of the blood-lusting, war-crying demi-lune that projected beyond them.

The real engagement began with the Spanish and Gallic horse and the Roman heavy cavalry, both of them being constricted by the river. Only a head-on charge could ensue, and the Romans – the armoured knights who were eager to prove their virtue and patriotism in front of the plebeian legionaries – had the disadvantage that, unlike their opposing numbers, they had not lived and fought in the saddle for a number of months, let alone years. 'Both parties pushed straight ahead,' writes Livy, 'and as the horses came to a standstill, packed together in the throng, the riders began to grapple with their enemies and drag them from their seats. They were fighting on foot now, for the most part. . . .' The Romans, only a week or so out of their winter quarters, and many of them soft from the city, were no match for their enemy: 'Sharp though the struggle was, it was soon over, and the defeated Roman cavalry turned and fled.' The heavy cavalry stormed through the gap left by the collapse of the Roman right wing. Consul Aemilius Paulus, who had been in command, escaped unharmed in this savage action and rode to the centre where he put himself at the head of the legionaries 'cheering on and exhorting his men'. He was of the old Roman stock, conservative but prepared to fight even where he himself would not have given battle. On the Carthaginian right the Numidians had now come into action against the allied Roman horsemen, the Africans using the free scope of ground beyond them to avoid any head-on clash but wheeling about and attacking their enemy in shifts and dips and glides like birds of prey.

Meanwhile the main bodies of the two armies, the sweating infantry, had come into collision. Hannibal, 'who had been in this part of the field since the commencement of the battle', regardless as always of his own safety, led on the very troops whom he had doomed to sacrifice. The thin line of Spaniards and Gauls could not hold for very long against the steady, bludgeon-like blows that the dense mass of the advancing legions threw against it. Slowly but surely the cusp of the crescent yielded and fell back, first an indentation, and then a U-shape. The legions, close-packed from the start and without the mobility that their open maniple formation normally gave them, now began to pour in behind one another so that they were like a stream of armour bursting through a collapsing dyke. But on either side of the yielding centre the iron walls of the Africans stood firm. Unlike the legionaries who had headed the attack, and unlike the legionaries who followed them (compressed together, shoulder to shoulder, scarcely able to raise their sword arms), the Africans had so far taken no part in the fighting.

On the Carthaginian right wing the Numidians had triumphed over the Roman allied cavalry, ill-matched as the latter were against the most skilful horsemen in the world, and were now pursuing the enemy as they scattered. Among those who fled was Consul Gaius Terentius Varro, the man whose misplaced confidence had led to this bloody encounter on the field of Cannae. All the while the Roman legions continued to drive in Hannibal's centre. They had penetrated so far that the African infantry on the wings projected on either side like banks enclosing a moving river of armour. 'In the thick of the battle Lucius Aemilius Paulus fell as a result of many dreadful wounds. . . .' Hasdrubal, Hannibal's staff officer, who was at the head of the Carthaginian heavy cavalry, had meanwhile completely routed the Roman right wing and now swung his horsemen round behind the Roman legions, attacking the allied horse on their left. Already in disarray, or in flight before the Numidians, this thunder of heavy cavalry in their rear completed the collapse of the Roman left wing.

A trumpet sounded. The moment had arrived. Hannibal's tactic of double envelopment of the Roman legions was complete. The African troops, heavily armed, disciplined and fresh, made their move: 'those on the right wing, facing to the left, and those on the left wing, facing to the right.' Upon the struggling mass of Romans, now caught in the centre, the Africans moved in like the two sides of an enfolding vice. To complete this terrible trap into which the legions had plunged in pursuit of Hannibal's collapsing centre, their rear lines now found themselves assailed. The heavy cavalry, having completed the rout of the allied horse, had left it to the Numidians to pursue them as they fled, and had turned to take the Roman legions in the rear. Encircled, since the Spaniards and Gauls who had formed Hannibal's centre still fought on ferociously, contesting every foot of ground, the Romans were totally stricken by the closing in on them of the two wings formed by the Africans. Throughout that hot afternoon the plain below the hill of Cannae became a slaughter yard.

Livy writes that 'forty-five hundred foot and two thousand seven hundred horse were slain in an almost equal proportion of citizens and allies.' Appian and Plutarch give a total of 50,000 men, Quintilian 60,000 men, while Polybius puts the grand total of Roman dead at 70,000. The Carthaginians lost about 4,000 Gauls, 1,500 Spaniards and Africans, and 200 cavalry.

(Leonard Cottrell in *Enemy of Rome* comments: 'This ghastly toll of lives, the result of a few hours' fighting, is greater than the total number of men killed in the Royal Air Force throughout the First and Second World Wars. . . . More men were killed at the battle of Cannae than in the British Army during the murderous battle of Passchendaele in 1917, though that lasted for four months.') As well as Consul Aemilius Paulus, the two consuls of the previous year, Servilius and Atilius, were both killed, as was Minucius, the former Master of the Horse under Fabius. Eighty senators, two *quaestors* (state-treasurers) and twenty-nine military tribunes – more than half the total of those scions of noble Roman blood – died on that day. The body of the Roman confederacy was savaged beyond repair, and as Livy was to write many years later, 'No other nation could have suffered such a tremendous disaster and not been destroyed.'

XVI

HIGH TIDE

Terentius Varro, together with a small number of allied cavalry, rode to Venusia thirty miles away. Polybius comments that 'he disgraced himself by his flight and in his tenure of office had been most unprofitable to his country'. The astonishing thing is that when he did ultimately reach Rome, he was met by a great throng who congratulated him on not having despaired of the Republic. It was this flexibility – the sheer strength and vitality – of Rome's political institutions that was in the end to defeat Hannibal. In Carthage the fate of an unsuccessful and cowardly general was well known – he was crucified.

Of the surviving infantry an unspecified number managed to reach Canusium, among them one of the military tribunes, the young Scipio. This was one witness of Hannibal's genius who was to study and profit by it. (Years later on the North African battlefield of Zama he was to demonstrate that he had absorbed the lessons well.) Ten thousand men who had been left to guard the Roman camp and, if possible, to attack and seize the Carthaginians' main camp, were caught after the battle, two thousand being killed and the rest taken prisoner. The loot from the Roman camp and from the field of Cannae was considerable: arms and armour, horse trappings, silver and gold, horses and baggage. It is said that the gold signet rings, taken from the Roman knights who had fallen in battle, alone amounted to three bushels in weight. Hannibal, as usual, attempted to reclaim the bodies of his leading antagonists, but only that of the consul Aemilius Paulus could be identified, and this was given honourable burial.

At this moment of triumph, when it seemed that their enemies were irrevocably broken, it was hardly surprising that there were those among the Carthaginians who felt that the time had arrived for the march on Rome. Even less surprising was it that this sentiment should be voiced by Maharbal, a cavalry commander without equal, who was justified in feeling that much of the success obtained by the Carthaginians since entering Italy could be attributed to his superb horsemen. It is the nature of a good cavalryman to be hot-blooded and full of *élan*, and Maharbal now called upon his leader to make use of the opportunity that such an outstanding victory gave him. 'On the fifth day from now,' Livy has him saying, 'you shall dine as victor on the Capitol hill. My horsemen will go before you, and the Romans will know you have come even before they know you are coming.' Hannibal replied that, good though such words were to hear, yet he must have time to consider. At which Maharbal's famous and angry response rings down the ages: 'Hannibal, I see that the gods give a man many gifts, but not all. You know how to win a victory, but not how to use one!' Hannibal had no option. His army was not large enough to invest a city the size of Rome and starve it out, and he had no siege machinery.

'The Carthaginians by this action [at Cannae] became at once masters of almost all the rest of the coast,' wrote Polybius, 'Tarentum immediately surrendering, while Argyrippa and some Campanian towns invited Hannibal to come to them. . . . The Romans on their part owing to this defeat at once abandoned all hope of retaining their supremacy in Italy, and were in the greatest fear about their own safety and that of Rome, expecting Hannibal every moment to appear.' The reasons that he did not are known, but at the time it seemed inconceivable to the Romans that he would not follow up his triumph. The first news that reached the city after messengers had been sent out to see what had happened at Cannae was that the army had been destroyed and both its consuls killed. (It was not yet known that Terentius Varro was gathering 'something resembling a consular army' at Canusium.) There was no sign of a Roman camp, and the enemy appeared to be in possession of the whole area. It was as if those proud new legions, which had marched south to destroy Hannibal once and for all, had vanished from the face of the earth.

Hannibal's treatment of his prisoners differed slightly on this occasion, since he did not automatically allow the allies to return free to their homes. He separated the one from the other, but offered both allies and Romans their freedom on payment of ransom – the Roman payment being fifty per cent higher than that of the allies. He had more than enough prisoners and slaves already and, despite the wealth garnered from the battlefield, he may have felt that now was a good time to acquire as much money as possible with a view to the future payment of his troops. He took care once more to impress on the allies that his war was not against them but against Rome, and allowed a delegation of ten Romans to leave for their city in company with a Carthaginian noble, Carthalo. Whatever Hannibal's expectations, he was to be disappointed: Carthalo was not allowed into Rome and was told to be clear of the city's territories before nightfall. If Hannibal had hoped by his magnanimity to be given an opportunity of discovering the state of Roman morale, the Senate was equally determined that he should learn that there had been no weakening. After much debate it was decided that the delegates should be sent back to Hannibal with a message that Rome had no intention of ransoming her captured soldiers.

In this hour of disaster Rome showed that tough and enduring face which was to make her the head of a great empire. Although she could well have used these soldiers, it was felt and proclaimed that it was a Roman's duty to die rather than yield. The city embraced the Spartan code. There was hardly a mother within the walls of Rome who had not lost a husband or son in the campaigns of Hannibal: they were not allowed to go outside their houses in mourning. Fabius Maximus, 'the delayer', once more asserted the old Roman code, taking charge of morale as well as the work on the defences. Public mourning was forbidden, rumour and gossip were eliminated by the imposition of silence in public places, all bearers of news coming from outside the city were immediately brought before the praetors to reveal their information (but not allowed to discuss it afterwards), and sentries were posted at the gates to prevent anyone from leaving the city. The necessity for these stringent measures was reinforced when the last piece of grim news came through: a consular army in the north of Italy, under the consul-elect Lucius Postumius, had fallen into an ambush set by the Boii and had been massacred.

Livy, looking back at this moment in Roman history, accurately assesses the situation:

> The year before, a consul and his army had been lost at Trasimene, and now it was not merely one blow following another, but a calamity many times as great as before. Two consuls and two consular armies had been lost [at Cannae] and there was no longer any Roman camp, or general, or soldier. Hannibal was master of Apulia, Samnium, and well-nigh the whole of Italy. . . . Would you compare the disaster off the Aegatian islands, which the Carthaginians suffered in the sea-fight, by which their spirit was so broken that they relinquished Sicily and Sardinia and suffered themselves to become taxpayers and tributaries? Or the defeat in Africa to which this very Hannibal afterwards succumbed? In no single aspect are they to be compared with this calamity, except that they were endured with less fortitude.

Hannibal could not invest and destroy Rome, but Cannae did enable him to reap the fruits of victory in political terms. A number of towns in Apulia opened their gates to him, including Arpi and Salapia, while all Bruttium, with the notable exception of the Greek cities, and nearly all Lucania left the Roman confederacy to join the Carthaginians. Most of Samnium came over, to be followed in due course by Capua in Campania – the second largest city in the whole of the Italian peninsula, richest after Rome itself, and the most important among the confederation. Capua was capable of fielding an army of some 30,000 foot and 4,000 horse and seemed designed to be the capital of this new coalition of states which, under Hannibal's control, might form an Italian bloc stretching from the river Vulturnus on the west to Mount Garganus on the Adriatic coast.

What was significant, however – and it can scarcely have escaped Hannibal's notice – was that not one of the Latin colonies in the area had opened its gates to him and that the Greek cities likewise maintained their allegiance to Rome. The latter was of the most consequence since it was the Greek 'naval allies', as they were termed, who provided the backbone of Rome's fleet. Their ports of Neapolis, Rhegium, Tarentum and Thurii were not only prosperous in themselves but essential for control of the Tyrrhenian Sea, the approaches to Sicily and, indeed, the whole western Mediterranean. Polybius was anticipating when he referred to 'Tarentum immediately surrendering'. It was months before this great southern seaport fell into Hannibal's hands, and for the moment he still had no real access to the sea. He did, however, manage to get his younger brother Mago back to Carthage with the news about Cannae and a picture of the general situation in Italy. Mago marched through the 'toe' of Italy, the Bruttian tribes welcoming anyone who freed them from the interfering dominance of Rome, and embarked presumably in some Carthaginian vessel that had detached itself from a fleet which had already been nervously probing the defences of Sicily.

Hannibal badly needed reinforcements, particularly with regard to cavalry and to trained North African infantry. The brilliant hand-picked force with which he had left Spain two years before had suffered severe losses – excluding even the many men lost in the passage of the Alps – and the Gauls and other allies were no substitute for professional soldiers. Hannibal also needed money; mercenaries had to be paid, and the spoils from Cannae and the political successes that stemmed from it were not without a reverse side to the coin : Hannibal now needed men to reinforce garrisons, money to bribe suitable citizens, and above all a siege train. With his army of conquest he had made a brilliant showing that would never again be repeated in the history of warfare. Now he was faced with something that neither he nor his father, and certainly none of the senate in Carthage, had ever envisaged : the requirements of consolidation. Having no means to reduce walled cities, and having no spare troops to garrison them even if they yielded, he was faced with an insoluble problem : he could not hold down a whole country.

Hannibal's thinking – the Carthaginian thinking – was out of date. Having done the impossible, crossing the Alps to attack the Roman state from overland, and having successfully defeated them in the north, Rome should have surrendered. Having marched south and annihilated a consular army at Lake Trasimene, Rome should have surrendered. Having marched further south and completely destroyed the armies of the Republic, Rome should then have surrendered. Hannibal and the Carthaginians were thinking in terms of the past. Over the centuries first of tribal and then of extra-territorial warfare, the Romans had learned that one battle does not make a conquest. Hannibal was a commando-leader and he had achieved his objectives. No one had told him – nor had he ever foreseen – that he would now be required to command an army of occupation.

XVII

THE KINGDOM OF THE SOUTH

Hannibal's brother Mago might have expected that his reception in Carthage would be warm and appreciative, at the very least. He came to report to the elders of Carthage, and to what amounted to their senate, that their general Hannibal, son of Hamilcar, the founder of their empire in Spain, had avenged the wrongs of the first war against Rome, and that the nation which had humbled them by the terms of an infamous peace treaty was now beaten to its knees. He had evidence from the battlefield – the gold rings of the Roman knights among other things – of the extent of the victory that had just been won.

If he brought outstandingly good news, Mago had also some requests to make. Hannibal badly needed reinforcements in terms of trained infantrymen, more Numidian horse, and money. The opposition party in Carthage, led by one Hanno, a descendant of the Hanno who had been eclipsed by Hamilcar Barca, and a representative of one of the richest families in Carthage, was prompt with objections against sending Hannibal assistance. If he had won such great victories, why did he need more money and men? If he was making these demands when most of Italy was in his grasp, what would he have asked for if he had been defeated? Now, surely, after so conclusive a victory was the time to make peace, for it seemed doubtful whether the position would ever be bettered for obtaining good terms.

Though often discredited by subsequent historians, the peace party did have a point to make – and one which later events would justify. It is not surprising, however, that it was overruled and the decision was taken to send Hannibal substantial reinforcements. The bulk of these, some 20,000 infantrymen, were to come from Spain while, from immediate Carthaginian territory, it was agreed to send him 4,000 Numidian horse and 40 elephants. In the event, the major reinforcements never reached Italy. The position in Spain had seriously weakened during the two years that Hannibal had become master of the Italian arena. After the defeat of Hanno in 218, Publius Cornelius Scipio and his brother Cnaeus had gone on to drive Hannibal's brother Hasdrubal back south of the Ebro, and the Romans had also gained control of the sea along the Spanish coast. Throughout 216, while Hannibal had dominated Italy and concluded the humiliation of Rome at Cannae, the Romans had been consolidating their hold on northern Spain, as well as fomenting tribal unrest in the south. Hasdrubal, even though reinforced from Carthage, was hard put to it to maintain Carthaginian suzerainty as far south as the Guadalquivir, with the result that he could spare no troops to send to assist Hannibal in Italy.

On the face of it, however, as the year 216 drew to a close it seemed to the ruling Carthaginians that the prospects of ultimate victory were good. There was a revolt in Sardinia against the Romans and this could be fostered; northern Spain could yet be regained; Hiero, ruler of Syracuse, the ally of Rome, was dying, and in due course events there might offer the chance of regaining the whole island – or as much of it as suited them. Hannibal's successes put heart into a Senate that was always inclined to judge things largely by the prospect of immediate financial return. Three expeditionary forces were fitted out, one for Sardinia, and two for Hannibal in Italy. Only the smallest of these ever reached him – the Numidians and the elephants – for Spain, main source of Carthage's wealth, was destined to receive the lion's share. It is significant that the reinforcements Hannibal was to receive as a result of the Carthaginians' decision had to land at Locri, a small port in the far south-west of Italy, because no major port was in his hands.

Intent on capitalising on his victory, Hannibal was in touch with Philip V of Macedon, a perspicacious and energetic ruler who had a long-standing grievance against Rome for her interference in Adriatic affairs, and who saw in the Carthaginian successes in Italy a chance to improve his own position in Greece. For him, as for so many others in Greece and the East, Rome was the enemy, the principal threat to independence of action, and he well understood the old saying 'My enemy's enemy is my friend'. In the summer of 215 he and Hannibal were to sign a treaty (preserved by Polybius) in which both parties, while in no way committing themselves, agreed on an alliance against Rome.

The Roman senate had no cause to feel anything but grave alarm in the latter months of what must be called 'The Year of Cannae'. The misery and gloom which shrouded the city took the people back from the straightforward atmosphere of the Republic into something darker, something that cried out from the very roots of an old peasant stock whose pragmatism had never quite overlaid the religion and the superstitions of the Etruscans whom they had conquered so many years before. The sacred Sibylline Books were consulted and an embassy was sent to Delphi to ask the advice of one of the oldest oracles in the Mediterranean world. Just as some two thousand years later, in the midst of more sophisticated wars, people have felt that their errors and sins have brought this calamity upon themselves, so the temples were crowded then, and every effort was made to uncover the reason for the wrath of the gods – and to appease it. Two Vestal Virgins, who might at other times have gone undiscovered in their sins of the flesh, were found to be unworthy of their celibate title : one committed suicide and the other was buried alive. The Romans, mindful though some of the educated were of the rationalism of Greece, even turned back to the darkest and oldest of gods (such as those whom the Carthaginians still worshipped) and reverted to expiation in human sacrifice: two Greeks and two Gauls were buried alive to satisfy this ancient thirst for blood.

'After the appeasement of this outbreak, however,' writes B. H. Warmington in *Carthage*, 'that fierce determination which had marked the Romans in the worst days of the First Punic War returned. As for the direction of the war, the voters from now on regularly chose candidates who had the support of the senate, since two of the consuls who had been chosen against its wishes were at least partly responsible for the defeats at Trasimene and Cannae. Tremendous efforts were demanded of themselves and the allies; the war tax was doubled in 215, by 212 there were twenty-five legions in the field, and all the while a fleet of 200 ships with 50,000 rowers was kept in being.' Rome, which had refused to ransom its soldiers captured at Cannae, now showed its iron mood: prisoners were released from jail on condition that they joined the legions and were prepared to fight for their country, and several thousand young and healthy slaves were bought from their owners and given their freedom on condition of their enlistment.

Temples and private houses were stripped of arms and armour that had been kept as battle trophies from earlier wars, and all craftsmen and artisans capable of working in metal were conscripted into the manufacture of armaments. The city had not forgotten its duty by the gods and it did not forget its duty by the material requirements of a war to the death. Another dictator, Marcus Junius Pera, was appointed, with Tiberius Sempronius Gracchus as his Master of the Horse. At the Trebia, at Trasimene and at Cannae the Romans paid bitterly for a policy of aggressive action. They now showed that they were wise enough to have profited by the lesson. Quintus Fabius Maximus, 'the delayer', had shown them the right course of action and henceforth they were to take it.

Hannibal now set about establishing, as far as he could, that kingdom in the south which the victory of Cannae seemed to have placed in his grasp. Capua was, of course, his primary consideration, for this rich, though politically divided, city seemed to offer a capital from which he could conduct his war on Rome. The city had not come over to him without considerable dissension among its leaders, but perhaps the decisive fact which led to them doing so was a Roman demand that the Capuans help them with money, grain and troops. The Capuans seem to have been a self-indulgent people and they shirked the burden of attaching themselves to a hard cause — especially when the army of Hannibal stood at their gates. On the other hand, they soon made it clear to the Carthaginian that their friendship did not imply any very active collaboration. He might not call upon any elements of their armed forces, although Capuans were allowed to volunteer for service with him, and in the whole area of Campania only local officials might have any jurisdiction. Similarly Carthaginian laws and customs were only to apply to the army of Hannibal but had no authority over the Campanians. Nevertheless Hannibal, who had hoped for the great port of Neapolis as his headquarters, but had been deterred by its closed gates and strong walls, had found a suitable and basically well-disposed capital city for his conquest.

It was apparent that the whole concept of the war on which he had acted was false. It was not enough to conquer dramatically upon the field, and then to dictate a peace that would confine Rome to her old boundaries and restore the Mediterranean world to the *status quo* that prevailed before the First Punic War. By refusing to yield even after their resounding defeats, the Romans had introduced a new element into warfare and were not abiding by 'the rules' which had long obtained among ancient civilisations. Hannibal has often been compared to Napoleon, but one of Napoleon's innovations was to unleash upon the eighteenth century kingdoms of Europe a new concept – total or 'people's' war. It was the Romans who now did this to Hannibal, by refusing to accept that defeat upon the battlefield implied defeat in the war. He had time during the winter of 216 to realise that he was faced with something quite novel: a war of attrition against a politically well-balanced republic. The Alexander of the Afro-Semitic world was faced with a problem that had never confronted the Greek Alexander in his campaigns against the kingdoms of the East.

North-east of Capua, dominating that fertile plain, rises the 1,800 foot head of Mons Tifata (Monte Virgo) which was to serve as one of Hannibal's main bases for the years to come. It had the great advantage that its summit was a plateau suitable for grazing horses and other animals, and that it commanded not only the plain to the west but also the valley of the Vulturnus, leading eastwards through the passes into Samnium and Apulia. It might be well enough for the troops and even Hannibal himself to winter in Capua, but it is doubtful (and he had good cause, if Livy is to be believed) that he ever trusted the citizens of Capua to any great extent. To suggest, as later Roman writers did, that the army, and even Hannibal himself, was 'corrupted' by soft living in the first winter in Capua is to imply that the Roman generals and armies who encountered him during the years to come were of very indifferent quality.

The year 216 was the high tide of Hannibal's success in the Italian peninsula, yet it was not until the autumn of 203 that he was finally to leave these shores. Throughout those years, despite one or two reverses, he was to maintain his hold over all this land with an army composed of dwindling numbers of North Africans and Spaniards and mainly of Gauls and natives of Bruttium and other southern provinces, where the influence of Rome had never been deeply felt. Notwithstanding the two thousand years and more that have intervened since the kingdom of the south was held by Hannibal it is possible to feel that his shadow still lies across all this land. 'Africa comincia a Napoli' ('Africa begins at Naples'), say modern Romans when they wish to disparage all this territory to the south. It is probable that the phrase originated during those later centuries when the Moors/Saracens/Africans and Ottoman pirates devastated the whole of this area. It is tempting, however, to think that the memory of Hannibal, which bit so deeply into the Roman consciousness during the classical period, has never been effaced.

XVIII

THE LONG STRUGGLE

At the beginning of the year 215 Hannibal was holding Mons Tifata, from which point he commanded all the Campanian plain. The Romans, who despite all their losses had eight legions in the field, were principally concerned with watching the routes north. Thus, Quintus Fabius Maximus, no longer dictator but now appointed one of the consuls for the year, was stationed with his army no more than ten miles to the north of Capua at Cales. The second consul, Tiberius Gracchus, was near the western coast at Sinuessa guarding the Appian road to Rome at a narrow point where the hills constrained it to the coast. At Nola, south-east from Capua and guarding the cities and ports that lay around the Bay of Naples, was the proconsul Marcellus with two legions. In Apulia, protecting Brundisium and Tarentum – since it was rightly feared that Hannibal might attempt to seize one or other of these valuable seaports – was stationed a fourth army under Marcus Valerius. All important routes were guarded and other smaller armies kept watch in Sicily and Sardinia, both areas where it was expected that the Carthaginians might make a landing. Rome was fully extended, and Hannibal, confident after his success of the previous year and his negotiations with King Philip of Macedon as well as with Syracuse in Sicily, could afford to wait developments. In the words of Arnold in *The Second Punic War*: 'Seeing the result of his work thus fast ripening, Hannibal sat quietly on the summit of Tifata, to break forth like the lightning flash when the storm should be fully gathered.'

During this year Neapolis was attacked on three occasions, but once again the weakness of Hannibal's position – his lack of siege equipment – was plain for all to see. The Romans were not slow to take note that any well-walled and well-defended city was secure against the Carthaginians. No doubt a corresponding feeling of relief was felt throughout Rome itself, even though so large a part of Italy was still denied to them. The inland towns of Casilinum and Nuceria fell to him, but by investment and not siege, and even the small Greek town of Petelia (Strongoli) in the south-west of the Gulf of Taranto managed to hold out for eight months before surrendering. With it soon went Cosentia and the useful port of Croton, once the dominant Greek city on the Gulf, whose defeat and extirpation of its rich rival Sybaris in 510 B.C. has passed into history.

By the end of 215 the Carthaginian army in Bruttium (modern Calabria) had overrun this whole south-western area of Italy, only Rhegium (Reggio) on the Strait of Messina holding out in its loyalty to Rome. As with the other important ports like Neapolis and Cumae, against both of which Hannibal had been unsuccessful, Rhegium owed its resistance not only to the strength of its landward walls but also to the fact that it could be supplied by sea, and the Roman fleet had complete mastery of that all-important narrow channel which divides Italy from Sicily. In the last years of the war, when the strength of the Carthaginian army was declining and the tactics of 'the delayer' were everywhere being applied against him, the region of Bruttium was to prove Hannibal's final redoubt in the Italian peninsula. In these comparatively early stages it provided a recruiting centre for the Carthaginians, now that they were so far separated from their Gallic allies in the north. Hanno, who was in command in the south, is said to have raised an army of some 20,000 out of Bruttium, mainly from the hardy mountain natives who disliked Rome and who had no feelings against the Carthaginians, as did the Greeks of the coastal towns.

Although unperceived by anyone at that time, the high water mark of Hannibal's success had been reached, and – so slowly as to be imperceptible for some years – the inexorable tide of fortune was beginning to withdraw from him. The atmosphere in Rome is well depicted by Livy, who, although writing so long after the events, had earlier and contemporaneous sources to draw upon:

Prodigies in large numbers – and the more they were believed by men simple and devout, the more of them used to be reported – were reported that year: that at Lanuvium ravens [always a bird of ill omen] had made a nest inside the temple of Juna Sospita; that in Apulia a green palm took fire; that at Mantua a lake, the overflow of the river Mincius, appeared bloody; and at Cales it rained chalk, and at Rome in the Cattle Market blood; and that at the Vicus Insteius an underground spring flowed with such volume of water that the force of the torrent overturned the jars, great and small, that were there and carried them along; that the Atrium Publicum on the Capitol, the temple of Vulcan in the Campua, that of Vacuna, and a public street in the Sabine country, the wall and the gate at Gabii, were struck by lightning. Other marvels were widely circulated: that the spear of Mars at Praenestra moved of itself; that an ox in Sicily spoke, that among the Marrucini an infant in its mother's womb shouted 'Hail Triumph!'; that at Spoletum a woman was changed into a man; that at Hadria an altar was seen in the sky, and about it the forms of men in white garments. . . .

The year drew to a close with the advantage if anything on the side of the Romans. An experienced old soldier, Torquatus, had successfully put down a Carthaginian-inspired rising in Sardinia; Claudius Marcellus, operating from his base on the hill above Suessula, had warded off Hannibal's attempts on Nola; and the capture of Philip of Macedon's ambassadors by the Roman fleet in the Adriatic had put the Romans on their guard against any immediate action arising from the alliance between Hannibal and Philip. On the other hand, the death of Hiero, ruler of Syracuse and an old and faithful ally of Rome, promised a new avenue of the war, for the kingdom was left to his grandson, a youth of fifteen, who opened communications with Hannibal and promised him the whole of the island in return for his assistance.

With the close of the campaigning season, Hannibal once more moved his troops over to the east coast of Italy and took up winter quarters at Arpi in Apulia. Mons Tifata was an admirable summer camp but unsuitable for wintering, and it is probable that he did not wish to inflict his army upon the inhabitants of Capua for a second time running. Capua, whose secession from Rome had seemed such a triumph, was to prove a millstone around Hannibal's neck, for without his help the city could not defend itself and he was to be called upon constantly for assistance in the ensuing years. Despite the continuing brilliance of his tactics the overall strategy now adopted by Rome was superior, and this year clearly marks the date from which he was compelled to follow a defensive pattern. This hardly suited his aggressive genius, although he was to show that even in this uncongenial role he was a master. It is significant that, although the Romans would continue to follow him wherever and whenever his army moved, they did not attack him when he was on the march. They had seen too much of his exceptional ability in extricating himself from what had seemed untenable positions.

This conflict in the Mediterranean basin and the lands surrounding it – the heartland of western civilisation – was soon to engulf the whole area. Within a year of the beginning of the war Spain had become a cockpit disputed between the two antagonists; Hannibal's invasion of Italy had brought Carthage and Rome into direct conflict for the first time on Roman soil; Sicily was now to become a major theatre of war; and Philip of Macedon's alliance with Hannibal was ultimately to draw the states and kingdoms of Greece into the Roman sphere of influence. In this war, the Hannibalic War, the four quarters of the Mediterranean were to one degree or another all to become involved.

The Semitic and African world to the south had challenged the European world to the north – involving the west, from Spain right up to the Rhône valley. The passes of the Alps had been stormed, and the Gauls both of Gaul itself and of northern Italy had been dragged into the conflict. Soon the First Macedonian War would start, when Marcus Valerius would cross the Adriatic and destroy the army that Philip was preparing for the invasion of

Italy, and burn the Macedonian fleet. Throughout the Mediterranean, ship-yards were permanently busy for the next ten years as, from Spain to Carthage itself, to Italy and to Greece, the powers sought to establish their dominance of the sea – that sphere which can be neglected by no adversary, but especially in a theatre where all are dependent on maritime communications and, ultimately, naval supremacy. For the year 214 the senate decreed that the Roman fleet should amount to 150 warships, the shortage of manpower for the navy being made good by taxing the rich on a sliding scale for the provision of sailors and their pay. Livy writes: 'The sailors furnished in accordance with this edict went on board armed and equipped by their masters, and with cooked rations for thirty days. It was the first time that a Roman fleet was manned with crews secured at private expense.'

The most important effect of these savage years was the slow but systematic devastation of the whole of southern Italy. As territory changed hands, so the new conqueror – whether Carthaginian or Roman – either plundered it to feed his troops or despoiled it to deny sustenance to the enemy. In 215 Fabius Maximus laid down that all crops of grain must be brought from the fields within the nearest walled cities by early June. Failure to do so would bear the penalty of the destruction of the farm concerned and the forced sale of all the farmer's slaves. The following year Hannibal, infuriated by the lack of response of the Neapolitan cities to his cause, ravaged all the lands around them and carried off the cattle and the horses. In the same year Fabius destroyed the crops and farms in the territory of the Hirpini and the Samnites, as a warning to all of what might be expected by those who showed friendship for the Carthaginians. In the course of the conflict the whole face of southern Italy was to be changed, the peasant farmer practically eliminated, and the path set for the long future of latifundia – vast estates owned by absentee landlords and worked by slaves.

The strength of Rome lay not only in the stability of her political associations, but also in her manpower. She proved this by putting under arms for the year 214 the better part of 250,000 men – the allies making their full contribution. Hannibal, with his dwindling forces which cannot have amounted, at the unlikely maximum, to more than 100,000 – most of them Gauls, Lucanians or Bruttians – was now confronted by no less than twenty legions. It was true that these had to be spread throughout the whole of Italy as well as Sicily, but it was a formidable war effort on the part of Rome which Carthage could never match.

Rome's fury at the defection of Capua knew no bounds: she was determined to threaten this 'capital' of the Carthaginian and to bring the Capuans, duly chastened, back within the fold of the alliance at the earliest possible moment. Appealed to by the Capuans, who were terrified by the threat ready to be applied against them, Hannibal moved from Arpi, brought his army down to the city, skilfully evading the consul Tiberius Gracchus at Luceria, and returned to his headquarters on the plateau of Mons Tifata. Livy writes: 'Then, leaving the Numidians and Spaniards to defend the camp and Capua at the same time, he came down with the rest of his army to the Lake of Avernus, with the pretext of sacrificing, in reality to attack Puteoli and the garrison which was there.' The strange thing about this statement of Livy's is that he implies Hannibal needed a pretext to attack Puteoli. He had already attacked or threatened many of the cities in Italy – and he needed no excuse for any of his other actions, which had already led to the slaughter of tens of thousands of men. Why then, one must ask, this visit to Avernus?

Avernus was one of the most sacred places in Italy. The lake, one and a half miles north of Baiae, was near the important Greek-founded cities and ports of Neapolis and Cumae. It was over 200 feet deep, being formed from the crater of an extinct volcano. Like the sacred lakes of South America, to which human sacrifices descended, Lake Avernus was dark, deep, and – to simple minds – not only mysterious but instinct with a very special *numen*. Surrounded by high banks, covered by a dense and gloomy forest sacred to Hecate (a threefold goddess associated with the moon, but predominantly a deity of the underworld), Avernus was the entrance to that mysterious lower world through which both Odysseus and Aeneas were believed to have passed. Mephitic vapours rose above the waters and legend had it that no bird could fly in safety over the lake, whence its name which in Greek meant 'Birdless'. The exact entrance to the underworld itself was supposed to be the cave of the Cumaean Sibyl – the last of whom had sold those Sibylline books to King Tarquin which Rome, as now, was wont to consult in moments of the gravest distress. Hannibal's reason for making his way here was probably rather similar; he had much blood on his hands and he wished also to know what the future held for him.

Men consult oracles when they are a prey to doubt and they wish to obtain some divine indication of what direction they should take, or a confirmation that the course they are holding is the right one. For the first time since he emerged upon the stage of history it seems possible that Hannibal was uncertain. Educated by a Greek tutor, he will have been familiar with Homer from his boyhood, and no doubt there was some prescribed ritual at a temple nearby which will have paralleled that adopted by Odysseus:

> With my drawn blade
> I spaded up the votive pit, and poured
> libations round it to the unnumbered dead:
> sweet milk and honey, then sweet wine, and last
> clear water; and I scattered barley down.
> Then I addressed the blurred and breathless dead . . .
>
> (*Trans. Robert Fitzgerald*)

It seemed that Hannibal's sacrifice in the gloomy regions of the dark lake had borne fruit when a small group of noblemen from Tarentum came to visit him. They told him they represented a party in the city which was favourable to the Carthaginian cause and that, if he would bring his army south within sight of Tarentum's walls, there would be no delay in its surrender. Not only was Tarentum the largest and richest port in the deep south of Italy; it was also ideally situated to serve as a communications centre, and a base if the Carthaginians could bring a fleet up from North Africa. Furthermore, in the event of Philip of Macedon moving a fleet and army across the Adriatic to invade Italy, Tarentum would serve as a disembarkation port and a supply centre. But the time was not yet ripe, and although Hannibal moved later in the year – after he had seen the corn harvested and safe within the walls of Capua – the provident Romans had forestalled him. The walls were manned against him, and once again Hannibal retired to winter on the Adriatic coast.

XIX

THE FALL OF TARENTUM

Whatever the dark gods at the gate of Hades may have told Hannibal it can hardly have been comforting – if the truth were spoken. Not only did that year see him without the capture of Tarentum, but his forces suffered their first, and only, disastrous blow that they were ever to suffer on Italian soil. Hannibal had sent orders for Hanno with his Carthaginian reinforcements and his newly recruited army from Bruttium to march north and join him in Campania. With this enlarged army he no doubt intended to try conclusions again with Neapolis or Cumae: the absence of an efficient seaport was bedevilling his whole campaign. Fabius, however, had ordered Tiberius Gracchus to advance from his position at Luceria to Beneventum and his son to take over Luceria in his stead. Hanno, who was marching north by way of Beneventum, was forestalled by the arrival of Gracchus and a pitched battle took place in which Hannibal's general was heavily defeated.

Although the Roman legions were largely composed of slaves (promised their freedom if they fought well), they were more than a match for Hanno's as yet untrained Bruttian recruits, and a relative handful of Carthaginian infantry and Numidian horse. Hanno himself escaped but the relief army upon which Hannibal had been counting was largely destroyed. Gracchus' victory was to give new heart to the Romans and led to their blockading and finally retaking Casilinum. Subsequently a number of small towns in Samnium and Lucania were attacked and captured by Fabius, Marcellus and Gracchus: they paid the penalty for their defection to the Carthaginian with many lives and the harsh confiscation of property. Hannibal could command the respect, confidence and admiration of the mixed troops who followed him over the years, but he could not command the wholehearted support of Rome's Latin confederation. The stern will and discipline of Rome were shown by the fact that, although Gracchus had decisively defeated Hanno, it was felt that not all of the legionaries had fought as well as they should. For the rest of that year they were ordered to take their evening meal standing up.

'Soft Tarentum' and 'unwarlike' was how the poet Horace was to describe the great southern port years later in the days of the Emperor Augustus. Certainly this city, which in its Grecian heyday had been the most prosperous in all Magno Graecia, was unlikely to provide a strong resistance against a determined attack. Here, at the head of the Gulf of Taranto, the indolent Ionian Sea and the prevailing south wind did not nurture a hardy race. In 281 B.C. when the Tarentines had been resisting the power of Rome, they had done so only with the help of Pyrrhus, king of Epirus, whose activities on Italian soil had given the Romans an early foretaste of what they were to endure at the hands of Hannibal.

Standing on low, flat land, Tarentum was unusual in the nature of its harbour. The main basin was large and protected to seaward by two islets, but there was also a small landlocked basin – the Little Sea – running deep inland with a narrow entrance. Hard by the mouth of this basin was a small eminence, no more than about 70 feet above the surrounding town, but sufficiently strong for it to have been turned into Tarentum's citadel. The Little Sea protected one side of the city, the Mediterranean another, and the third landward side was heavily walled and fortified. It was not the kind of place that Hannibal would have dreamed of attempting under normal circumstances. The Tarentines, however, unlike their fellow Greeks of Neapolis and Cumae, were suspected by the Romans, probably in view of their earlier conduct, of being untrustworthy allies. For this reason they had been forced to send hostages to Rome as surety of their good behaviour. Some of these were unwise enough to make an attempt to escape back to their city and, when recaptured by the Romans, were put to death with great cruelty – something which made the anti-Roman party in Tarentum even more hostile. They came to the conclusion that they would fare better under the Carthaginian, whose generosity to other towns and cities such as Capua was well enough known by now.

With the opening of the campaigning season in 213 B.C. Tarentum began to seem even more desirable to Hannibal, for he had the misfortune of losing the important communications centre of Arpi to the consul Fabius and – a rare blow to morale – some of the Spanish garrison had even deserted to the Romans. Informed that there was a pro-Carthaginian party inside Tarentum, Hannibal moved south but remained far away from the city. In this position he was potentially threatening not only Tarentum but also Brundisium, the two most important ports in southern Italy and the only ones, with the exception of Rhegium on the Messina Straits, still remaining in Roman hands. Hearing of his arrival in the area thirteen young Tarentine nobles, led by a certain Philemenus, left the walled city, whose gates of course were closed by night, and made their way to Hannibal's camp on the pretext of going on a hunting expedition. Captured by the sentries on the outskirts of the Carthaginian camp, Philemenus explained their political sympathies, and the beginning of a plot for the betrayal of Tarentum was hatched. To make their absence seem plausible upon their return, Hannibal allowed the young men to take back with them some cattle which they could say they had found straying and had rounded up. The same pretext was used on a number of other occasions. Philemenus being well known as a keen hunter, his return with cattle or game – some of which he was always careful to give to the Roman sentries – was accepted as quite normal.

Hannibal, who had pretended to be ill as an excuse for his unusual inactivity and accordingly had kept to his tent, waited until all the preparations for the seizure of Tarentum had been made. He had promised Philemenus and his fellow conspirators that the Carthaginians would neither garrison the city nor demand any tribute from its inhabitants. His army would be forbidden to plunder, with the agreed exception of those houses which would be pointed out to Hannibal as belonging to Roman or pro-Roman citizens.

Once Philemenus' nightly routine of going out to hunt had become so established that the Roman sentries thought nothing of it, and willingly opened the gates when they heard him whistle upon his return, the moment was ripe for Hannibal to act. Taking ten thousand infantry and some cavalry with him, and sending eighty Numidian horsemen to scout in advance, he left the main body of his army and moved up to a point about fifteen miles distant from Tarentum. The Numidians were ordered to kill any people that they encountered, so that no one should learn of the advance of Hannibal's troops. At the same time they were to raid the countryside haphazardly, thus confirming the Romans in their belief that they were no more than a foraging party and did not herald the advance of an army. Livy recounts the events of that night:

Hannibal's guide was Philemenus with his usual load of game. The rest of the traitors were waiting as previously arranged. . . . As he approached the gate a fire signal was given by Hannibal as had been agreed and from Nico [another leading conspirator inside the city] the same signal blazed; then on both sides the flames were extinguished. Hannibal was leading his men silently to the gate. Nico and his men attacked the sleeping sentries in their beds, slew them and opened the gates [the main Teminitis entrance]. Hannibal with his infantry column entered. . . . Meanwhile on another side of the city Philemenus was approaching the postern gate by which he was accustomed to come and go. His well-known voice and the now familiar signal aroused the sentry as Philemenus was saying that they had a boar so large they could scarcely carry it. While two young men were carrying in the boar, he himself followed with a huntsman who was unencumbered. As the sentry was marvelling at the size of the animal he was looking towards the men who were carrying it, and Philemenus ran him through with a hunting spear. Then about thirty armed men rushed in and, cutting down the rest of the sentries, broke open the adjacent gate. The Carthaginian column burst in and made their way silently to the forum, where Hannibal joined them. He then despatched two thousand

Gauls, divided into three units, through the city, each group being accompanied by two Tarentines to act as guides. Hannibal ordered them to occupy the principal streets and, when the uproar began, to kill the Romans everywhere but to spare the citizens of Tarentum. The guides were told to warn any of their own people whom they met to be quiet and fear nothing.

Already there was a great uproar (as is usual in a captured city), but what it was all about no one quite knew for certain. The Tarentines thought that the Romans must be plundering the city, while the Romans thought it was some kind of uprising treacherously started by the townspeople. Their commander, roused early in the uproar, escaped to the harbour where he was picked up by a skiff and rowed round to the citadel. Further confusion was caused by the sound of a trumpet from the theatre. This was a Roman trumpet stolen by the traitors for this very purpose and, being unskilfully sounded by a Greek, no one could tell what signal was being given and to whom.

When the day broke the Punic and Gallic weapons were recognised which ended the uncertainty of the Romans, and at the same time the Greeks, seeing slain Romans everywhere, realised that the city had been captured by Hannibal. The Romans who had not been slaughtered had fled to the citadel and, while order was gradually being restored, Hannibal ordered all the citizens, except those who had followed the Romans in their retreat to the citadel, to assemble without arms. Then he spoke to them with friendly words, reminding them of how he had released their fellow citizens who had been captured at Trasimene or Cannae. He inveighed against the haughty rule of the Romans and then bade each citizen to go to his home and write upon the door the word 'Tarentine'. After the assembly had been sent away and all the doors had been marked, Hannibal released his troops to plunder the houses of the Romans, and the booty was considerable.

Hannibal's commando tactics, aided by his fifth column within the walls, secured for him a great port and a prosperous city, though his success was somewhat nullified by the fact that the Roman garrison and their sympathisers still held the citadel, and were not to be dislodged from it. An attack on it failed, and Hannibal was forced to try to seal it off by an earthwork. This proved ineffectual, for the position of the citadel on its promontory commanding the entrance to the inner harbour meant that the garrison and its other inmates could be reinforced and fed from the open sea, where the Roman fleet had naval superiority. Furthermore, all the Tarentine ships were now bottled up in the inner harbour, the Little Sea, and it looked at first as if they were permanently trapped. Hannibal solved this by having the ships dragged onto the land and then moved through the streets of Tarentum on wheels, before being launched again into the outer harbour.

The betrayal and the capture of the city, and even the ingenious method of freeing the ships, all bore the stamp of Hannibal. The fact that Tarentum fell by treachery was one of the arguments later used by the Romans to accuse Hannibal of 'Punic faith' or double-dealing. It only remains to be said that, throughout the whole of the history of warfare, the betrayal of a city from within by a party favourable to the besiegers has always been a common practice. The early history of Greece abounds in accounts of just such stratagems. There is nothing in any way peculiarly 'Punic' about it.

Leaving the citizens themselves to cope with the problem of the garrison in the citadel, Hannibal moved out his troops (as he had promised the Tarentines he would do) and shortly afterwards took them back to winter quarters. Metapontum, on the Gulf of Taranto and slightly to the west, soon came over to him while Thurii, another Greek port on the far side of the Gulf, fell to an army under Hanno and Mago, the townspeople opening the gates to the Carthaginians. Despite the loss of Arpi, the year finally had proved favourable to Hannibal, and the only large ports in southern Italy, below the Bay of Neapolis, that still remained in Roman hands were Brundisium on the Adriatic coast and Rhegium on the Messina Straits.

Polybius' comment that, 'Of all that befell both the Romans and the Carthaginians, the cause was one man, and one mind – Hannibal's', was clearly justified. Almost the whole of the Mediterranean world, with the exception of Greece where Philip of Macedon still hesitated, was now engulfed in flames. The main event in Sicily had been the accession to the kingdom of Syracuse of the young Hieronymus, who had at once declared for the Carthaginians – only to be almost immediately murdered by the pro-Roman party. This in its turn had provoked the Syracusans who favoured Carthage to kill or expel the rich merchants and others who favoured Rome. It is significant that here, and elsewhere in Italy itself, it was the popular party in its hatred of those who had grown wealthy through their Roman connections who favoured Hannibal. The poor and the dispossessed saw in him a leader who would free them from the heavy hand of Rome, but who would not thereafter concern himself overmuch, if at all, as to how they governed their cities. It is, perhaps, curious to see the autocratic warlord welcomed by the plebeians but we can see it happen time and again throughout history.

In Spain the war had been going well for Roman arms, to such an extent that one of the principal allies of Carthage, the Numidian king Syphax, now changed allegiance and declared for Rome. Since the Carthaginians depended so greatly on the skill and superiority of the Numidian horse this was a bitter blow, but one which was to be offset by further changes of political allegiances. The war had now spread to North Africa and another Numidian king, Gaia from eastern Algeria, was encouraged to take arms against his fellows and prevent the Romans from securing a foothold on the continent. Gaia's son, the young prince Masinissa, was to play a large part in the later story of Hannibal's campaigns. In combination with Hannibal's brother Hasdrubal, who had been compelled to take his troops to Africa to put down this threat in his rear, he crushed the rebellious Syphax, thus permitting Hasdrubal to return to Spain to meet the Roman threat in that quarter.

The war now exploded in Sicily. There can be no doubt that Hannibal, although he was constantly engaged in Italy against the ever-increasing tide of Roman arms, never failed to realise how important to his cause could be a Carthaginian triumph in that rich and powerful island to the south. Sicily had been for centuries the bone of contention between Greek and Carthaginian, and it had been the loss of Sicily to the Romans – through no fault of his father Hamilcar – which had led to the humiliating peace that had concluded the First Punic War. Two emissaries of Hannibal, Hippocrates and Epicides, had now been entrusted with the government of the great city and port of Syracuse after the expulsion of the pro-Roman party. It was essential for his overall strategy that the Carthaginians not only should retain their hold over Syracuse but also should gain control over the major part of the island. With the ports and harbours that had once been theirs – particularly in the west – they had a chance of breaking the Roman stranglehold upon the sea between Sicily and Carthage itself. The real difficulty lay in that, once the Romans had gained the upper hand over the Carthaginians in that sphere which had formerly been synonymous with the name of Carthage, they were never to relinquish it. Because his city, the Queen of the Sea, was never able to reinforce him properly, nor challenge the Romans successfully, all the years that Hannibal was to spend in Italy were in the end to prove unavailing. The influence of seapower upon history has never been more clearly demonstrated than in this great war between Carthage and Rome.

XX

SICILY

Syracuse had once been the most prosperous and important city in the central Mediterranean. In the fifth century B.C. at the time of the Graeco-Persian wars – wars which determined the fate of the West – Syracuse had been able to field more heavily armoured infantrymen and more ships than all of Greece. Now, although still of consequence, it had become something of a backwater, but a backwater that was enriched by the money and the artistic treasures of the greatest era of its parent Greeks.

Romans who visited the city were dazzled by the beauty of its architecture, by the visible evidence of wealth, by its vast theatre and its superb situation. The alliance of its former ruler Hiero had given the Romans not only a promise of stability in an always bedevilled island but also an acquaintance-ship with the rich treasures of colonial Greece. The Great Harbour, about five miles in circumference, had witnessed the destruction of Athenian powers in 413 B.C. The small harbour lying between the island of Ortygia and the capital was capable of housing a fleet. Its importance to the Romans as a naval base in the war against Carthage was obvious enough, while its loss, if it should be occupied by a Carthaginian fleet, would have been a dangerous blow to Rome and of the greatest value to Hannibal. If the Carthaginians could secure and hold Syracuse they had a lifeline to their capital and a major supply base for Hannibal's army.

It was for these reasons that the consul Claudius Marcellus had been sent to Sicily. In the confusion that followed the death of Hiero, a number of towns went over to the Carthaginian cause, notably Leontini a little north of Syracuse, commanding the richest and most fertile area in the island. Marcellus was a tough and distinguished soldier whom Hannibal had learned to respect as the man who had several times blocked him in Campania whenever he moved from Mons Tifata. Completely fearless, Marcellus in his first consulship in 222 had personally engaged a Gallic chieftain and killed him with his own hand. He had then dedicated his spoils, the *spolia opima*, in the temple of Jupiter Feretrius – the third and last time in Roman history in which such an outstanding offering was ever made. Ruthless to the defeated and in the imposition of military law, Marcellus was loved by his own troops for his concern about their welfare. After retaking Leontini, where he had some two thousand of the opposing troops beheaded as rebels against Rome, he moved south to invest Syracuse by land and sea. The Romans were masters at siege warfare and Marcellus had every reason for confidence. The Syracusan defences were overextended, particularly to the north of the island-fortress of Ortygia, where a large triangular area, only lightly inhabited, was enclosed by massive walls that would have required many more men for its defence than the Syracusans possessed.

Hannibal was fully aware of the importance of this struggle that was taking place to the south of him and had been in correspondence with Carthage about the necessity of landing an army in Sicily to lend a hand in the insurrection. With Sicily in Carthaginian hands the Roman dominance of the Strait of Messina could be challenged – thus reversing the process of the First Punic War and providing the secure base from which he could overcome those adamant cities on the Bay of Neapolis. So long as Sicily was basically pro-Roman his own position in southern Italy was always threatened. Some later historians have referred to the misuse of Carthaginian ships and manpower in the Sicilian campaign, arguing that they would have been better employed as reinforcements for Hannibal. It is very doubtful if that is how he himself saw the matter. Hannibal was not only a master tactician but also a considerable strategist: Sicily was the key to his ultimate success in Italy, since it now looked as if the help that he had been expecting from his brother Hasdrubal would not be forthcoming. With Tarentum secure and with the Romans unwilling to challenge him anywhere on the battlefield, it seemed that he could maintain his position in Italy for years if need be (which he was in fact to do). What he needed now was a success in the south: Sicily, with its rich land as a granary and its excellent ports for the use of the Carthaginian fleet. With this firm base behind him he would be able to move north in due course, after securing Neapolis and Cumae and eliminating the Roman naval threat in his rear, and come to grips with the heart of the adversary – Rome and the Latin confederation, which it was now clear would never be broken on a single battlefield.

These were the reasons why the Carthaginian fleet when it came did not make its way to the great harbour of Tarentum, but brought up instead on the long beaches of southern Sicily where, over many miles of barely inhabited territory, the overstretched Roman fleet could keep no permanent watch and ward. The harbour of Heraclea Minoa at the mouth of a small river was chosen as the disembarkation point, and here the admiral Himilco brought ashore 25,000 infantry, 3,000 cavalry and 12 elephants – a large enough force, it might have seemed, to secure all the south of the island before moving on to the relief of Syracuse. All seemed to go well at first and the principal city in the south, Agrigentum (Girgenti), fell to the invaders. But generals of the calibre of Hamilcar and his sons were always rare among the Carthaginians, and this army was in due course to come up against Marcellus.

The siege of Syracuse, undertaken with such confidence, proved to be protracted : largely because of one man. Among the inhabitants of the city was the great Greek mathematician and scientist Archimedes. Educated in the Alexandrian mathematical school, at a time when Euclid was teaching there, Archimedes (a friend, if not a relative, of Hiero) had enriched the city with his gifts of intellect, as well as constructing for the ruler numerous unusual engines of war. (Like Leonardo da Vinci, centuries later, he paid for the leisure and freedom to speculate, with practical work that could ensure the security of his patron.)

Marcellus had decided to attack the city from the seaward side of Achradina, the suburb of the old city on the northern side. Ortygia itself appeared to be almost unassailable.

Archimedes had supplied the ramparts with an artillery so powerful that it overwhelmed the Romans before they could get within the range which their missiles could reach; and when they came close they found that all the lower part of the wall was loopholed, and their men struck down with fatal aim by an enemy whom they could not see, and who shot his arrows in perfect security. If they still persevered and attempted to fix their ladders [to the seaward side of the walls], on a sudden they saw long poles thrust out from the top of the wall like the arms of a giant, and enormous stones or huge masses of lead were dropped from these upon them by which their ladders were crushed to pieces and their ships almost sunk. At other times, machines like cranes were thrust out over the wall, and the end of the lever, with an iron grapnel affixed to it, was lowered upon the Roman ships. [Livy's description inspired numerous artists in later centuries.]

As soon as the grapnel had taken hold, the other end of the lever was lowered down by heavy weights and the ship raised out of the water until it was made almost to stand upon its stern; then the grapnel was suddenly let go, and the ship dropped into the sea with a violence which either upset it or filled it with water. . . . The Roman soldiers, bold as they were, were so daunted by these strange and irresistible devices, that if they saw so much as a rope or a stick hanging or projecting from a wall, they would turn about and run away crying that 'Archimedes is going to set one of his engines against us.'

It was one of the first examples in the history of warfare of a superior enemy, in terms of numbers and of purpose, being thwarted and overcome by superior technology. 'So the genius of one man, Archimedes, defeated the efforts of innumerable hands.'

The Roman quality of dogged perseverance, which was to win them their empire, finally triumphed over Greek scientific ingenuity and those walled defences, which had made the Syracusans confident that theirs was the 'unconquerable city'. Repulsed in his sea-attack, Marcellus turned his attention to the landward side and – on a night when it was known that the Syracusans would be celebrating a great feast of Artemis – overran the weak fortifications in the north and swooped down on the city. (It never paid to relax when matched against the Romans, as countries from Persia to Britain were to learn in the centuries to come.) The struggle that followed was long and complicated. A Carthaginian fleet that had been in the harbour withdrew in an irresolute manner when it seemed that it might be trapped there by the Roman ships to seaward. Part of the Carthaginian army that had landed in the south was unable to reinforce the city and was compelled to take up quarters in the marshy delta of the Anapus river that fed into the Grand Harbour. As had happened before in the long history of Syracuse, the fever-ridden delta of the Anapus took its toll of the army encamped there and thousands of soldiers and two Carthaginian generals died. Hannibal's emissary, Epicides, who had been conducting the defence of the city, realised that all was lost and fled south to Agrigentum.

Late in 212 B.C. the marble and golden city fell to Marcellus and his Romans – men who had absorbed the courage of Sparta, without having the wit of the Athenians, but who possessed an organised discipline that most Greeks lacked. Allcroft and Masom in *A History of Rome* summarised the conclusion of the siege of Syracuse thus – the conclusion, it might be said, of centuries of Greek colonisation of Sicily, that great island which had seemed to the first Greek navigators the perfect 'new-found-land' and rich beyond all their expectations:

> In the autumn a Spanish officer opened the gates of Ortygia and Achradina, and the Romans were masters of Syracuse after a siege of more than two years. The usual atrocities marked its downfall; the city was pillaged, and most of its treasures of art carried off to Rome. Archimedes was cut down by a Roman soldier. The war in Sicily lasted two years longer owing to the energy of Mutines, a Libyan officer, who waged a guerilla war with the Romans, until the repeated slights of a jealous colleague led him in revenge to betray Agrigentum, 210 B.C. After this the island became once more a peaceful province, whose destiny it was to provide corn for its masters and submit patiently to the extortions of the governors, tax-collectors, and money-lenders of victorious Rome.

(The pattern of the island, one might say, was shaped for all its future history, and the nature of the Sicilian temperament irrevocably fixed into a mould of resentment and a determination to evade any conqueror's law by whatever means possible.)

Marcellus had given orders that Archimedes was on no account to be harmed (or so he said later), but legend has it that the great mathematician was so engrossed in working out some problem in a sand tray that when soldiers burst into his chamber and he disregarded their shouts to declare his identity he was run through with a spear. He was not Syracuse's only major loss, for innumerable art treasures of the city were now despatched to Rome. It has been said that this first major introduction of Greek art was to some extent responsible for the growth of the subsequent Roman admiration and emulation of Hellenic culture. In much the same way, many centuries later, the loot from Constantinople was to adorn Venice and fertilise the imagination of that city's artists and craftsmen.

The consequences of the fall of Syracuse were strategically very damaging to Hannibal. With the Romans in possession of the Great Harbour, and with their hold upon the Messina Strait strengthening their control of the sea approaches to Sicily and Italy, Hannibal and his army were even further cut off from their mother city of Carthage. Unless reinforcements could reach him from Spain by way of the Alps he was more or less marooned in Italy. Only his military genius, and the fear that his previous successes had instilled into the Romans, could preserve him from defeat.

XXI

THE MARCH ON ROME

In the spring of the following year Hannibal was largely concerned over the fate of Capua, where four Roman armies had been deployed with the intention of reducing the city by blockade rather than by assault. The usual appeals for help had already reached him from the Capuans. Since he himself was still in the region of Tarentum, he had sent Hanno from Bruttium to Beneventum to try to relieve the city. Hanno, having brilliantly evaded the army of Gracchus in Lucania, as well as that of Nero on his flank, had managed to slip through and set up a fortified camp which he turned into a grain store. The Capuans were asked to send every waggon and beast of burden available to take away the grain that he had collected for them. Fatally subject to inertia and ineptitude, the Capuans only managed to produce four hundred waggons, at which Hanno exclaimed: 'Not even hunger, which excites dumb animals to exertion, can stimulate the Capuans to any diligence.'

The Capuans were sent back with orders to produce further transport but by the time they returned with two thousand waggons, the Romans had got wind of the project and were ready and waiting. While Hanno was away with a foraging party, they attacked the camp and, despite a spirited resistance by the remaining Carthaginians, the position was stormed and the grain, the waggons, and other stores were captured. Hanno and his party managed to get away and retired in disgust to Bruttium. Capua, through no fault of its Carthaginian allies, was still left without supplies.

On hearing the news Hannibal despatched two thousand Numidians to go to the relief of Capua – something which was achieved by these astonishing desert horsemen by evading all the cordons around the city and managing to enter Capua by night. Heartened by this evidence of support, the Capuans rode out when the confident Romans were gathering in the corn outside the city. At the head of them rode the Numidians. Fifteen hundred Romans were killed in this sortie and the rest, demoralised by the unexpected arrival of Hannibal's great cavalry arm, took refuge behind their fortifications. At the same time they suffered a further shock. Gracchus, who was on the point of leaving his province to come and reinforce the blockade of Capua, was drawn into an ambush and killed. Hannibal, with his traditional attention to the courtesies of war, had his body given honourable burial.

He had sent his Numidians ahead only to act as an advance force, and it was not long before the consul, Fulvius Flaccus, was apprised of very unwelcome news. Mons Tifata was swarming with men, and its flat top was once again occupied. Hannibal, moving from southern Italy with extraordinary speed (faster than the Roman cavalry who had been summoned from Lucania, comparatively close at hand), had appeared upon the scene once more. He entered Capua in triumph, the two consular armies withdrawing before him — evidence of the awe still felt by the Romans at his presence, as well as of some unspoken agreement among them to adhere to the policies of Fabius Cunctator, even though the latter no longer commanded high office. Hannibal could not, however, quarter his army on the town because of the lack of supplies and when the Roman armies withdrew, he followed the one under Appius Claudius which was heading for Lucania as if to threaten southern Italy. As soon as the Carthaginian army had moved away Flaccus returned to invest Capua; not long afterwards Claudius gave Hannibal the slip and also returned to the city. By the end of the year six Roman legions were at Capua to begin the Roman practice of circumvallation : surrounding the besieged place with earthworks and trenches that prevented the inhabitants from leaving, as well as relief forces from entering.

Hannibal started back to Tarentum, where the Roman garrison in the citadel was still holding out; he was hoping, no doubt, that over the winter months he could succeed in dislodging them where the Tarentines had failed. The Tarentines! The Capuans! The great Carthaginian must have despaired of the quality of these wartime allies. . . . It was so evidently true that only the weak-spirited, only those with a grudge against Rome, ever came over to him. No members of the Latin confederacy deserted their old alliance and, if the Gauls and the Bruttians fought well on his side, they were undisciplined and semi-savage peoples who could not be used against Rome until they had been honed by training with his Carthaginian officers and men — and then only in a rough fashion to provide 'cannon fodder' while the real infantry and cavalry did the professional work.

Hannibal rounded off a year which, if it had not been very satisfactory for him, had certainly been an unhappy one for Rome. On his route back to Tarentum he came across a Roman army barring his path. Superior in cavalry — and superior largely because of the quality of his Numidians — he deployed them carefully on the wings. The Romans, advancing in their old-fashioned (as it had now become) manner, confident in the strength of their armoured legions, were cut to pieces, and the general, Marcus Sentenius Paenula, was killed. As if this was not sufficient for a foreign invader on his march back to winter quarters after the conclusion of a successful campaigning season, Hannibal heard that Herdonia, on the east coast in Apulia, was being besieged by the brother of the consul, Fulvius Flaccus, and turned his army north-eastwards across the breadth of Italy. He arrived to catch the unsuspecting Romans in the rear and, having laid a typical Hannibalic trap on the flank towards which he reckoned the Romans might turn, annihilated the enemy. Two thousand – or less – of this army escaped, and Hannibal secured his territorial position, then turned south again to ensure his troops adequate supplies and good quarters for the winter. Two Roman armies had been destroyed and two generals killed – all in a cursory campaign. Could any country, could even the senate of Carthage, have demanded more of one man – unsupported and far from home?

The following year 211 was to prove one of the strangest and most alarming in Roman history. Hannibal was torn between his desire to capture the citadel at Tarentum, which was still preventing the Carthaginians from using the port as their supply and fleet base for the Italian campaign, and the need to hold Capua. As Livy writes:

However, regard for Capua prevailed, a city on which he saw that the attention of all his allies and enemies was concentrated, and one destined to be a striking example, whatever might be the result of its revolt from the Romans. Accordingly, leaving in the land of the Bruttii a large part of his baggage and all the heavy-armed, with picked infantry and cavalry he hastened into Campania in the best possible condition for a rapid march. In spite of his swift movement thirty-three elephants managed to follow him. [He had managed the same thing before, in his march up the east bank of the Rhône.] He encamped in a closed valley behind Tifata. ... As he approached, he first captured the stronghold of Galatia, overpowering its garrison, and then directed his march against the besiegers of Capua. And sending word in advance to Capua, stating at what time he proposed to attack the Roman camp, so that they also, making ready for a sally, might at the same time burst out of all the gates, he inspired great alarm. For on one side he himself attacked, on the other all the Capuans, cavalry and infantry, sallied out, and with them the Carthaginian garrison commanded by Bostar and Hanno.

In the ensuing battle the weakness of Hannibal's overall position was clearly demonstrated: he could not carry a defended position. Although his hardy Spanish infantrymen broke through the Roman lines they were unable to force their way into Capua, and were cut off and killed. The Carthaginian cavalry remained, as it always had been, supreme in the field but this was insufficient when it came to attacking Roman legionaries in their entrenchments. Hannibal did all that he could to provoke the Romans out into an open battle, but they were not to be drawn. They had learned their lesson in the first two years of his campaigns in Italy. Polybius, himself a cavalry commander, acknowledges at this point that even this powerful arm was useless when it came to dislodging a tough and dug-in enemy. Furthermore, the co-ordinated operation with the Capuans proved a dismal failure, his allies being easily repulsed by the Romans, who were determined to make this renegade city pay the price for its desertion from the Latin alliance. Hannibal threw all the forces at his disposal into his attack on the Roman lines, quite apart from his Numidians and Spaniards who 'burst into the Roman camp unexpectedly'. The elephants charged with them and 'on their way straight through the camp were wrecking the tents with a terrible noise, and making the beasts of burden break their halters and flee.' Livy concludes: '. . . the elephants were driven out of the positions by the use of fire. However it began or ended, this was the last battle before the surrender of Capua.' As the Romans had found out, the elephants had their weaknesses; fire was one, and the other was to let them blunder through the lines and then attack them in the hindquarters.

With the benefit of hindsight, it would seem that Hannibal had made a strategic mistake in his attempts to relieve Capua. He had brought against the Roman positions a weight of forces that would have better been deployed against the garrison at Tarentum, thus freeing that great harbour for the Carthaginian fleet. On the other hand, elephants and numerical superiority meant little against a fortified citadel, with an internal water supply and a good store of grain. This was why citadels, garrisons and castles survived for thousands of years in the history of war. Only explosive projectiles and scientific mining methods put paid to the 'strong point'. Quick enough to sense his mistake after this failed combined operation to relieve Capua, Hannibal withdrew. There was only one strategic move left to him, one that has been used by many great captains, including Napoleon (who learned so much from Hannibal). This was to take his forces away and threaten the major piece upon the chessboard – Rome. He must have known, in view of his failure against lesser walled cities, that it could only be a threat and no more, but could the Roman legions surrounding Capua be completely confident that the capital would survive the attack of the great Carthaginian?

Hannibal's march on Rome, an event so terrifying that it was still being recalled by poets and historians centuries later, raises the interesting question as to what route he took. Livy is confusing, saying that he used the great Via Latina on the later stages of his march, while he has Fulvius Flaccus taking the more westerly Via Appia and reaching Rome before him. Polybius – often more trustworthy when it comes to military matters – shows Hannibal taking his army right up through Samnium to the east and descending on Rome from the north-east. Knowing from his other manoeuvres Hannibal's fondness for doing the unexpected, this route seems the more likely. Sir Gavin de Beer makes a further point: 'Marching through Samnium to Sulmo, and then through regions hostile to Rome, Hannibal passed by Alba Fucens where his passage is reflected by two rough-carved stone elephants, unmistakably African from the large size of their ears.' Burning and pillaging as he went, and with the Numidians harrying the countryside in advance of his army, Hannibal created a panic such as the city had never known before. He finally encamped on the right bank of the river Anio, only three miles from Rome – the desert horsemen, the Carthaginian heavy infantry, the wild Gauls and Bruttians, all visible to watchers on the walls.

After an inconclusive cavalry skirmish, in which Flaccus seems to have come off best, the two armies confronted one another, with the city as the prize at stake. But, as Livy tells the story, 'after the armies had been drawn up . . . a great downpour mingled with hail so confused the battle lines that, holding on to their arms with difficulty, they returned to camp.' It happened that the land on which the Carthaginian was encamped was up for sale and, even while Hannibal's army was occupying it, it is said that the deal went through – and with no reduction in price. Such tales may have been untrue – they flatter Romans of later generations by displaying the confidence of their ancestors – but the fact remained that at no time can the Roman defence have felt that the city was in any great danger. It was always the same story – without siege equipment Hannibal could not take Cumae or Neapolis, so it was impossible for him to capture what was then probably the most heavily-fortified and well-defended capital in the Mediterranean world. After a further delay, when violent weather again caused both armies to withdraw to their camps, Hannibal moved back to a position six miles away. He had seen Rome; it is just possible, as legend has it, that he had hurled a javelin at the Collina Gate to mock the impotence of its defenders. But he never entered the city of his enemies, and he was never to see it again. (An unlikely enthusiast for Hannibal was Sigmund Freud, who idolised the Carthaginian so deeply that for many years he was unable to enter Rome – because Hannibal had never set foot there.)

Hannibal's attempt to relieve Capua by threatening Rome had failed. No Roman army had moved up from Capua to check his threat; the two consuls were in Rome and with them two, and possibly more, legions behind those strong fortifications. He made the most of his march, however, plundering all the countryside around, ransacking the ancient shrine of Feronia, where gold and silver offerings dating from immemorial times went to pay for the service of his mercenaries. (It has always to be remembered that Hannibal's magnificent polyglot army had to be paid; it was no citizen body like that of Rome and had no allegiance except to one man.) Capua, it was clear, was lost, and Hannibal knew that well when he turned back from Rome. Inevitably he was followed on his march, and some of his 'tail' loaded with baggage and plunder was cut off. Failing at Rome, he maintained his usual indomitable spirit, turning back on the Romans and, in a night attack, mauling them so severely that they never harassed him again on his march. In many respects he resembled a great and noble animal out of Africa which was always strong enough to swing back and savage the predators at its heels.

Hannibal moved eastward towards the Adriatic and then made a feint at Tarentum, where the indomitable Roman garrison was still holding out, before moving rapidly south-east, right through Bruttium and arriving quite unexpectedly at Rhegium. It is probable that he had picked up some fresh troops who had wintered in Bruttium, yet his march remains one of the fastest and most memorable in the history of warfare. Nevertheless, even though he arrived so suddenly at the city that he captured a number of the inhabitants still working outside in the fields, treating them with kindness in the hope of making a favourable impression, Rhegium closed its gates and remained faithful to Rome. Despite his astonishing series of marches, despite his trouncing of the Romans in the night action and the rapidity of his movements, which had them always confused as to his intentions, the spring campaign of 211 had achieved nothing. Capua was doomed to fall, and with it Hannibal's dream of an Italian federation independent of Rome. Politically he had failed, and the Carthaginian hopes of isolating Rome and then destroying her almost at leisure were shattered.

Once the Capuans heard that Hannibal had withdrawn from Rome and moved south they recognised their fate. A decree of the Roman senate that the lives of any Capuans who surrendered to Rome would be spared was disbelieved, those who had been active in the conspiracy realising that nothing but death awaited them. Surrounded by the legions, on the verge of starvation, there was nothing for them to do but open the gates. Twenty-eight of the senators who had voted against the resolution committed suicide by poison and the sword. They were right in their estimation of the Roman desire for vengeance, and seventy who had been compromised in the decision to receive Hannibal were executed, along with many other leading citizens. The secession from Rome was viewed as what indeed it was, collusion with the enemy. Although Capua was not sacked, all its public buildings and lands were pronounced the property of the Roman people. Capua as an independent entity ceased to exist, and the Roman masters of Campania would from now on see that those rich and fertile lands were worked for the benefit of its Roman masters. All Italy, save for the deep south and Bruttium, trembled; and the cities and farming towns that had received the Carthaginian forces, in some of which Hannibal had placed small garrisons, became pro-Roman once more and rededicated to hostility against the invader. At a blow Hannibal was deprived of his connecting links with Samnium and Apulia and more or less confined to Bruttium and the southern coastline. Even here, with his failure before Rhegium and his inability to reduce the garrison at Tarentum, he was left with little scope for manoeuvre. Without an adequate port and with the Romans controlling the sea, he had little hope of ever receiving reinforcements.

The fall of Capua and the capture of Syracuse seemed to signal a disastrous year for Carthaginian fortunes. The only good news that can have reached Hannibal in the area that was to become his ultimate fortress in Italy was the triumph of his brother Hasdrubal in Spain – a triumph so great that it almost eclipsed these other losses. The two Scipios had advanced into the heart of Spain, far south of the Ebro, at first achieving considerable success. Publius Cornelius Scipio in particular was adept at winning the allegiance of many Spaniards and incorporating them into an alliance with Rome. But the return of Hasdrubal, after dealing with the Moroccan revolt, and his linking up with Hasdrubal Gisgo and Mago was fatal for the Scipio brothers' fortunes. Hasdrubal's influence over the Celtiberians soon proved its worth and the Scipios found themselves with overextended lines of communications, and more or less abandoned by their new Spanish allies. Apparently unable to join forces, the two Roman generals were engaged in separate actions. Their armies were cut to pieces and both the Scipios were killed. The disaster to Roman arms and the death of these two distinguished generals did much to reverse the balance in the overall pattern of the great Hannibalic war against Rome. Meanwhile Hannibal himself, although unsupported, remained undefeated in the Italian homeland. A constant threat to Rome and a constant concern to her generals, he was to remain there for a further seven years.

XXII

UNENDING WAR

The tempo of the war could only slacken. The losses sustained by both sides were sufficient to make them weaken as much from loss of blood as from faltering determination. The army that Hannibal had brought into Italy over the mountains must long since have changed its temper and construction; nine years cannot have failed to have taken a great toll of those veterans of Spain, France and the Alps, who had once gazed down with expectancy upon the rich prize of Italy.

There are no records, and one can only presume that, after so many engagements, the original strength of armoured Carthaginians had been heavily depleted – even though victorious in all their major battles. It is clear that the Numidian horse had been reinforced by transports from Africa. This light brigade of cavalry remains in evidence to the end of the long war but, curiously enough, there is no further reference to the heavy brigade of horsemen – although it is possible that Polybius and Livy merely assumed that they were always present. The main body of the infantry had certainly changed beyond all measure, Spaniards being replaced by Gauls, and they in their turn by Bruttians. There must also have been many defectors from the Roman camp – deserters (not the best of soldiers), Etruscans who had long hated the city that had overthrown their own state and, since the fall of Capua, Campanians who no longer dared to return to their own land. It was a heterogeneous force to lead against that formidable compound of states that Rome had annealed. Hannibal, with the fall of Capua, had also lost allies and there was little or no likelihood of their being replaced. Rome had shown how ruthless was her judgement against defectors, and only another victory of the immensity of Cannae could convince the states of Italy that Hannibal was the potential ruler of the whole peninsula.

Rome was also feeling the effort of sustaining so long a war. War-weariness was clearly evident on the Roman side and the burden of heavy taxation, to which there seemed no end, contributed to a general atmosphere of defeatism. As Livy puts it:

> Complaints began to be heard among Latins and their allies in their gatherings: that now for the tenth year they had been exhausted by levies of troops and their pay; that almost every year they fought in a disastrous defeat. Some, they said, were slain in battle, others carried off by disease.

The townsman who was enlisted by the Romans was lost to them more completely than a man taken captive by the Carthaginians. For with no demand for a ransom the enemy sent him back to his native town; the Romans transported him out of Italy. ... If the old soldiers should not return to their native places, and fresh soldiers continued to be levied, soon no one would be left. Accordingly, what the situation itself would soon refuse must be refused the Roman people, without waiting to reach the extremes of desolation and poverty. If the Romans should see the allies unanimous to this effect, surely they would think of making peace with the Carthaginians. Otherwise never, so long as Hannibal lived, would Italy be rid of war.

Twelve Roman colonies out of the thirty that comprised the Roman state revolted in 209, informing the consuls that they had no means left to furnish further soldiers or money. In order to pay the armies, even the sacred treasure of Rome, to which recourse might be had only in the very gravest of emergencies, had to be distrained upon for its gold. The senators were urged – and responded – to bring in the private gold, silver and jewels of their families in order to replenish the coffers of the State. Never in its history had Rome been reduced to such penury, and it looked as if the threat posed by Hannibal and his army was in no way likely to recede.

Although towns which had turned to the Carthaginians were restored to the Roman allegiance – Salapia in Apulia, for one, and Meles and Narronea in Samnium – the fearsome shadow of the invader still overhung great areas of Italy. When the Romans were rash enough to engage him, as happened at Herdonia, they learned the usual bloody lesson. Here the proconsul Fulvius Centumalus had been encamped against the town, while treating with a pro-Roman party within the walls. When Hannibal heard of the threat, he moved up from Bruttium by forced marches and engaged the two legions under Centumalus; his cavalry struck at the rear of the legions while his heavy infantry held them in the front. The result was another of those mortifying Roman defeats which, until the end of the war in Italy, made every Roman general tremble for his reputation when confronted by the Carthaginian. Marcellus, who had returned from his victory over Syracuse in Sicily, was one of the consuls for the year 210 and was the one Roman general for whom Hannibal evinced any real respect, saying of him: 'Marcellus is the only general who, when victorious, gives his enemy no rest, and, when defeated, takes none himself.' Hannibal's dry turn of phrase is revealed in a comparison he is said to have made between Fabius 'the delayer' and Marcellus: 'Fabius was a schoolmaster whom I respected, but Marcellus was a worthy foe: the one would not let me do any mischief, but the other caused me to suffer it.'

Marcellus was to share part of the campaign of 209, in which Hannibal was to lose his last important holding in Italy, the city-port of Tarentum. The other consul for the year was old Fabius Maximus, who for the first time was to gain an ascendancy over the man who had successfully challenged him on previous occasions. While Fabius brought his forces down from the north and proceeded to march on Tarentum, Marcellus harassed Hannibal and dogged his footsteps on his march in true 'Fabian' style. Apart from these two armies, Rome fielded that year a further one under Fulvius Flaccus, to reduce towns in Lucania and Samnium which had shown favour to the Carthaginians.

Hannibal's opening campaign, which had so very nearly succeeded, had been designed to break Rome's spirit by a series of massive victories in the field. He had achieved the victories, but still Rome had pugnaciously refused to yield. His second, and political, campaign had been designed to break the spirit of Rome's allies and, in doing so, to shatter the Latin confederacy upon which Rome must necessarily lean for money and manpower. Yet, after nine years and more of war, eighteen out of the thirty allies remained faithful to Rome and the twelve who had just renegued had done so only because their manpower was exhausted and their treasuries empty. Two major factors had always plagued Hannibal since he had realised that he must fight a war of attrition on enemy soil. The first was the lack of a siege train and the second the lack of trained heavily-armed infantry, which could only come from Carthage itself or Spain. The Roman command of the sea, established in the First Punic War, had clearly demonstrated that a state like the Carthaginian, dependent so largely upon overseas trade, must command the sea or perish. (This was a lesson that British statesmen and commanders, educated in the classics, had well absorbed by the time of their eighteenth century wars with France.)

It was astounding that Hannibal with his small body of Carthaginian officers and his dwindling corps of professional soldiers had been able to use the manpower of rough Gauls and primitive Bruttians to such effect. At the same time, while his own army, however well Hanno and others had recruited replacements, declined in strength, the Romans drew upon the powerful numbers of the large and relatively prosperous land of Italy. Only a major reinforcement of ardent and trained soldiers could give Hannibal back the initiative he had had when he entered Italy, and which he had subsequently confirmed at Cannae. This reinforcement must either come over the Alps from Spain or by sea from Carthage into southern Italy. The Romans of the Republic had learned much from their early mistakes in the field against a genius of war and had now permanently adopted the tactics of attrition against him. They had also learned a great deal of the necessary overall strategy for dealing with a war encompassing a large area – in this case the whole Mediterranean basin. While they were engaging the enemy in Spain they calculated that the first thing to do in the Italian peninsula was to prevent Hannibal from receiving any reinforcements from Greece or Carthage. The key to this was Tarentum, where the Roman garrison in the citadel had denied full usage of the port to the Carthaginian.

While Marcellus followed Hannibal's army and tried to lure him north-ward towards Apulia, distracting him sufficiently to make him turn aside on at least two occasions, Fabius Maximus moved swiftly towards the ancient Greek seaport. In the long run it was little matter that Hannibal turned back and fought off Marcellus, compelling his army to withdraw to their quarters at Venusia. Marcellus had achieved his object and, while Hannibal was en-gaging him, the army of his fellow consul Fabius had arrived before the walls of Tarentum. Like the citizens of Capua, the Tarentines had not over-exerted themselves in the Carthaginian cause (both had merely hoped for an easier and less-taxed life) and had signally failed against the Roman-held citadel. It is clear that Hannibal that year was expecting reinforcements from North Africa, for he was now distracted from the problem of Taren-tum by a siege of the port of Caulon in the south-east corner of Bruttium, carried out by troops now freed from concerns in Sicily. After mauling Marcellus so badly that he had been compelled to retire, Hannibal marched right through the heart of Bruttium and lifted the siege of Caulon.

He would have done better to have looked first at Tarentum, but one can only assume that he had designated Caulon as the disembarkation point for the Carthaginian troops, since it was an insignificant and obscure port in the deep south, well within friendly territory. There were spies everywhere in those days, and just as the Carthaginians had their own agents within the very walls of Rome so in every port where merchants came and went there must have been sharp eyes that provided information to one side or another in this struggle for the Mediterranean world. With their hold over the Messina Strait and their occupation of Syracuse the Romans were in a good position to know when and where a Carthaginian fleet was to be expected. Hannibal received no reinforcements that year by sea or by land. He was now to lose his last and only major port, Tarentum.

Leaving Caulon restored to Carthaginian hands and sympathisers, he marched right back along the 'foot' of southern Italy and round the great Gulf of Tarentum – to reach the city just after it had fallen. Despite his diversion against Marcellus to the north, and his further diversion to relieve Caulon in the south-east, he was only five miles from the city when Taren-tum was betrayed from within. The troops of Fabius Maximus, who had never been able to face Hannibal with any confidence upon the field, gazed out from the walls and mocked their enemy. Carthalo, the Carthaginian commander, had been killed in the fighting after the Romans had broken in, as had the two Tarentines principally responsible for the city's original betrayal. As he came within sight of the walls Hannibal is said to have been told by a scout what had happened and is credited with the cool comment: 'So the Romans also have a Hannibal. They have taken Tarentum as we did.'

Tarentum was to stand as a further monument to the Roman determination that all should know that receiving the Carthaginians was sadly unprofitable. As Livy recounts:

> Soldiers slew men everywhere, whether armed or unarmed, Carthaginians and Tarentines alike. Everywhere Bruttians also were slain, many of them, either by mistake or old, inbred hatred of them, or to blot out the thought of treachery, that Tarentum might be thought to have been captured rather by force of arms. Then from the slaughter they dispersed to plunder the city. Thirty thousand slaves are said to have been captured, an immense quantity of silver, wrought and coined, of gold three thousand and eighty pounds, statues and paintings, so that they almost rivalled the adornments of Syracuse.

It is noticeable that Livy, writing of the history and greatness of his city and her rise to power, does not omit such details of that iron ruthlessness which finally ensured the Roman empire. When Hannibal captured the city, he had been careful to ensure that there was minimum bloodshed and that only the houses of pro-Roman Tarentines should be looted.

He now proceeded to withdraw in the direction of Metapontum, across the bay from Tarentum, where he arranged for a number of distinguished citizens to go to Fabius and offer to betray their city if the Romans would move against it. Hannibal had his army concealed on either side of the route to Metapontum and there can be little doubt that if Fabius had moved, he would have fallen into a typical Hannibalic trap – from which neither he nor his army would have escaped. On this occasion, however, the Romans were saved by their religious observances, for Fabius, a man of the old school, would never march without taking the omens, and the priest on each occasion, after inspecting the sacrifice, found them unfavourable and warned Fabius that he must be on guard 'against the ruse of an enemy'. Knowing the reluctance of Fabius to make any move that could expose his men to unknown dangers it is more than probable that he himself had a hand in interpreting the sacrifices. His suspicions were confirmed when the citizens from Metapontum returned on a second occasion to inquire why the Romans delayed from moving against their city and, being arrested and threatened with torture, confessed the plot.

The loss of Capua and now the loss of Tarentum were accurately read by Hannibal as the disasters that they were. He is said to have remarked to his officers, 'Unless we can acquire new strength we have lost the war in Italy.'

He had hoped that Tarentum would serve as a disembarkation port for reinforcements from Carthage as well as for use by his Macedonian ally. With its loss he had even less hope of enticing Philip to move troops across the Adriatic to support the invasion of Italy. He remained undefeated in the field, but this in itself meant little. He could only look towards Spain and his brother Hasdrubal – and the news from Spain was bad.

XXIII

SCIPIO THE YOUNGER

The man who now emerged as one of Republican Rome's greatest soldiers came from an illustrious patrician family to which Rome was ultimately to be more indebted than to any other for the empire of the world. As their family tomb has revealed, the Scipios had been men of the greatest distinction in Roman history since the early fourth century B.C., consuls following consuls in a long line of merit on the field of war and in civil affairs.

Publius Cornelius Scipio was the son of the Publius who had recently been killed together with his brother Cnaeus during the fighting in Spain. As a youth of seventeen he had saved his father's life when the latter had been wounded at the battle of Ticinus, Hannibal's first major success in Italy. Two years later, after the disaster at Cannae, he had been one of the few survivors who had never lost heart and who had helped to rally the others and persuade some of the young noblemen not to flee the country in despair as they were preparing to do. His background was in some respects similar to Hannibal's – aristocratic and rich, powerful and intelligent – and he had had the opportunity from the time that Hannibal burst into Italy to study his great opponent's strategy and tactics. Another curious point of resemblance which was to display itself was that where the Barca family, ever since the arrival of Hamilcar in Spain, seem almost to have treated the land as a private province of their own, the Scipios also acquired a somewhat similar and accepted association with that strange, hot land – probably sealed by the blood of the two brothers who had recently died there. Scipio the Younger had been elected *aedile* (one of Rome's magistrates) three years after Cannae although he was extremely young for the position and was strongly opposed by many of the tribunes, on the surface because of his youth, but largely because they pursued the interests of other patrician families. In 210 Scipio, although only in his middle twenties, was elected to take the command in Spain. There were some who felt almost immediately that they had been rash to appoint such a young man to so important a post (he was about the same age as Hannibal when the latter had mustered his army for the invasion of Italy), yet the decision was soon seen to have been one of the wisest that Rome ever made.

The character of Scipio was complex and of a degree of sophistication that was little understood by his Roman contemporaries, or even by later historians such as Polybius and Livy. Like Hannibal he had been educated in the culture of Greece and he had the same intellectual curiosity and text-book knowledge of warfare, among other things, as Hannibal had had at his age – although less of the latter's experience in the field.

> Scipio [writes Livy] was remarkable not only for his real abilities, but thanks to a certain skill had adapted himself to their display, doing much of his actions before the public either as if they were prompted by visions in the night or inspired by a certain superstition, or in order that men might carry out his commands and advice, as though emanating from an oracular response. ... From the time when he put on the manly gown, there was not a day on which he did any business public or private without going first to the Capitol, and after he had entered the temple, sitting down and usually passing the time there alone in seclusion. This custom, which he maintained throughout his lifetime, confirmed in some the belief, whether deliberately circulated or by chance, that he was a man of divine race.

Two modern historians, Dorey and Dudley, have assessed him perhaps more sympathetically, describing his superior intellectual gifts, his natural courtesy, genuine culture, and real sympathy for people of other races. 'That he stood so clearly apart from the ordinary Roman nobles is the reason why he excited so much jealousy among them. As a soldier his greatness is un-disputed. He was one of the greatest creative thinkers in the field of warfare, and the tactics that he developed made the Roman army supreme for many centuries. He was also an outstanding field commander with a wonderful sense of timing, and could carry out complicated manoeuvres with success in the face of the enemy.'

He had learned much from Hannibal, and the major lesson was to be flexible in his thinking and not to approach every issue or every battlefield in the old Roman mould of unyielding consistency. In the event, the ap-pointment of Scipio to the important command in Spain fully justified the senators' faith in him. Within a year of his arrival in Spain he had struck such a blow at the Carthaginian empire that he had directly changed the course of the war. The Romans, dispirited on so many accounts – loss of prestige, virtual bankruptcy, immense taxation, and consciousness always of the dark shadow of Hannibal looming over the land – were to be uplifted by almost unbelievable news: Cartagena, New Carthage, capital of Cartha-ginian Spain, had fallen to the forces under Scipio. At one blow he had de-prived the Carthaginians of their finest harbour in Spain, the administrative capital of their Spanish empire, and the main source of their wealth and power in the West.

Arriving in Spain at the end of 210 with 11,000 reinforcements, Scipio at once moved down to Tarraco (Tarragona). Throughout that winter he met as many representatives of the Spanish tribes as possible, men who were confused by the constant shifts of fortune in the war between Carthage and Rome, but who seem to have been reassured by Scipio's confident air and invariable good manners. Like Hannibal himself, he seems to have possessed an innate ability to get on with the native people of other countries : not for these two patricians the arrogance of ordinary generals or the bluster of plebeian politicians. Thus Scipio's brilliance, it was soon revealed, lay not only in the field of warfare but also in a statesmanlike approach to the local inhabitants. The Spanish tribes, passionate, proud, and sensitive to slights, already bore the unmistakable mark of the nation that has evolved in the peninsula over the centuries. During that first winter Scipio learned to understand their nature, to make friends among their chiefs, and to lay the first stone in that mighty and prosperous province which would ultimately be Roman Spain.

In the spring of 209 he crossed the Ebro with 30,000 men and marched south on Cartagena, his army being accompanied down the coast by a Roman fleet. It was a well-planned amphibious operation and Scipio did not move without good prospects of success. He knew from his informants that the Carthaginian forces were divided into three, and that all were far apart : one under Hasdrubal near Saguntum, another under Mago in the interior, and the third under Hasdrubal Gisgo far to the south-west in Gades. This separation of command was not only due to rival ambitions among the leaders, but was also prompted by the very nature of the country itself. There was at that time no single area in which a large concentration of men could be based and live off the land. 'Spain', as Henry IV of France was to remark centuries later, 'is a country where large armies starve and small armies get beaten.' Scipio moved with the assurance that Wellington was one day to display when confronted by French marshals similarly rapacious and at odds with one another.

The garrison of Cartagena, small but confident because of the supposed impregnability of the city, launched a brave sally against the investing Roman army but was repulsed. The Roman fleet blockaded them from the sea, and Scipio, making use of local knowledge, had learned that a lagoon which protected the Carthaginian capital to the west could be forded through certain shallows when the wind was from the north, something which lowered its level by a foot or more. Over-confident about the protection afforded by this lagoon, the Carthaginians had left the walls on that side far less well fortified than those at the landward end of the peninsula on which Cartagena then stood (the neck of this peninsula has long since been filled in and is no longer discernible). Having tested the strength of the main walls and found that they were too high and too well defended for a successful assault, Scipio waited until a strong northerly was blowing, then, while the garrison was kept involved on the landward side, had part of the army attack Cartagena across the lagoon. The manoeuvre was successful, the Romans burst into the city and soon had the gates open for the main body of their army.

The Carthaginian commander withdrew to the citadel while the town was delivered to the usual rapine and massacre. Then, seeing that the situation was hopeless both by land and by sea – the investing fleet had drawn in to destroy and capture the vessels in the harbour – he surrendered. New Carthage, the capital of the rich province of Spain which had so largely funded Hannibal's war-effort, was lost. At this moment Scipio's control over his troops, so unlike that of Marcellus at Syracuse, was immediately exerted: the troops were called to heel and from then on Scipio displayed that courtesy towards the conquered, especially the Spaniards, that was to become the hallmark of his success. 'Of male free men about ten thousand were captured. From that number Scipio released those who were citizens of New Carthage and restored to them their city and also all the property which the war had spared to them.' Livy goes on to record how several thousand trained artisans were declared slaves of the Roman people but were encouraged to carry on working with the prospect of freedom in the near future if they exerted themselves in the armament industry. (They were also very necessary to keep the docks and shipbuilding industry going.)

Cartagena was a great prize in every way. Quite apart from the plunder that was divided among the Roman soldiers, there was an immense amount of gold and silver that would go far towards replenishing the empty chests of the Roman treasury. There was also a vast store of barley and wheat, quantities of bronze and iron, and all the necessary reserves for maintaining a fleet – as well as the fleet itself. Eighteen Carthaginian warships were captured and Scipio enrolled many of the slaves to serve as oarsmen. Sixty-three merchantmen with all their cargoes intact also lay in the harbour. The Romans had indisputably extended their control over the seaways of the Mediterranean, and now dominated the western and central areas as well as the Adriatic and the Ionian. Among the large amount of war material which fell into Roman hands were over a hundred of the largest type of catapults, as well as rock- and spear-hurling instruments and all the equipment for a large siege train – something which Hannibal had lacked throughout his years in Italy, and which the Carthaginians had never been able to transport across the Roman-dominated sea.

Scipio was able to make good political capital out of the Spanish hostages who had been held in Cartagena as surety for the good behaviour of their tribes. 'On learning the names of their states he made a list of captives, showing how many belonged to each people, and sent messengers to their homes, bidding that each man should come and recover his own children.

If ambassadors of any states happened to be there, he restored their hostages to them directly.' When the sister-in-law of Indibilis, prince of the important Ilergetes, fell weeping at his feet beseeching him to ensure the safety of her beautiful young daughters, Scipio 'handed them over to a man of proven uprightness' and ordered him to protect them as if they were his own. 'Then', Livy goes on, 'there was brought to him a grown maiden of such beauty that, wherever she went, she drew the eyes of everyone.' Scipio's fellow officers knew well enough that he was fond of women and thought they were making him a most suitable present. Scipio, however, did not forget that he was not only the conqueror of Cartagena but the man upon whom future policy towards Rome's new subjects in Spain might be founded. Having inquired about the girl's parentage and found out that she was betrothed to a young Celtiberian of some consequence, he had him summoned into his presence and entrusted to him his future bride, stipulating that he wanted no thanks but that he should be a friend of the Roman people. Her parents in the meantime, having thought to ransom her, brought Scipio a large sum of gold : he in his turn gave it to the young nobleman as a wedding present. This, and similar actions, played a large part in securing the transfer to the Romans of the allegiance of the tribes who had hitherto provided so many of the men for the Carthaginian army. Large numbers of tribal levies who were serving in Hasdrubal Barca's army deserted the Carthaginians over the next few months.

Having shown his ability as general and statesman Scipio now turned to the immediate practical aspects of war. He had observed in Italy and again in Spain the advantages of the Spanish sword, which could be used both for cutting and thrusting, over the Roman *gladius*, suitable mainly for thrusting. During that winter, while the armouries of Cartagena resounded to the clang of hammers, Scipio exercised the legions in more flexible tactics than the old Roman frontal attack, which relied so much upon the sheer weight of the legions. He had seen that fail at Cannae. At the same time he did not neglect the fleet, and the oarsmen and marines were exercised regularly in sham battles whenever the weather permitted.

Most of the other Roman generals in the war so far had been blinded by the brilliance of Hannibal and by the fact that he was roaming at large throughout the length and breadth of Italy. To them, Hannibal was the enemy. Scipio, on the other hand, knew that it was Carthage, and that the North African city must be brought to her knees in her own territory before the war could end. The first step towards achieving this desired aim was to deprive her of her empire in Spain; to cut off her supplies from the silver and other mines, and to transfer the allegiance of the hardy fighting men of the country from Carthage to Rome. Hannibal, despite his unquestioned brilliance on the battlefield, was no more than a distraction. Scipio, like all great commanders, took a far-sighted view of the aims and objects of a war. The capture of Cartagena was not just a victory to be acclaimed in Rome when the spoils and tribute arrived : it was the beginning of the end.

XXIV

DEATH OF TWO CONSULS

It was ten years since Hannibal had swept down into Italy to shatter the Roman armies, and cause the first doubts to grow among their allies that Rome was the master and future ruler of the Mediterranean. By 208, however, with the impetus of his assault long since spent and the cracks in the Latin confederation made good, Hannibal looked upon a very different scene.

Capua was lost, and Tarentum too. The towns in Samnium and Campania that had forsworn the Roman alliance and turned to what had seemed to be the rising star of Carthage were now denied to him, and such others as had at one time thought of following their example were taking due note of the way in which Rome punished any backsliders. He had no ports worthy of the name to maintain sea-links with Carthage, and the all-important island of Sicily was irretrievably lost. Sardinia had never managed to break free of Rome and all the approaches to Italy were watched and guarded by triumphant Roman fleets. Philip V of Macedon, who had been almost convinced after Cannae that it would be worth his while to lend assistance to the conquering Carthaginians, had long since been reminded of the Roman control of the Adriatic. (He was now heavily engaged in Greece against the Aetolians who, with the support of Rome, were to keep him occupied at home until the threat from Hannibal was over.) Hannibal could certainly derive no comfort in the news from Spain, where his brother Hasdrubal was to be mauled at Baecula that year by the young Scipio. He had little to sustain him and his troops but the knowledge that he was still in Italy after so many years – and still undefeated. Yet the year 208, which must have looked ominous to the Carthaginian, was to close with an extraordinary reversal of Roman fortunes.

The consuls for the year 208 were the tough old soldier Marcellus, now in his fifth consulship, and Titus Quinctius Crispinus, who had been Marcellus' right-hand man in the capture of Syracuse. Each was in command of two legions. Crispinus began that year's campaigning with an attack on Locri, one of the few ports remaining to Hannibal in the south, where he might still have hoped to receive reinforcements by sea from Carthage. Forced to give up the siege by Hannibal, he retreated northwards to the town of Venusia where he and Marcellus encamped with their armies only a few miles apart. Willing to bring them to battle if, as he had grounds to suspect, the Romans might have sufficiently recovered their nerve to meet him on the open field, Hannibal set off north after them. On his way he heard that a legion from Tarentum had been sent out to march down to Locri and renew the siege, with the hope of capturing the city-port in his absence. He set a typical Hannibalic trap beneath the 1,000-foot high hill of Petelia, concealing his horsemen and infantry on either side of the route – the kind of snare into which he had earlier hoped to lure the troops of Fabius. The Romans, presuming that Hannibal was away to the north, advanced carelessly and without any scouts sent ahead, and learned the lesson which it might have been thought had long been absorbed by all intelligent commanders – 'Never underestimate the Carthaginian.' The trap was sprung; 2,000 Romans were killed, 1,500 were taken prisoner; and the rest fled back to Tarentum, happy to see the gates of the city opened to let them in.

When Hannibal finally reached a position not far from Venusia and the Roman armies he pitched camp and prepared for what promised to be a set engagement. As Livy puts it, 'both consuls were alike in a fierce spirit and went out daily into the battle-line with no uncertain hope that, if the enemy should risk battle, with two united consular armies, it would be possible to finish the war.' Between the two armies lay a small wooded hill which the Romans, who had been in position long before Hannibal's arrival, should certainly have seized. The master of warfare wasted no time; overnight he sent forward a number of squadrons of his Numidian cavalry to see if the hill was occupied and, if not, to conceal themselves there and lie up without making a move during daylight hours. He had already decided from its shape and size that the hill was more suitable for some form of ambush than as a camp for the army.

As usual his thinking was somewhat in advance of his opponents'. 'In the Roman camp', writes Livy, 'there was a general outcry that the hill must be occupied and defended by a fort, in order that they might not have the enemy upon their necks, as it were, if the hill should be occupied by Hannibal.' Not knowing what had already happened to the legion out of Tarentum, nor aware that the troops under Hannibal were full of fight and confidence, nor remembering from the past that only the ignorant or the foolish ever treated the presence of Hannibal without considerable care, Marcellus and his fellow consul Crispinus decided to ride out and take a personal look at the hill. Perhaps the news from Spain and the general situation in the Mediterranean had buoyed them up with careless confidence. Taking no more than 220 horsemen with them, along with a few infantrymen and some staff officers including Marcus Marcellus, the son of the consul, they rode out of camp. As they left the earthwork Marcellus gave orders for the soldiers to be ready and, if the hill was found suitable for establishing a camp or lookout post, they were to move up immediately. The signal to do so never came.

The Numidians, who had been waiting in case they might be able to catch a few men who had gone in search of fodder or firewood, were astonished to see the red military cloaks and the glittering armour of senior officers moving across the small plain towards them and entering the wooden slopes. Immaculately-disciplined, they waited until the whole party was within their grasp and then, like dark shadows, from the rear of the Romans and on each side of them the horsemen from North Africa made their move. 'Those who, facing the enemy, had to rise up from the hillside itself, did not show themselves before those who were to cut off the road in the rear turned the enemy's flanks. Then they all sprang up from every side and, raising a great shout, made their attack.' Marcellus was almost immediately struck by a spear and fell dying from his horse, Crispinus, wounded by two javelins, just managed to escape, while the young son of Marcellus, also wounded, joined him in the flight of the survivors – a few staff officers and a handful of Etruscan cavalry who seem to have had little heart for the engagement.

The sudden outcry from the wooded hill had brought both armies to the alert, the Romans being the first to know from the bloodstained survivors what had taken place on that bright summer day. Hannibal, as soon as he was told the news by one of the Numidians, moved his army forward and occupied the hill. He himself rode through the wood until he found the body of Marcellus; he had it cremated with due honours and sent the ashes to the dead man's son in a silver urn. He had respected Marcellus as an opponent when alive and he paid him, when dead, as was always his custom with fallen opponents, the marks of respect due to a man worthy of honour.

While the severely wounded Crispinus took charge of the consular armies and moved up into the mountains 'to a high place that was safe on every side', Hannibal considered his next move. He now had in his possession the ring of the dead consul : his seal and authority for any message that might be sent. Hannibal at once thought of Salapia on the Adriatic coast of Apulia; Salapia which had broken away from its Carthaginian alliance and reverted to Rome. He needed a secure garrison on the east coast, for it would seem that he had heard from his brother Hasdrubal in Spain that the latter intended to break out, cross the Alps, and join him for a final onslaught on Rome. The events of that year were to confirm Hasdrubal in his pessimism about the Carthaginian position in Spain and he saw clearly that only a combination of Hannibal and himself, and their two armies, the one full of fresh blood and eager for conquest, the other wise in experience, could save Carthage by striking direct at the heart of Rome.

To Salapia, then, Hannibal addressed a message, authenticated by the seal of Marcellus, saying that Marcellus would arrive on the following night and that the gates of the city were to be open to receive him. It was an ingenious ruse and might have worked, but for the fact that Crispinus, dying though he was, had anticipated him and had sent messengers to all the nearby city-states telling them that Marcellus was dead, and to trust no message that came bearing his seal. The men of Salapia sent back Hannibal's messenger, a Roman deserter, saying that all would be ready for Marcellus when he arrived. When Hannibal neared Salapia by night he sent forward an advance party of Roman deserters, all speaking Latin and all bearing Roman arms, marching like the legionaries they had once been and designed to convince the people of Salapia that the consul was following. The sentries on the gate, hearing them call out, pretended to be ready to welcome them, and raised the portcullis. But when several hundreds of the deserters had entered the town, the portcullis was dropped behind them and the advance party was massacred.

Foiled for once by an intelligence as sharp as his own, Hannibal abandoned the attempt to secure the city for the long-awaited arrival of his brother from Spain, and withdrew to the south. He had learned that Locri was once again under siege and it was all-important to him that he should keep this communication-link with Carthage open. The ever-versatile Numidian horse arrived in advance of Hannibal's marching columns, took the besieging Roman army in the rear, and Locri was saved.

Titus Quinctius Crispinus died shortly afterwards of the wounds he had received in that fatal ambush on the wooded hill. 'So two consuls – and this had happened in no previous war – losing their lives without a notable battle, had left the state as it were bereft.' At Trasimene and at Cannae Hannibal had killed one of the consuls then in office, and he had killed many Roman generals, knights, innumerable staff officers and other valuable citizens of Rome. But now, in the year that had seemed to open with the gloomiest of prospects, he still bestrode the landscape of Italy – an implacable, avenging figure whom the Romans had never defeated.

Across the Mediterranean in Spain his brother Hasdrubal, who had been eager to join Hannibal in Italy for several years, had his choice resolved for him. If he had wavered in the past, torn between the necessity of preserving the Carthaginian empire and of helping Hannibal strike the enemy in his heart, he was now to receive the blow that produced decision. At Baecula (Baelen), guarding the all-important silver mines of Castulo, Hasdrubal was brought to bay by Scipio. The Hannibalic War, like all others, revolved around metals and money – metals for war materials and money with which to keep troops in the field and to pay for the support of allies. Hamilcar had founded his Spanish empire to replenish the treasury of Carthage after the disastrous peace following the First Punic War, and it was the mineral wealth of Spain that had emboldened Carthage to support Hannibal's astonishing venture against the Roman state. Hasdrubal's last battle in Spain was significant for the reason that he was defeated by Scipio's use of a tactical approach that no Roman commander in the past would have thought of, nor possibly even Scipio himself if he had not been present at Cannae.

Hasdrubal had taken up a position beneath the town of Baecula on a ridge which had a small river below it. To get at his enemy Scipio had to ford the river and then make a frontal assault up a slope: two disadvantages which earlier Roman commanders would have accepted, relying on the weight of the legions to steamroller their way through the enemy's defences. Scipio, however, had observed that on either side of the plateau there were dried gulleys descending from the top. After his troops were across the river he suddenly shifted the main weight of his attack, sending a large body of lightly-armed troops up the slope to meet the enemy head on, while he and his second-in-command took the heavily-armed legions up the gulleys on either side. In doing this he emulated Hannibal at Cannae, having his light troops and his Spanish allies bear the brunt in the centre, while his heavy veterans closed in on the sides for the kill. 'And no longer', writes Livy, 'was space left open even for flight ... the gate of the camp was obstructed by the flight of the general and chief officers, while in addition there was the panic of the elephants, of which, when terrified, they were as much afraid as of the enemy. About eight thousand men were slain.' The fact remained that Hasdrubal, who had proven himself on many a battlefield, managed to get away with the hard core of his army – all his heavily-armed troops, as well as his cavalry, and 32 elephants besides. Like Hannibal himself, and like Scipio, he was ruthless in sacrificing his local troops when it came to the major issues. And for Hasdrubal, having decided that Spain must be at long last abandoned, even if only in the short-term – the all-important goal was to move his forces to Italy.

In the autumn of 208 Hasdrubal took his troops over into Gaul, having evaded the Romans in eastern Spain by following the upper valleys of the Tagus and the Ebro. The subsequent fame of Scipio seems to have eclipsed the fact that he let Hasdrubal escape and thereby allowed his country to be more exposed to danger than at any time since Hannibal himself had crossed the Alps. To quote O'Connor Morris: 'He must have known – for the rumour had spread far and wide – that Hasdrubal's object was to leave Spain and to co-operate with his brother in Italy: the Roman general's first object should therefore have been to take care that Hasdrubal should not elude him; if he was not sufficiently strong to strike his enemy down, he should certainly have dogged his advance to the Pyrenees, and not have let him reach Gaul unobserved and intact. He did nothing of the kind, and made an immense mistake and it is simply untrue that he was obliged to confront the Carthaginians in great force on the Ebro, for Mago and Hasdrubal Gisgo, when Hasdrubal had gone, betook themselves, the one to the

Balearic islands, the other to Portugal, hundreds of miles distant; they were clearly unable to face the Romans in Spain.'

It is unfortunate that our ancient authorities did not enlarge upon this march made by Hasdrubal, the second greatest of that 'Lion's brood' of Hamilcar's sons who had threatened and terrified Rome for so long. His was an epic journey worthy of his brother. Evading Scipio, he left the Romans vainly watching the eastern passes of the Pyrenees while he and his Carthaginian infantry, his Spaniards, his Numidian horse, and the plodding African elephants, moved far to the west, passing by the Bay of Biscay and the great grey ocean which few Mediterranean men had ever seen. Before he left for Gaul he conferred with Mago, and this younger brother went to the Balearics in order to raise a force of those formidable 'slingers' who were later to cross by sea to Italy. The three sons of Hamilcar Barca, it was planned, would then meet for the first time in many years and execute that vengeance upon Rome which their vows to their father and the smoking altars of Carthage had long demanded.

XXV

THE METAURUS RIVER

Hannibal and Hasdrubal both knew that, with the declining situation in Spain, the year 207 must prove decisive in the war against Rome. Only by the junction of their armies and the total defeat of the Romans – something more devastating even than Cannae – could the object of the long war be achieved. From the very beginning the great enterprise was to prove hazardous and, on later reflection, almost impossible. The Romans commanding the centre of Italy had the benefit of interior lines of communication and were able to place their forces so that one part kept an eye on Hannibal to the south while the other faced to the north and the expected arrival of Hasdrubal. In those days of primitive communications the great obstacle between the two brothers was the length and breadth of Italy.

Hasdrubal wintered in Gaul, far to the west where no friends of Rome or of Massilia were to be found, and then probably crossed the Rhône fairly high up, near Lyon. Although it was no secret that Hasdrubal was intent on joining his brother in Italy no attempt, in any case, could have been made to stop him once he had cleared the Pyrenees and moved into Gaul. Massilia was far away and the Gallic chieftains were as hostile to Rome as they had ever been. Although, on Livy's authority, Hasdrubal had escaped from Baecula with no more than 15,000 men it is unlikely that he set out for the Alps with less than double this number. (Hannibal far away in the south may have been able to muster an army of 40–50,000 – but most of these second-rate troops.)

In the spring of 207 as soon as the snows melted Hasdrubal set out : he was not delayed in any way as his brother had been, nor apparently was he harassed by hostile tribes. Crossing the territory of the Arverni (Auvergne) he very probably followed the course of the river Isère and almost certainly did not take the difficult route that Hannibal had done. Both Livy and Appian state that he did, but it seems most unlikely, since the basin of the Isère leads into the Mont Cenis pass and the Roman historian Varro seems without any doubt to place Hasdrubal's pass as distinct from Hannibal's, and to the north of it. The Col du Mont Cenis would fit this well, and the suggestion that Hasdrubal followed in his brother's footsteps is no more than metaphorical. In any case, as Livy points out, the Alpine tribes who had thought that Hannibal was intent on their own poor territory had now learned about 'the Punic war, with which Italy had been aflame for eleven years, and realised that the Alps were no more than a route between two very powerful cities which were at war with one another. . . .' There was no reason any longer for them to attack the Carthaginians en route, nor to deceive them with information that might lead them into high and treacherous passes. Hasdrubal moved towards Italy at the right time of the year, with an assurance that is borne out by the fact that no mishaps are attributed to his expedition.

The Romans were well aware that this year was crucial. The Republic steeled itself, and indeed showed itself in so noble a mood that even generations later it was always regarded as an inspiration. Although the news that Hasdrubal was on the march produced scenes in Rome that were reminiscent of the panic inspired by Hannibal in the early stages of the war, the senate never faltered in wise and sensible measures to defend the state. Men had by now become so inured to war that they were hardened and trained to cope with all its vicissitudes. In some respects also they could take comfort from the general situation: Scipio had undoubtedly gained the upper hand in Spain; there was no threat from Sardinia, and the war in Sicily had finished satisfactorily. Hannibal's inactive ally, Philip of Macedon, was on the defensive in Greece and preparing to sue for peace; and throughout the Mediterranean Sea the Roman navy rode triumphant. Rome's allies had scented the change of wind and those who had earlier shown themselves faint-hearted or treacherous had now learned their lesson. It was with some confidence, then, despite the double threat of Hannibal and Hasdrubal, that the Romans faced the year. Evidence of this, and of their available manpower, is shown by the fact that no less than twenty-three legions were raised. Of these only eight were required for foreign service: two in Sicily, two in Sardinia, and four in Spain. The remaining fifteen were all in Italy, representing 75,000 Roman citizens to which must be added an equal number of allies. It is hardly surprising, though, that Livy remarks that the number of young men fit for service in the field was beginning to dwindle.

More difficult than mustering troops was finding the men to command them. Fabius Maximus was now a very old man and Marcellus, the 'Sword of Rome', was dead. The losses sustained over the years, and particularly at Cannae, were only too perceptible in the ranks of Rome's leaders. After much debate Claudius Nero and Marcus Livius were finally elected consuls, the former taking command of the southern army facing Hannibal at Venusia and the latter of the northern army at Senegallica on the Adriatic coast. Fulvius Flaccus, victor at Capua, supported Nero with an army at Bruttium, and another army was at Tarentum. In the north Lucius Porcius Licinius commanded an army in Cisalpine Gaul while Terentius Varro (still popular with the masses despite all) held the unstable region of Etruria.

Early that spring Hasdrubal moved south, almost certainly earlier than had been expected. If the army which he brought with him from Spain was not exhausted as Hannibal's had been, nor needing rest to anything like the same extent, it was not of the same quality nor was it strong in that arm which had played such havoc with the Romans, the superb horsemen of North Africa. Nevertheless, reinforced by several thousand Ligurians who had risen to join them, and stirring once again the rebellious spirit in the Cisalpine Gauls, Hasdrubal moved like an ominous thundercloud over the land of Italy. Crossing the Po and mastering the Stradella pass, he marched against Placentia. Here he faltered and lost time, laying siege to this faithful Roman colony which had closed its gates against him, having taken note of the fact that, like Hannibal, he had no equipment to conduct a siege. Hasdrubal has been blamed by some historians for delaying at Placentia, instead of bypassing it and marching on to rendezvous with his brother before the Romans could collect all their forces together. He was faced, however, with the fact that Placentia seemed a very strong garrison to leave in his rear and – even more important perhaps – the local Gallic tribes were slow to rise in his favour. He needed to wait until sufficient Ligurians had reached him and as many Gauls as possible had been recruited. Finally, drawing off from Placentia, he marched by way of Ariminum over to the eastern seaboard. Porcius, who did not have sufficient troops to withstand him, retired. Such were the opening moves that spring in the north.

Hannibal, who had been wintering in Apulia as usual, moved first into Lucania to raise further troops and then back to his old stronghold in Bruttium, no doubt to pick up as many reserves as possible from this area that had long been faithful to his cause. According to Livy, the Roman troops from Tarentum fell upon his levies while they were on the march and in the ensuing struggle he lost about 4,000 men, the burdened Carthaginian troops being cut down by the unencumbered legionaries. Meanwhile the consul Claudius Nero with an army of 42,500 moved from Venusia to block Hannibal's march from Bruttium to Lucania. 'Hannibal hoped', says Livy, 'to recover the towns which had gone over to the Romans out of fear', but he also had to march north so as to effect a meeting with his brother. The confusion of the Carthaginian movements was due to the primitive communications of the times: Hannibal knew no more than that Hasdrubal should by now be across the Alps and Hasdrubal, who was already in Italy, knew no more than that Hannibal was somewhere in the south. The Romans, on the other hand, working from their interior lines of communication and supply systems, were in an admirable position to keep their two enemies apart and to tackle them one at a time with their superior forces.

At Grumentum in Lucania the armies of Nero and Hannibal first met in a battle notable for the fact that the Roman consul, 'imitating the arts of his enemy', concealed part of his troops behind a hill so as to fall on the Carthaginian rear at a suitable moment in the engagement. It was now that Hannibal felt the need of his trained Punic and Spanish troops and Numidian horsemen, who had never reached him from Carthage. His motley, semi-trained forces – outnumbered by the Romans – were no match for Nero's disciplined legions. Furthermore it was the consul's intelligent use of Hannibal's own style of tactics, frowned on as 'un-Roman' by Livy though this was, that secured him the victory. Hannibal lost, we are told, 9,000 men, 9 standards and 6 elephants. Even so, it seems to have been an indecisive engagement for, far from retreating, Hannibal continued his march northwards towards Canusium in Apulia, and it is significant that Nero, while dogging his heels, was unable to prevent him from moving as and when he pleased.

Hannibal at this juncture was naturally more than anxious to make contact with his brother. The latter had now reached Ariminum and intended to make for Narnia in Umbria, coming down the Via Flaminia along the Adriatic coast. It was essential that this information should reach Hannibal as soon as possible, so that the latter could sweep up north and the two armies be joined for the battle that would decide the fate of Rome. Six horsemen, four Gauls and two Numidians, were accordingly chosen to ride through the land of Italy, heavily occupied by Roman and allied troops, to take the news of Hasdrubal's arrival to his brother and to acquaint him with the desired rendezvous. It might have been thought that such information could be contained in a simple verbal message which could easily have been memorised by the horsemen. But Hasdrubal seems to have written a letter or letters – despatches, in fact, which contained not only the position of his own army at the time, and the request for Hannibal to meet him at Narnia, but possibly also the entire composition of his army.

The contents of Hasdrubal's letter to his brother were never disclosed, nor available for subsequent historians, so this is nothing but surmise. The fact remains that when, in due course, the information fell into Roman hands it was sufficient to enable them to move with triumphant success against Hasdrubal. Codes certainly existed in those times, yet it seems that Hasdrubal transmitted his information in ordinary Punic – something that was easily translated, Punic having for so long been one of the great trading tongues of the Mediterranean.

The messengers achieved the first part of their mission successfully, passing right through central Italy without falling foul of the armies that were everywhere moving to the defence of the Republic. Then disaster befell them. Ignorant of Hannibal's movements, they moved south from Apulia and were intercepted in the region of Tarentum. (Hannibal at this time was down in Bruttium and it is unbelievable that his brother did not know that Tarentum itself had long since fallen to the Romans.) So, at this moment, incalculable chance or fortune, the one thing against which no man can be forearmed, took a hand. Hasdrubal's letter was immediately transmitted to Claudius Nero, who acted with masterly speed and decisiveness. Passing the information on to the senate, he advised them to close the roads to Narnia, call out every available man and withdraw the legion that was at Capua. Nero, although he had previously failed against Hasdrubal in Spain, rightly reckoned that he was the more vulnerable of the two brothers, and it was he who at the moment posed the more immediate threat to Rome. Without waiting for the senate to confirm his choice of action, he decided to leave his army where it was, blocking Hannibal, and take a select force northwards to reinforce Livius and Porcius. His legate Catius assumed command of the 30,000 men who were left holding Hannibal in check, while Nero under cover of night took 6,000 legionaries and 1,000 cavalry on a forced march north.

His action was brilliant, showing all the marks of a man who had learned from Hannibal that it is dash and decision which often win great battles. He had already displayed something of this quality in his prior engagement with Hannibal but now, acting completely against all Roman conventions (leaving his designated place as consul), he took to the road with his chosen levies. Horsemen were sent ahead of the marching columns to arouse all the villages and townships that lay in their way to have food, water and everything made ready for men upon whom depended the life or death of the Republic. Livy gives a spirited account of that famous march: 'They were marching everywhere between lines of men and women who had poured out from the farms on all sides, and amidst their vows and prayers and words of praise. . . . They vied with each other in invitations and offers and in importuning them to take whatever they wished in food or in beasts.' The men marched day and night, arms piled on carts that accompanied them, while messengers spurred ahead to Livius to tell him that his fellow consul was on the way to join him.

Hasdrubal, expecting that his letter would by now have reached Hannibal and that the latter would be hastening to meet him, lay confronting the army of Livius and Porcius. The Romans had shown no sign as yet of wishing to give battle, and Hasdrubal no doubt thought that the longer he could stay in a holding position the more time was afforded for Hannibal to come up behind the enemy and take them in the rear. He had crossed the Metaurus and then moved south towards the small river Sena (Cesano) which lay between his position and that of the Romans, only about half a mile distant. The area was part of the Umbrian plain and, although more wooded then than now, was good campaigning country. The Metaurus, in those days when the Apennines were dense with trees, was probably a larger river than it is today, and the banks and cliffs which overhang its northern side were undoubtedly more of an obstacle. Claudius Nero is said to have come within reach of his fellow consul after only seven days on the march, an average of thirty miles a day – something which, even with all the aid along the way, seems hardly possible. Certainly he moved amazingly fast, as fast as Hannibal on any of his forced marches, and he was up in the intended battle area long before any news of his approach could have preceded him. Waiting out of sight until nightfall, Nero now joined his fellow consul Livius, he and his troops moving in to share the tents of the soldiers already assembled there. When dawn came there would be no evidence from freshly erected tents that the Roman army had been augmented.

On the next day a council of war was held, the praetor, Porcius Licinus, being present together with the two consuls. Livy records that 'the opinions of many were inclined towards postponing the time for battle, until Nero should refresh his troops, worn by the march and lack of sleep, and at the same time should take a few days to acquaint himself with the enemy.' Nero, however, was adamant: he was determined to attack at once, pointing out that 'his plan, which rapid movement had made safe,' must not be nullified by any delay. He was acutely aware that Hannibal might discover his absence from his own army, and attack at once. If Hannibal yet again achieved one of his astounding victories, he would certainly follow Nero's route north and the Roman army would find itself caught between the two Carthaginian brothers. Livius somewhat reluctantly agreed and the Roman forces began to deploy themselves for battle.

While the Carthaginian troops also began to move into their determined places – both opposing armies being no more than half a mile apart – Hasdrubal decided to take a final look at the Roman dispositions. Livy writes that 'riding out in front of the standards with a few horsemen, he observed among the enemy old shields which he had not seen before and very lean horses; and he thought the numbers also larger than usual. Suspecting what had happened, he promptly sounded the recall and sent men to the river from which the Romans were drawing water, that some Romans might be captured there and scanned to see whether any chanced to be more sunburned as though from a recent march.' At the same time he sent horsemen off to ride round the Roman camps and check whether the earthworks had been enlarged or whether any new tents had been erected. Deceived by Nero's subtlety in having no changes made and having his own men billeted with those who were already there, they reported back to Hasdrubal that all was as before. They had, however, noticed one unusual thing – when the orders were being given by trumpet, one had sounded as usual in the praetor's camp but, instead of only one sounding from the camp of the consul Livius, there had been two distinct trumpet blasts. Hasdrubal, familiar for years with the routines of his Roman enemy, deduced at once that this meant that two consuls were present. If two consuls, then possibly two consular armies or at least a vastly enlarged force awaited him.

The presence of the second consul also suggested the terrible thought that his brother and his army might have been defeated. The Romans would never leave Hannibal unwatched by one or other consul if he were still alive. Hasdrubal succumbed to the fear that all was lost in the south. That night he gave the order for his troops to withdraw and take up a new position on the banks of the Metaurus.

From the moment that Hasdrubal determined on this retreat in the face of the enemy all, indeed, was lost for him. His native guides deserted, his troops lost heart, and the Gallic levies – undisciplined, untrained, and always prone to drunkenness – became completely disordered. Confused in the darkness, ignorant of the countryside, the Carthaginian army straggled back in the direction of the river. If Hasdrubal had intended to take up a strong position on the northern bank he was to be foiled by the condition of his own troops, and by the fact that the Romans followed hard on his heels. Hasdrubal was a brave and experienced general, and it is unlikely that he had no future plans beyond trying to bring the Romans to battle on the line of the Metaurus. Dorey and Dudley suggest that 'he could have marched north-east and then back into the Po valley, but this is not very likely. Probably he intended to turn left towards Rome, by-pass the Roman armies at the Sena, reach friendly communities in Etruria or Umbria and then find out what had happened to Hannibal.' Claudius Nero had not realised, when he had so cannily concealed the presence of his troops from the watching Carthaginians, that his own presence would be disclosed to them by the sound of a trumpet, and he certainly could not have guessed that the report of this would cause Hasdrubal to withdraw. The fear of Hannibal uniting his army with his brother had spurred Nero on his march to the north, and the fear that Hannibal was lost had caused Hasdrubal to withdraw precipitately.

With the dawn of the following day Hasdrubal drew up his troops as well as he was able on the south bank of the Metaurus – concentrating his best troops, the Carthaginians and the Spanish veterans, against Livius. His drunken and demoralised Gauls were sited on a small hillock, where he hoped that they would enjoy some protective advantage against the Romans under Nero on his right. Other Spanish troops and Ligurians were in his centre, where he had also placed his ten elephants, hoping that the weight of their attack would break down the troops under Porcius, who commanded there. In the event, the elephants proved a liability. The Romans had learned by now that, when wounded by spears (the formidable *pilum*), the elephants would turn tail and run amok among the ranks behind them.

The battle was fierce and prolonged on Hasdrubal's right, where he and Livius were engaged, the Carthaginians, Spaniards and Ligurians fighting courageously and well. But on the left the Gauls, in their protected position, scarcely moved, and Nero found it hard to attack them. In the centre the elephants caused as much confusion among their own troops as among the Romans, and the issue remained undecided. Eventually Nero, judging that the real contest was on the other wing and that it was there that the battle would be won or lost, once again used his initiative and acted completely against all conventional military practice. Abandoning his attempts to draw out the Gauls, he moved his troops right round behind the Roman battle-line and fell upon the Carthaginian right wing. This new weight of fresh legionaries pouring in against them caused Hasdrubal's seasoned troops to fall back. The battle suddenly became a rout. Panic-stricken men struggled to cross the Metaurus, while the whole of Hasdrubal's right wing collapsed in ruins. Realising that all was lost, Hannibal's brother spurred his horse into the Roman lines and died, sword in hand – 'a heroic gesture', says Polybius, but Hasdrubal was worth far more to the Carthaginian cause alive. It is probable that the despair he felt was induced not only by his defeat, but also by the fear which had earlier driven him to withdraw his army – the fear that his brother lay dead somewhere in the south of Italy.

Livy gives the fanciful figure of 56,000 men killed on the Carthaginian side (anxious, perhaps, to provide the Romans with a suitable vengeance for Cannae), while Polybius gives 10,000. The latter is more likely to be accurate, for it is doubtful if Hasdrubal had more than 60,000 men in the first place, many of whom had already deserted, while the Gauls, who had hardly been engaged, withdrew safely in a body. The Roman dead are given as 8,000. Such was the battle of the Metaurus, a battle that sealed the fate of the Carthaginian attempt to defeat the Romans in their homeland. On that day the balance of power in the Mediterranean shifted for ever.

Nero, who by his action in the battle and by his first swift move to re-inforce his fellow consul had shown that he was an outstanding general both tactically and strategically, wasted no time now all was over. He was well aware that the main threat to Rome was past – the danger of two armies under two sons of Hamilcar uniting on Italian soil. But he knew that the seemingly permanent threat still lay with Hannibal in the south. He hastened back from the victory at the Metaurus and took command again of his legions in Apulia. Hannibal's troops remained facing his own (Nero's absence had not been remarked), and no word had reached the opposing armies of the great battle in the north.

The first news of the disaster was when some Roman cavalry spurred up to the Carthaginian's outposts at night and threw a dark object towards the sentries. When it was brought to Hannibal in his tent he looked at it and said, 'I see there the fate of Carthage.' It was the head of his brother Hasdrubal.

XXVI

THE EBBING TIDE

With the death of his brother Hannibal had lost his last hope of defeating Rome. The severed head had signalled the end of that brave endeavour to bring the greatest military power in the Mediterranean to its knees by striking at the heart of the Roman homeland. For the first time in twelve years Hannibal had lost the initiative in the war. He withdrew into Bruttium, that wild and mountainous area from which he had drawn the bulk of his recruits in recent years, and where he still retained the two small seaports of Croton and Locri. The temptation to return to Carthage must have been almost irresistible, for Hannibal could see that the loss of Hasdrubal and his army meant that the war in Italy was drawing to a close. He knew, too, that Spain was likely to pass out of Carthaginian control and that the next stroke after that on the Roman part would be an invasion of the Carthaginian homeland. At the same time, he evidently concluded that his presence in Italy, weakened and relatively ineffectual though his army had become, tied down many legions and prevented the Romans from concentrating their forces and their fleet in an attack on Carthage itself. He must remain where he was, posing a permanent threat to Rome.

The news of the battle of the Metaurus river was received with a joy such as the city had not known in all those long years. It was, as the poet Horace remarks, the first day since Hannibal had swooped down out of the Alps that victory smiled on the Roman people. Both consuls were accorded a triumph, in which Claudius Nero was deservedly received with greater acclaim than his fellow, for it was clear that his initiative and brilliant dash — in defiance of all rules and regulations — had given them a victory of immense consequence. The threat to Rome was eliminated and it had already been seen that Hannibal on his own, unmatched as a general though he was, did not have the men or the equipment to endanger the city. Four legions were disbanded, and no further action was taken that year, save to keep watch and ward on the Carthaginian in his Bruttian lair. Philip of Macedon, sensing that the curtain was coming down on the great Hannibalic enterprise, made his peace with the Aetolians, thus bringing to an end his short and uneasy alliance with the Carthaginian.

The year 206 saw no major operations in Italy, the two consuls, Quintus Metellus and Lucius Philo, contenting themselves with keeping Hannibal bottled up in Bruttium. The main centre of the war was now in Spain, where

Scipio continued to display his customary brilliance, decisively defeating Hannibal's younger brother Mago and Hasdrubal Gisgo at Baecula. In the previous year other armies under Hanno and Mago had been worsted and it was clear that the whole of Spain, of that Carthaginian empire founded by Hamilcar, was slipping from their grasp. This was evident enough to the Iberians and the Celtiberians themselves, who were nearly all rapidly allying themselves with the Roman cause. For those who resisted, such as the powerful chieftain Indibilis, the Roman reaction was swift and bloody. Fortress towns like Astapa and Iliturgi were destroyed, tribes which had conspired against Scipio's father and uncle were decimated, and Castulo, the stronghold where Hannibal many years before is said to have found himself a wife, yielded to Roman siege engines and Roman swords.

Scipio's actions in Spain anticipated the later history of the Roman empire (which he so largely helped to found) in 'sparing the defeated but beating the rebellious to the ground.' His discipline was not only extended to the wild tribes of Spain, for when a mutiny broke out in one of his legions it was put down with equal harshness, the leaders being promptly put to death. It was soon clear that, with the departure of Hasdrubal for Italy to join his brother, the unifying Carthaginian hand in Spain had been withdrawn. Carthaginian control over the country was lost even more quickly than it had first been imposed. Only Gades remained as a last outpost of Carthaginian power and, before the end of 206, even this ancient trading centre of the Punic peoples was preparing to welcome the Romans. Although it would be many years before all the tribes of the wild and mountainous Iberian Peninsula would be pacified (that euphemism for the sword) all Spain in effect was in Roman hands. After some thirty years the dominion that had been established by the Barca family was at an end.

Although Hannibal was to remain in Italy for a further three years and was never defeated on Italian soil, he now found himself deprived of the very base from which he had set out on his long march. Moreover he and his country had now lost Spain's silver and mineral wealth, and even the manpower which had so largely fuelled his giant enterprise. He was to find that the strategy which he had used against the Romans when he had decided to invade their country was to be turned against the Carthaginians. All along Scipio had seen that to debar the enemy from his source of power was the best way of defeating him, and had achieved this first objective with his success in Spain. He now prepared for his second objective – Africa.

Livy writes that Scipio 'considered the conquest of Spain insignificant compared with all that he had imagined in his high-minded hopes. Already his eye was upon Africa and the greater Carthage and the glory of such a war. . . .' His policy did not go unopposed in the senate and it is clear that there were two main parties in the debate: the one pressing for peace in

Italy first, and the removal of Hannibal, and the other for carrying the war overseas. The Fabians, led by the son of the old dictator, were in favour of an Italian policy – setting their own house in order before extending the war – while Scipio stood for expansion. His father and his uncle had died in Spain and he had now achieved its conquest, but looking further ahead he envisaged the conquest of Mediterranean Africa. Most of the senate were against him. In that thirteenth year of the war, the whole country was weary, its lands devastated, its manpower dwindling, and every citizen and ally staggering under an intolerable burden of taxation. The reason that Scipio managed to succeed in his ambitious plan was that his triumphant return to Rome, preceded by hundreds of pounds' weight of silver and many noble captives as evidence of his success, eclipsed the arguments of his opponents. On a wave of popular enthusiasm he was elected to a consulship for the year 205. He had in any case already begun to take soundings in Africa, thus anticipating the opposition.

Some months before his return to Rome, confident that all was over in Spain, Scipio had crossed to Africa to meet Syphax, the Numidian king, with a view to bringing him into an alliance with Rome against Carthage. In the harbour of Cirta (Constantine), adjoining Carthaginian territory, Scipio found enemy warships and no less a person than Hasdrubal Gisgo, against whom, with Hamilcar's son Mago, he had recently been engaged in battle. It was a strange meeting (possibly engineered by the wily Numidian king) but since it took place on neutral territory, there could be no question of any display of hostility between the visiting Romans and Carthaginians.

Livy writes that 'to Syphax it seemed a splendid thing – as indeed it was – that the generals of the two richest peoples of that time had come on the same day to ask for peace and friendship from him.' He invited them both to dine with him, and '. . . on the same couch even, since the king would have it so, Scipio and Hasdrubal reclined. Moreover, such was the genial manner of Scipio, such his inborn cleverness in meeting every situation, that by his eloquent mode of address he won not Syphax only, the barbarian unacquainted with Roman ways, but his own bitterest enemy as well. Hasdrubal plainly showed that in this 'social' engagement, Scipio seemed even more marvellous than in his achievements in war, and that he did not doubt Syphax and his kingdom would soon be in the power of the Romans; such skill did the man possess in winning men over.' The fact was, of course, that the intelligent Numidian could read the way the wind was blowing in the Mediterranean. 'So Scipio, after making a treaty with Syphax, set sail from Africa. . . .'

During that winter, while Scipio was being acclaimed in Rome, Hannibal's brother Mago was in the Balearic islands. After making a daring but ineffectual attempt to capture New Carthage he had despaired of the situation in Spain. He had left Gades and taken the Carthaginian fleet first of all to Pityusa (Ibiza), long a Carthaginian colony, intending to recruit foot soldiers and the famous Balearic slingers among the islanders. Even at this late stage in the war it is clear that Carthage had not despaired of winning it in Italy. Mago had received orders 'to hire the greatest possible number of young Gauls and Ligurians, to join Hannibal and not permit a war that had begun with the greatest vigour and even greater good fortune to decline now.' The senate in Carthage had sent him a large sum of money for this purpose. Mago's fleet was also laden with gold and silver from Gades, where he had plundered the temples and the treasury before leaving. He had even ransacked the famous and immensely wealthy temple of Melkarth (Hercules) which for centuries had been the last place where Phoenician sailors had made their offerings before voyaging out into the great ocean. That a Carthaginian, descendant of those Phoenicians who had founded this sacred shrine some nine hundred years earlier, should desecrate it is evidence of the despair that Mago and his men must have felt at the loss of Spain. Over that winter, although rebuffed in Mallorca, Mago managed to recruit some 12,000 soldiers and 2,000 horsemen in Menorca. With these troops he was to make an onslaught on the Ligurian coast in the spring of 205, in the course of which he captured the important towns of Savo (Savona) and Genua (Genoa).

At this stage in the complexity of the Hannibalic War, which embraced the whole of the central and western Mediterranean and all the adjacent lands, it is comparatively easy to see the objective of Scipio. His colleague for the year was Publius Licinius Crassus, to whom was entrusted the guard over Bruttium and Hannibal, while Scipio was allotted the province of Sicily with the provision that from there he might pass over to Africa 'if he judged it to be to the State's advantage'. This, despite the objection of the Fabian party to any more overseas involvements, was a clear invitation to him to take the war to the doorstep of Carthage, for all Sicily was now quiet and subservient to Rome. At the same time his opponents in the Senate did everything that they could to prevent him from acting – denying him the right to take overseas any legions from Italy itself because of the threat from Bruttium ('Where Hannibal is, there is the centre of the war'.) It was left to Scipio's own discretion whether he took the war into North Africa. If he failed, he would be found guilty of exceeding his instructions.

While it is possible to see the Roman goals at this moment in the long conflict, it is extremely difficult to understand those of the Carthaginians. There are no records for one thing, and Livy could not have known them, and Polybius – who may well have done so and who is more reliable as a historian – cannot help, for this section of his history is lost. The instructions to Mago to proceed to the Ligurian coast after enrolling a small hard core of an army in the Balearic islands, and then to proceed to Cisalpine Gaul and enlist more Gauls, as had Hasdrubal, suggests that a duplicate type of operation was planned – a swoop from the north to join up with Hannibal coming up from the south. On the other hand, poor though communications were in those days, it would be surprising if the Carthaginian senate did not have enough evidence of how this strategy had failed under Hasdrubal. They must certainly also have known (for Carthaginian spies were everywhere) that Etruria was disaffected and potentially ripe for rebellion against their ancient enemy, the Romans. If Hannibal's brother Mago could raise enough troops among the Ligurians and the Cisalpine Gauls to inspire this Etruscan revolt – and then consolidate it by joining up with the Etruscans – Rome would indeed be threatened as never before since Hannibal had crossed the Alps. At such a moment, Hannibal, moving up from Bruttium, would disclose the power of his generalship against the armies that watched him in the south.

Carthage and its rulers (and they, like Rome, had always two conflicting parties, one suing for negotiated peace and the other for war) did not fail Hannibal or Mago even at this late hour. During the course of the year 205 two main convoys were sent up from North Africa to Italy, the one designed for Mago and the other for Hannibal. It was evidence of Carthage's shipbuilding capability that, even after their steady humiliation since the First Punic War, they could still send fleets across the seas. The convoy designed to reinforce Hannibal in the south was never to reach him: eighty Carthaginian ships were captured that summer as they made their way across the quiet seas off Sardinia. Once again the Romans displayed their naval superiority and showed how well they understood the importance of seapower. The convoy to Mago, however, got through and reinforced him with 25 warships, 6,000 infantry, 800 cavalry and 7 elephants. He also received a further sum of money for buying the services of mercenary troops.

While his brother was raising troops in the north, Hannibal was still held inactive in Bruttium and little took place on this front except for desultory forays into Roman territory. The quality of Hannibal's men was now such that it is doubtful if he could have fielded an army capable of a major engagement. Proof of this can be seen in the circumstances under which he now lost Locri, one of his only two ports (and by far the best), to a seaborne attack launched by Scipio from his base in Sicily. Although Locri was technically outside his sphere of command Scipio realised that his fellow consul to the north could never fight his way down through Bruttium to capture the city, so he acted wisely and on his own judgement. Three thousand men were despatched from Rhegium under one of Scipio's officers, Quintus Pleminius, to attack Locri overland, at the same time as – in the usual fashion – a group of dissidents within the city prepared to hand it over. The small harbour of

Locri lay sheltered between two heights, both of which were defended by citadels. The Romans managed to seize one of these while the Carthaginians retreated into the other. On hearing the news Hannibal immediately marched down from the north, sending word ahead to the Carthaginians to sally out as soon as they saw his army approaching. Scipio, who had anticipated that Hannibal would move to the rescue of the town, meanwhile came round by sea from Messina in Sicily and disembarked troops, who waited in the town until the Carthaginian army came in sight. Instead of being met by the Carthaginian garrison, Hannibal found a Roman fleet in the port and fresh Roman troops drawn up for battle. His relief of Locri was foiled, and his raw troops were worsted in an early encounter. There was nothing left for him but to withdraw.

He had lost Locri, and now the only port remaining to him was Croton. For Hannibal's remaining two years in Italy this ancient Greek city became his main base. Once the home of the philosopher Pythagoras, and of the famous athlete Milo (six times victor in wrestling at the Olympic games), Croton was now little more than an unimportant provincial town with a small harbour. Its most famous feature was the great temple to the goddess Hera, known as Hera Lacinia after the promontory on which it stood. For centuries this had been one of the chief landmarks for sailors as they neared Italy from Greece, or as they took their departure south of the Gulf of Taranto for the Ionian islands. It was here, amid the *ex votos* of mariners, that Hannibal later had set up the great bronze tablet (mentioned by Polybius) on which was recorded in Punic and Greek the strength of his army when he had crossed the Alps, and his actions during the fifteen years he had spent in Italy.

It was at Locri that Hannibal and Scipio first encountered one another as commanders. Curiously enough, it was from the ranks of other survivors of the Roman disaster at Cannae (Scipio himself had been one) that Scipio now began to prepare his attack on Africa. In Sicily, which he intended to use as his invasion base, the excellent harbour of Lilybaeum (Marsala) in the west was the nearest point of departure for the area of Carthage. The two legions in the province had been formed out of the discredited soldiers of Cannae, who had been sent there in disgrace after their defeat, and whom the anti-Scipio faction in the Senate doubtless thought would prove unsuitable for any ambitious projects that Scipio might harbour. However, these legionaries, who had been strengthened by Marcellus' victorious veterans of Syracuse, were still smarting from their humiliation and wanted nothing better than to redress the past and take the war into the enemy camp. Scipio, who had suffered with them, understood their feelings and was exactly the right man to lead them. Furthermore, in the desire for vengeance on their ancient enemy, Scipio enjoyed the voluntary help of many of the communities in

Italy, a number of whom, such as the Etruscans, were no doubt eager to prove their loyalty to Rome now that it seemed clear that the Carthaginian cause was doomed.

Livy lists the places and details the spontaneous aid that was given the ambitious young consul as he prepared to carry the war into enemy territory: 'First the Etruscan communities said that they would aid the consul, each according to its resources. The men of Caere promised grain for the crews and supplies of every kind, the men of Populonium iron, Tarquinii linen for sail, Volaterra the interior fittings of ships, also grain. . . .' Arretium supplied 3,000 shields and an equal number of helmets; 50,000 javelins, short spears and lances; also axes, shovels, sickles, baskets and hand mills, sufficient to equip 40 warships; 120,000 packs of wheat, and supplementary pay for petty officers and oarsmen. A large quantity of grain came from Perusa, Clusium and Rusellae as well as fir trees for shipbuilding. Umbria and the Sabine district provided soldiers, while the Marsians, Paelignians and Marrucini volunteered in large numbers for the fleet. Camerinum sent a cohort of 600 fully armed men. Twenty quinqueremes and 10 quadriremes, ready and equipped, were launched 'on the forty-fifth day after the timber had been brought from the forests'.

In the spring of 204 B.C. Scipio embarked at Lilybaeum with 30,000 men in 400 transports escorted by 40 warships. No longer consul, but proconsul with command over Sicily, Scipio was taking the vengeance of the Roman Republic into Africa.

XXVII

RECALL TO AFRICA

During Hannibal's last years on the continent of Europe he had been able to do little more than ensure that the Roman legions remained in Italy. It was nothing but the fear of Hannibal himself that tied down so many thousands of men, for his army was by now a makeshift affair that in any other hands could have posed no threat to Rome. The focus of interest in the war had shifted first to Spain and then, after Scipio's brilliant generalship had driven out the Carthaginians, it was to be the turn of Africa. As it became clear that Carthage itself would soon be the object of attack and that Carthaginian power was everywhere weakening, the various tribes inhabiting the Mediterranean coastline of the African continent began to prepare to shift their allegiance away from their old master.

When Scipio left Africa after his meeting with the Numidian king Syphax, he could be pleased that he had achieved his object and that Syphax was now an ally of Rome. Scipio knew from the war in Spain and Italy that a fearsome and efficient part of the Carthaginian armies was provided by their Numidian horsemen. He hoped that he could count on this alliance to give his own invading army the cavalry in which the Romans tended to be deficient. Before he even left Sicily, however, he heard from Syphax that Scipio could count on no support from him and, indeed, Syphax carefully warned him not to invade or he would meet with disaster. What had happened was that, during Scipio's absence in Rome and Sicily, Hasdrubal Gisgo had won back Syphax's allegiance to Carthage by offering him in marriage his beautiful daughter Sophonisba. The Numidian king, 'while under the influence of the first transports of love', abandoned his Roman alliance and became the faithful servant of Carthage. Masinissa, the other powerful Numidian king and the deadly enemy of Syphax, after a long struggle for the throne of his Numidian kingdom, was then defeated by Syphax and forced into hiding. One thing only was certain when Scipio left with his invasion force for North Africa : he had lost the support that he had counted on from Syphax but, so great was the hatred between him and Masinissa, the latter might be counted upon to help the Romans if it meant revenge upon the man who had humiliated him.

In the spring of 204 Scipio's troops disembarked at Cape Farina (the Promontory of Apollo), the headland forming the western arm of the great bay on which Carthage lay. Close to hand was the town of Utica which

Scipio hoped to use as his main base and port for the African campaign. The arrival of the Roman fleet and army so close to their city caused a panic among the Carthaginians that may even have exceeded the state into which Rome had been thrown by the early exploits of Hannibal. Unlike the Romans they had no large standing army, having always depended heavily on mercenaries; they had no reliable allies, and no great general to hand, with Hannibal far away across the sea in Bruttium. One suspects that even so early in the African war there must have been voices raised to recall Hamilcar's son. The Carthaginians only knew by repute what Hannibal had achieved in Europe, but they must have remembered how his father had saved them before. In the meantime Hasdrubal Gisgo began to raise an army (of indifferent quality) while Syphax, still enamoured of his bride and therefore of Carthage, prepared to aid him with his cavalry. As might have been expected, the latter's arch enemy, Masinissa, now appeared in Scipio's camp, promising the help of his own Numidian horsemen. The hatred between these two North African kings is said to have been fuelled even further by the fact that Masinissa had also been a suitor of Hasdrubal Gisgo's daughter, Sophonisba, and, to echo Livy, 'Numidians surpass all other barbarian people in the violence of their appetites'. Sex, it seems, as well as politics played a part in the war.

Having achieved his objective, the invasion of Carthaginian territory with an adequate army and fleet, it might have been expected that Scipio would have acted with the same dash and determination that had given him New Carthage and then all of Spain. Instead he seems to have hesitated, almost as if he was daunted by the strangeness and vastness of North Africa. Unlike Hannibal in his crossing of the Alps, Scipio had been able to transport siege machinery in his ships from Sicily, and he had many trained siege engineers among his men who had assisted at the capture of Syracuse. But Carthage on its shimmering bay was undoubtedly much more formidable, and perhaps he did not know of the poor state of morale within the city and its inadequate forces. He never seems to have considered attacking it, but instead began the siege of Utica. It is also possible that Scipio was haunted by the memory of the famous Regulus who, after early successes in the same area during the First Punic War, had been decisively defeated and had died under torture at the hands of the Carthaginians. He had been warned of the fate of Regulus by the Fabians in the Senate and he knew how many of his enemies in Rome would be glad to see his hubristic plans laid low.

In any case Scipio decided to secure his base at Utica before moving to consider an attack on the capital. Even in this objective, however, he was unsuccessful: for nearly forty days the towers and walls of Utica were attacked by land and sea, yet still the defenders held out. Then the relieving force under Hasdrubal Gisgo and Syphax arrived – an army, according to

Polybius, larger than Scipio's and with a formidable amount of cavalry. Obliged to raise the siege, Scipio withdrew his forces into a camp on the headland, where he set up winter headquarters. The first year's campaign in the land of his enemies had not been a success and he was still held in check on the beachhead where he had landed so confidently earlier that year.

While Scipio was engaged in Africa, the two consuls for the year were in Italy, one, Cornelius Cethegus, watching Etruria and the north in case Mago should move, and the other, Sempronius Tuditanus, guarding Bruttium and Hannibal. Sempronius, ambitious and eager to try conclusions with the Carthaginian, marched down to threaten Hannibal's last stronghold, the town of Croton. In the first confused clash, while both armies seem to have been on the march, the Romans were worsted, losing about 1,200 men. Unwilling to take any further risks, Sempronius summoned up the proconsul Publius Licinius with his two legions. There were now four Roman and four allied legions moving on Croton, and Hannibal, whose forces by this time can have consisted of barely half that number, prepared to accept battle, the reason no doubt being that he could not afford at this stage to abandon the city and the port. With insufficient Numidian cavalry and practically no trained heavy infantry from Spain or Carthage, his unskilled army was forced to retreat within the walls of the city, losing, so Livy tells us, over 4,000 men. The consul could perhaps claim to have been the first man to have driven Hannibal from the field during all the years in Italy. But his objective, Croton, was still in the hands of Hannibal, who stayed behind the closed gates. He could afford to wait.

Had Hannibal been able to withdraw that year with whatever army and ships he could muster, his appearance on the coast of Africa would have changed the course of the war. The senate and people of Carthage would have rallied their spirits; his very name would have called in the tribesmen and the horsemen in their thousands; Roman morale would have slumped. Scipio had been unsuccessful at Utica and had done little except harry the surrounding countryside; the arrival of Hannibal over the sea behind him would have put the Romans at such a disadvantage that they might have been forced to evacuate. But no word came to summon Hannibal back to the city.

The role of Mago in this phase of the war is not well documented, but from such information as is available, it seems that Mago did not intend to make a conjunction with Hannibal but rather to divert Roman attention to the north, thus preventing the movement of a Roman invasion force to North Africa. His recruitment of Ligurians to his cause was successful, especially since he had shown how he could dominate the whole Gulf of Genoa by his occupation of the two major ports and his fleet's activity in that area. The Cisalpine Gauls, however, who had shown themselves somewhat reluctant to join Hasdrubal when he had come down through the Alps, were even less willing to join a cause that they now saw so far in decline. Their fathers had sprung to arms behind Hannibal, hoping to see Rome destroyed, but despite Hannibal's successes they had died all over Italy, and such few as still remained with him were pent up hundreds of miles away in savage Bruttium. The Gauls had witnessed the failure of Hasdrubal at the Metaurus river, and this youngest brother of the family, Mago, could hardly move them to risk the wrath of Rome. (They had also learned the benefits of those settled agricultural areas which the Romans made possible, and the simple Homeric warfare of their fathers had become less attractive.)

In the summer of 203 Mago seems to have crossed into the area of the Po, thus concentrating the attention of the Roman legions to the north. Clearly he hoped for a rising in Etruria against the Romans. Whatever the intention, Mago was engaged in a major battle with the Romans on Italian soil in 203. It seems to have been hard-fought, with considerable losses on both sides, but with the Carthaginian forces yielding the day. During this action Mago himself was seriously wounded, and withdrew with the other survivors into Liguria. This was to be the last major engagement in Italy between Carthaginians and Romans in the course of the war. On his arrival in Liguria, Mago found instructions awaiting him to return with his ships and men to Carthage. The mother-city, threatened by Scipio, was now on the defensive. The Italian venture was, to all intents and purposes, to be abandoned. Mago died of his wounds as his fleet passed Sardinia – that island of timber and minerals which was now under Roman control, but which had once been one of the largest of the many Carthaginian island-colonies that had threatened Rome.

During the winter of 204–203, while Hannibal remained in Croton and his brother Mago prepared for the spring offensive that led to his death, Scipio was busy in North Africa. He had failed to capture Utica, and the opening of his campaign had not yielded the success that he may have expected after his experience with the Carthaginians in Spain, but he had never ceased to work at his overall strategy – the defeat of Carthage with, as ultimate aim, the incorporation of the city's North African empire into that of Rome. (No man may claim more credit – or blame – for the nurturing of the Roman empire than Publius Cornelius Scipio, who has been hailed in the twentieth century by the British military historian B. H. Liddell Hart as 'greater than Napoleon'.)

Realising that the Numidian Syphax was possibly of more consequence than Masinissa, commanding more forces—and forces on which Carthage was largely dependent – Scipio decided to try to detach him from his allegiance. Throughout the winter envoys moved back and forth between the Roman and the Numidian, Scipio pretending to an authority which was never his – that of being able to make a peace treaty without any reference to Rome – and Syphax suggesting an end to the war by an agreement between Scipio and Hannibal that the one should leave Africa and the other Italy. The negotiations were protracted, for Scipio could easily divine that Syphax only wanted the Romans out of the way so that he could finally destroy his hated rival Masinissa and take over all his kingdom. When the Roman envoys went to visit the camps of their enemies they were always accompanied by senior centurions, disguised as grooms and servants, who took the opportunity, while their 'masters' were in conference, of making a careful study of the camps and the disposition of their enemy. Upon their return they reported that discipline was lax, morale low, and that the Carthaginians were housed in wooden huts, while the Numidians lived in reed tents, a great many of which were not even within the stockade of the camp.

By the early spring of 203 Scipio was ready for his offensive. He sent a message to Syphax that he was ready to conclude a treaty but that he had some opposition – which he hoped to overcome – from his senior officers, and this meant that he must, for the moment, break off negotiations. Syphax and Hasdrubal Gisgo took this to mean that in due course Scipio would be able to persuade his fellows of the good sense of a treaty, and they sent back a reply that for their part they were only too willing to agree to the terms that had been discussed. Scipio now knew not only the disposition of the enemy, but that their morale was low and that they eagerly sought peace. His whole behaviour was far from in accordance with that old Roman tradition of good faith, which their historians liked to contrast, unjustly, with so-called 'Punic' faith. Indeed, it would seem that the Carthaginians often behaved more scrupulously than the Romans. Hannibal's conception of the honours of the battlefield, for instance, always entailed paying the proper respects to the enemy dead, while Claudius Nero after his victory at the Metaurus river had descended to the level of cutting off the head of Hannibal's brother, preserving it, and then throwing it into Hannibal's lines at night.

Scipio, having induced a feeling of relaxation among his enemies, now began to move. He reopened the siege of Utica by land and sea, sending round his fleet – newly launched after the winter – to blockade, while the main engines of war were dragged from his camp for the land attack. All this was no more than a blind to distract the Carthaginians from his real intention, and possibly to convince Syphax and Hasdrubal Gisgo that he was continuing to play at a war that did not really threaten them, whilst waiting for his Roman opposition to be persuaded that a peace treaty should be sought. His clever diversion succeeded, and the Carthaginians and Numidians felt secure that he was doing no more than repeat his tactics of the previous year. Then Scipio struck.

One night, the Roman officers suddenly began to move their men out of camp as soon as the trumpet-call announcing nightfall had been sounded. Some seven miles lay between them and the enemy encampments, which they reached about midnight. Scipio's right-hand man, Laelius, was assigned together with Masinissa and his horsemen to attack the Numidian camp while Scipio attacked the Carthaginians. With the attentions of the Carthaginian and Numidian leaders concentrated upon Utica, and relaxed by the long-protracted peace negotiations as to their state of preparedness, their camps were vulnerable targets. Masinissa's Numidians had no difficulty in riding in amongst the camp of Syphax and setting fire to the reed huts — they were accustomed to living in them themselves and they knew how readily they would blaze. There was a wind blowing, possibly a southerly at that time of the year, and in a short while the whole encampment was on fire. As the drowsy occupants rushed out, thinking that no more than an accident had happened, they were cut down by Masinissa's horsemen. Alerted by their sentries of the holocaust in the neighbouring camp, the Carthaginians began to leave their wooden huts — unarmed spectators. As they did so, Scipio's Romans (many still smarting from Cannae) fell upon them. The Carthaginian camp too was burned to the ground, and the Carthaginians were killed in their thousands.

With this double blow, so brilliantly if somewhat treacherously executed, Scipio had destroyed the combined forces of the Carthaginian army. Hasdrubal Gisgo and Syphax themselves managed to escape, with only a few thousand men between them. Hasdrubal as commanding general had been guilty of grave negligence in allowing himself to be lulled into a sense of security. His experiences fighting against Scipio in Spain should have alerted him to the fact that the Roman was both a great strategist and a devious and hard-hitting commander in the field. He now followed up his night attack, pursuing Hasdrubal Gisgo and the remnants of his army, driving him out of a town where he had taken refuge and sacking several local settlements. There was fear and confusion in Carthage but, despite the urgings of the peace party, the resolution was taken to fight on. Carthage's immense wealth was used to give Hasdrubal and Syphax the money to set about forming another army. The arrival of four thousand Celtiberians, recruited from Spain, produced a fighting core for the new force, and within a short space of time Hasdrubal and Syphax had raised an army of some 30,000 men which they assembled in an area known as the Great Plains on the Bagradas river. Scipio wasted no time and, leaving a token siege force around Utica, marched rapidly after the enemy. When he caught up with them he destroyed this second army in a masterly set piece battle. Once again Hasdrubal and Syphax escaped in the general rout, the first to Carthage and the other to Cirta.

Scipio, even more than Hannibal, never relaxed after a success but followed up his advantage. He now moved against a number of North African towns, some of whom came over to him out of fear, and others because of old grudges against Carthage. Next Scipio began the siege of Utica – this time in earnest – with half his army, sending the other half under Laelius and Masinissa along the North African coast into Numidia. Masinissa was eager to try conclusions again with his enemy Syphax, both for the sake of Sophonisba and to recapture Cirta which, although now the capital of Syphax, had once belonged to Masinissa's father. In a hard fought battle he and his cavalry and the enduring Roman legionaries not only routed Syphax's army but captured him alive. Masinissa's triumph was complete, for not only did he regain Cirta but, exercising a truly North African sense of revenge, he also took his enemy's wife Sophonisba for his own. Scipio was later to reprimand him for this, since Syphax and his wife were both the prisoners of Rome, and to Rome they must go. Sophonisba, rather than be held captive to adorn a Roman triumph, took poison. The story of this young Carthaginian noblewoman, enmeshed in war and politics, is a curious and moving one. Bearing some resemblance to the stories of Dido and Cleopatra, it is yet another North African tragedy.

These successive disasters in the spring and early summer of 203 had thoroughly alarmed everyone in Carthage. The same Hanno who had commanded Hannibal's heavy cavalry at Cannae was put in charge of all defence, and Carthaginian envoys were sent to Rome to try to negotiate terms of peace. As a last blow to Carthaginian fortunes, an attempt to relieve Utica failed. All these disasters coming on the heels of one another now prompted a clamour at every level, from the council on the Byrsa to the homes, workshops and warehouses of the city – 'Recall Hannibal!' Unfortunately, as events were to show, they had left it a year too late.

Despite the naval superiority of Rome, three Carthaginian fleets managed to cross the Mediterranean between Italy and North Africa during that year. One carried the dying Mago back from the Ligurian coast with his mixed force of Balearic troops, Ligurians and Gauls; the second was sent up from Carthage to evacuate Hannibal; and the third was this same one, enlarged by such ships as Hannibal had in Croton, bringing him back to defend Carthage in her hour of need. The sea is wide, and in the days of primitive communications it was hardly possible for the Romans to keep an eye on all the shipping routes. Centuries later, even Nelson, who was consciously looking for Napoleon's fleet, failed to sight him as he sailed triumphantly towards Egypt.

Hannibal's fleet was clearly inadequate for his needs, and the army which he finally brought back with him to Africa probably numbered no more than 15,000 men (estimates range between 12,000 and 24,000). The Army of Italy was a strange composite. There can have been few if any of the veterans who had crossed the Alps with him some fifteen years before. The Bruttians, Gauls, and Roman deserters who now made up the large part of his troops were clearly not of the same quality, but they still willingly followed the same man, their one-eyed Carthaginian general. That he was short of transports is evident from the fact that he could not take back the horses which had helped him to so many of his victories and which he would sadly need the following year. All had to be killed so as not to leave them for the Romans.

In the autumn of 203 Hannibal looked his last on the small port of Croton and, beyond the old city, saw the rugged heights of the Sila range, dense with trees, a wild wolf landscape. For the last few years he had had to make this area his home, but once he had ranged all Italy; from the Po valley in the far north, to smiling Etruria, to the west coast and the Bay of Neapolis, where the Greek cities clustered, and then, many times, to the wilder shores of the Adriatic. He knew the land and its peoples as few Italians would ever know it: cities and townships, the frowning walls of Rome – where he had never penetrated – hot plains like Cannae, domesticated valleys, indolent Capua, peasants and charcoal burners, wild mountain men and tough, disciplined Romans – a whole world, which he had almost made his own. Now he was going home, to a city that he could hardly remember. Yet it was for Carthage that he had fought so long and suffered so much – for Carthage and for an oath taken by a boy on a smoking altar.

XXVIII

ZAMA

In the autumn of 203 B.C., before Hannibal had left Italy, the terms of a treaty proposed by Scipio to the Carthaginians had already been accepted by them and had been sent to Rome for discussion. In view of the long bitterness of the war, and the desolation that had been made of great areas of Italy, they were moderate. Firstly, all Carthaginian forces were to leave Italy, and Spain must be abandoned. All deserters, runaway slaves and prisoners-of-war must be returned to Rome. All Carthaginian warships save twenty must be surrendered. A very large quantity of wheat and barley must be supplied to feed the Roman troops and, finally, a heavy indemnity must be paid. It is not surprising that Carthage accepted terms that compared favourably with those of the First Punic War, and an armistice was concluded, pending a ratification of the treaty from Rome.

Scipio also sent Masinissa to Rome in company with Laelius, the former to obtain recognition of his Numidian kingship and the latter, who knew his general's mind, to enlarge on the proposed terms and act as spokesman for Scipio's interests in the treaty. It is significant that Masinissa should go to Rome for confirmation of his kingship. In the past, Carthage had been the natural seat of authority for all local kings and their tribes. Scipio's action is already asserting the dominance of Rome over North Africa. Furthermore he is presenting his Fabian enemies with a *fait accompli*, and making Rome responsible for North African affairs.

In the same year that Hannibal left Italy his old honourable opponent Quintus Fabius Maximus died, the man who had done more than any other to teach the Romans that the only way to wear down – and finally defeat – such a military genius was the way of 'the delayer'. The Romans, except on a few disastrous occasions, had followed the old man's precepts until they had kept Hannibal confined in the wild country of the south, and lastly in a narrow area around Croton. The news that Hannibal had finally left their land naturally brought rejoicing in Rome and an effusion of hope, but there still remained great anxiety, as Livy reveals.

Men could not make up their minds whether it was a fit subject for rejoicing that Hannibal, retiring from Italy after sixteen years, had left the Roman people free to take possession of it, and not rather a ground for apprehension that he had crossed over to Africa with his army intact. The place doubtless had been changed, they thought, not the danger. Fore-telling that mighty conflict Quintus Fabius, recently deceased, had often predicted, not without reason, that in his own land Hannibal would be a more terrible enemy than in a foreign country. And Scipio would have to deal ... with Hannibal, who had been born, one might almost say, at the headquarters of his father, the bravest of generals, had been reared and brought up in the midst of arms; who even in boyhood was a soldier, in earliest manhood a general; who, ageing as a victor [Hannibal was about forty-five], had filled the Spanish and Gallic lands and Italy from the Alps to the Straits with the evidence of his mighty deeds. He was in command of an army whose campaigns equalled his own in number; was toughened by enduring such hardships as one could hardly believe human beings had endured; had been spattered with Roman blood a thousand times and carried the spoils, not of soldiers only but of generals. Many men who would encounter Scipio in battle had with their own hands slain Roman praetors, generals-in-command, consuls; had been decorated with crowns for bravery in scaling city-walls and camp defences; had wandered through captured camps, captured cities of the Romans. All the magistrates of the Roman people did not at that time have so many fasces [those symbols of authority] as Hannibal was able to have borne before him, having captured them from fallen generals.

This account, while showing in what great awe Hannibal was still held by the Romans, errs in its description of his army. Livy, or his authorities, is speaking of the army that marched over the Alps, and that had long since disappeared. Hannibal was now in command of the ragged composite force that had held Croton for the past few years. Nevertheless, his arrival in Africa, bringing any army at all, had such an effect upon Carthaginian morale that the Barcid party began almost immediately to seek for a renewal of the war.

Hannibal landed at Leptis near Hadrumetum (Sousse) where he set up camp for the winter and began to reorganise his forces and recruit more soldiers and horsemen. Here he was joined by the remnants of Mago's army and learned that his youngest brother was dead. There can be small doubt that Hannibal would have accepted Scipio's peace terms as being the best thing for Carthage, even though he can have had little knowledge of the political factions and intrigue in the city. But he was astute enough to know that the overall Carthaginian position was hopeless in view of the loss of Spain, the increasing power of Rome by sea and by land, and the native man-power that fuelled their legions. He had defeated the Romans many times in battle, it was true, but he knew that the Romans were hardy and brave soldiers, knew too that they were already – dangerously – beginning to learn from his tactics, and were adopting more flexible methods on the battlefield.

In his early years in Italy he had profited from the out-of-date system where-by the consuls were automatically in charge of the legions and, since they were changed every year, never had the time to learn professional expertise or adapt their tactics. He had also been able to make use of known divisions and differences of temperament between two consuls. But he saw quite clearly in the emergence of Scipio the shadow of the future, where individual generals, in like manner to himself, would emerge – men totally dedicated to war, learning by experience on the battlefield, and familiarising them-selves with not only the nature of the battle terrain but also the quality and the racial character of their adversaries.

Whatever Hannibal may have thought about accepting the peace con-ditions, the war faction in Carthage, making use of his name and fame, had now got the upper hand. In the winter of 203 B.C. a food-convoy from Sicily destined for Scipio's forces was caught in a storm and driven ashore in the area of Carthage, and Carthaginian warships were sent out to capture it and bring the provisions into the city. This was in clear contradiction of the truce, and Scipio despatched envoys by sea to register a protest. On their way back the ships carrying the envoys were treacherously attacked by Carthaginian triremes, sent to lie in wait for them, and they narrowly escaped with their lives. Scipio rightly saw this as a declaration that the truce was over and that war was renewed. Here indeed was evidence of Punic faith, although it is very doubtful if Hannibal, seventy miles away in Had-rumetum, had any knowledge of it. It was an act of folly, something to which he was not prone.

Scipio reopened the war and attacked such towns in the area as were still under the jurisdiction of Carthage. Throughout the summer of 202, while Hannibal, realising that a major battle was now inevitable, continued to train and gather more recruits for his army, Scipio laid siege to Carthagin-ian towns, showing no mercy when they fell and enslaving the inhabitants. He was determined to show the Carthaginians that those who broke treaties had put themselves outside the normal considerations of war. He, too, was fully aware that the final test was yet to come and that Carthage could not be forced to yield until he and Hannibal had met on the field of battle and established conclusively the outcome of the war. Masinissa, having returned from Rome confirmed in his kingship, was away in Numidia consolidating his hold upon the country; he received an urgent summons from Scipio to muster all the men he could and join the Romans.

Hannibal now received orders from Carthage to march and challenge Scipio before it was too late. The council and the city were deeply worried by the devastation of their land that was going on unchecked, and at the loss of tribute-paying cities and townships: they were witnessing the destruction of the fertile hinterland which for centuries had maintained the great mercantile city on the sea. Hannibal refused to be hurried and replied that he would fight when he was ready. He had good reason for his response since he was still waiting for reinforcement of his cavalry arm, in which he was singularly deficient, and he knew well enough how large a part the Numidians had played in all his successful actions. He was trying to replace this deficiency by training up elephants, and at the time of the final engagement he had some eighty of them in his army. These were, however, young animals, which had never been in action and, as events showed, were more of a liability than an asset. The fact was that even though the Romans themselves used the elephant to some extent in later centuries, it was already an obsolescent weapon of war. Elephants had achieved successes in the past through their formidability when unleashed in great waves upon primitive people and undisciplined lines of infantry. But the Romans in Italy had already taken their measure and had discovered that, when assailed by flights of the formidable *pilum*, they were likely to turn tail and run down their own army. Semi-trained elephants, which were all that Hannibal was able to muster, were to prove the truth of this in the crucial battle.

Some historians have commented that Hannibal made a tactical error in relying upon them, but the fact was that he was compelled to do so through his shortage of cavalry. He did, however, late in that summer receive some useful reinforcements in the shape of 2,000 horsemen from a Numidian prince, Tychaeus, who was a rival of Masinissa and who no doubt hoped to do to Masinissa what the latter had done to Syphax, and then take over the kingdom for himself. These North African rivalries and intrigues, difficult as they may be to unravel from this distance in time, nevertheless played a great part in the battle that was to decide the fate of the western world. The army that Hannibal finally led out to engage Scipio was even more heterogeneous than usual: Balearians, Ligurians, Bruttians, Gauls, Carthaginians, Numidians, and (strangely enough at this late moment) some Macedonians sent by King Philip, who perhaps at last had realised that the defeat of Rome was all-important for the freedom of his own country.

Leaving Hadrumetum, Hannibal marched west in the direction of a town called Zama, which is probably to be identified with a later Roman colony Zama Regia (Jama) ninety miles west of Hadrumetum. Reports had reached him that Scipio was engaged in burning villages, destroying crops and enslaving the inhabitants of all this fertile area, upon which Carthage depended for its grain and other food. It can only have been this driving necessity that made Hannibal march after Scipio, for on the surface it seems more logical for him to have taken his army in the direction of Carthage and interposed himself between Scipio and the city. But the latter's systematic destruction of towns and villages, and his present activities in the Carthaginian hinterland, clearly precluded the ability of the city to feed a further

40,000 or so men, together with their horses and elephants, as well as its own teeming masses. The main cause, then, for the battle taking place where it did arose out of a matter of supplies to the capital. Scipio knew what he was doing, and had quite deliberately drawn Hannibal away from the city so as to decide the outcome of the war in an area selected by himself. It is an ironical fact that the great Carthaginian did not know his own country, not having seen any of it since he was nine years old, whereas Scipio and the Romans were by now well acquainted with the Carthaginian terrain. But Scipio was not without his worries: his army, probably somewhat smaller than Hannibal's, although well trained and experienced in the climate and conditions of North Africa, still lacked its cavalry arm. He desperately awaited the arrival of Masinissa and his Numidians, without whom he could hardly engage in a major battle – particularly against an opponent such as Hannibal.

On reaching Zama, Hannibal, as was natural enough, sent forward spies to try to discover the nature and number of the Roman army: in particular he must have been concerned to find out just how strong was Scipio's cavalry. These men were detected and brought before the Roman general, who had them entertained, shown round the camp, and then released to report back to their master. Some historians have doubted the likelihood of this, instancing among other things that the same story is told by Herodotus about Xerxes and the Greek spies prior to the great Persian invasion of Greece. There is nothing inherently improbable about it, however, and the fact that it is vouched for by Polybius gives it a certain authenticity. Scipio no doubt wished to let his enemy know that he was supremely confident about the outcome of the impending battle. There was something else which that astute Roman must have wished to be reported back to Hannibal: Masinissa and his Numidians were not in the camp. It was this, of course, which Hannibal wished to find out more than anything else, and the news that Scipio was weak in cavalry must have been encouraging. What he did not know of course, and Scipio undoubtedly did, was that Masinissa and his Numidians were only two days' ride away.

Unaware that Masinissa was closing up, and thinking that he was still busily engaged in trying to establish his somewhat precarious hold over the Numidian kingdom, Hannibal possibly felt that he was in a position of superiority to the Roman. This would be a good moment, then, to try to negotiate and see whether he could not obtain favourable conditions for Carthage – terms similar to those which Scipio had previously given the Carthaginians but, if anything, somewhat improved. Accordingly he sent a message to Scipio asking him for a personal meeting to discuss terms, something to which the latter agreed. Apart from anything else, there must have been considerable personal curiosity on both sides about the nature and even the appearance of their opponent. The two men had never seen each other before, although on three occasions over the years they had been close on the field of battle. First of all, the young Scipio had been present at the battle of the Ticinus, just after Hannibal had swept into Italy (when Scipio had managed to save his wounded father from the battlefield); secondly, he had been at Cannae and had witnessed the full genius and wrath of the Carthaginian unleashed like a storm against the Roman legions: thirdly, he had initiated the successful move against the port of Locri in southern Italy, when he had thwarted Hannibal's attempts to recover it. He had had three opportunities, then, to confront the great enemy of Rome and on each occasion had had the perspicacity to observe exactly how Hannibal reacted in a given situation. The Carthaginian, on the other hand, engaged in the responsibilities of high command, had never been conscious of the pair of keen young eyes that watched him, as it were, from the sidelines. It was as if an ageing chessmaster was soon to meet a student who had secretly for years been studying his 'games', detecting his weaknesses, and determining to improve upon the master's play. Hannibal, for his part, knew only by report of the young man's triumphs in the Spanish war, although he was sufficient strategist and tactician to appreciate just how brilliant was the capturer of New Carthage and the victor in several engagements over men as able as his dead brother Hasdrubal, his dead brother Mago, and Hasdrubal, the son of Gisgo. He had observed how the Romans were changing, learning how to shake free of the old consular command and acquire flexibility on the field of battle, and he was probably as curious as Scipio to meet his opponent face to face.

The factitious accounts of both Polybius and Livy, composed so many years after the events, must be considered suspect, but there can be no doubt as to the outcome of the meeting between these two great commanders – two of the most distinguished soldiers not only of the ancient world, but of all time. Hannibal, apart from the ability to speak Punic, various Hispanic dialects and Gallic, could also speak Greek and Latin fluently: Scipio, apart from Latin, was also educated in Greek. The two men could well have chosen either Latin or Greek as their lingua franca but (like many modern leaders) they preferred to make use of interpreters so as to give them flexibility and time for making their responses. If we ignore the rhetoric of Livy, the substance of their encounter was brief and to the point. Hannibal offered Scipio 'the surrender of all the lands that were formerly in dispute between the two powers, namely Sardinia, Sicily and Spain', together with an agreement that Carthage would never again make war on Rome. He also offered all the islands 'lying between Italy and Africa', i.e. the Aegates islands off western Sicily, the Lipari islands, places like Lampedusa, Linosa, Gozo and Malta – but not naming the western Balearics, which had proved so useful to Carthage. He made no mention of indemnities, nor of the handing over of nearly all the fleet, nor of the return of Roman prisoners and runaways.

Scipio could hardly have been impressed by the offer, pointing out that 'if, before the Romans crossed to Africa, you had retired from Italy, there would have been some hope for your propositions. But now the situation is manifestly changed. . . . We are *here* and you have been reluctantly forced to leave Italy. . . .' Scipio could not accept lesser terms for the Carthaginian surrender than had been agreed by Carthage before their recent betrayal of the treaty. There was no more to be said.

Scipio had gained some invaluable time by his meeting with Hannibal: all along he had been aware that Masinissa and his Numidian horsemen were spurring across the land to be at his side when the great encounter took place. The delay had rendered the arrival of Masinissa in time for the battle almost certain. It was Hannibal who was dazed by the immensity of Africa, and not Scipio, and it was Hannibal – accustomed for so many years to the relative size of Italy – whose intelligence service had been deceived by the absence of Masinissa's cavalry in Scipio's camp, and by the lack of knowledge about events in Numidia. The meeting between Hannibal and Scipio has been compared to that between Napoleon and Alexander I of Russia two thousand years later. 'Mutual admiration struck them dumb,' wrote Livy. One doubts that Hannibal was struck dumb, but he was certainly reassured, while Scipio, for his part, knew that the great expatriate Carthaginian was willing to make peace, and the knowledge that your adversary has anything other than victory in his heart is always a considerable comfort in any contest.

On the day after this historic meeting, Masinissa's troops reached Scipio – there were some 4,000 Numidian horsemen and 6,000 infantrymen in all – and the Roman prepared to give battle in a place of his choosing. Much debate in subsequent centuries has never satisfactorily established the exact location of the battle of Zama, although certainly it derived its name from the fact that the town of Zama was the only well-known point of reference. It is almost impossible to define a specific place in an area of North Africa which was then unmapped, and where one cannot estimate how the land may have changed during two thousand years, yet the research of several scholars seems to place the battle at twenty miles south-east of Naraggara (mentioned by Livy) and thirty miles west of Zama. The site is distinguished by the fact that there are two eminences of rising ground overlooking a flat plain, one having a spring and the other being waterless (both mentioned by Polybius and Livy). Scipio, who had chosen the battlefield, naturally selected the place with the spring for his camp, while Hannibal's men found that they had some distance to go to fetch water. Since it was the hot autumn of North Africa this in itself may have had some bearing on the subsequent battle.

Scipio's forces, although somewhat smaller than those of Hannibal, had two great advantages over the latter's mixed and hastily trained army: the majority of them were disciplined Roman legionaries and, with the arrival of Masinissa, Scipio had superiority in cavalry – the finest horsemen in the world. Scipio could be confident that his Romans would not panic at the elephant charge, upon which it was clear that Hannibal must be counting for the opening phase of the battle, and he took careful steps to see that its effect would be minimised by his unusual disposition of the infantry. Instead of placing the maniples (units of 120 men) in the normal fashion like a chequer board, with the maniples of the second line covering the intervals between the maniples of the first line, and so on, as was standard practice, Scipio placed them one behind the other so that there were open lanes running right through the army. These gaps he filled with his light-armed troops so that they could harass the elephants when they charged and at the same time could take refuge behind the armoured legionaries when necessary, leaving the lanes clear. On his left wing he deployed the Roman cavalry under Laelius, and on his right the Numidians under Masinissa.

Hannibal's dispositions were governed by the fact that shortage of cavalry made him dependent on the elephants: all eighty were ranged in front of his army, the hope being that they would smash the Roman front line troops and cause general chaos in Scipio's dispositions. Behind them Hannibal placed his mixed infantry – Gauls, Ligurians, Balearians and Moors, his intention being, as in other battles, to let the Romans expend their first impetus upon these rough-and-ready troops while keeping his best infantry fresh in reserve. As a second line he placed the Carthaginian and Libyan levies, and behind them what remained of his Army of Italy, the 'Old Guard', held back until the end. On his right wing, facing the Roman cavalry, were the Carthaginian horse and on his left, facing Masinissa, his own Numidian horse.

On that unrecorded day in autumn the last great battle began: the elephant charge thundering across the plain between the two camps. Quite apart from the awe-inspiring sight of those great animals bearing down upon the infantry lines, and their effect upon horses which were unused to their sight and smell, the elephant drivers relied upon the trumpeting of their charges to strike fear into the heart of any enemy. Unfortunately for them, in this case, the Romans reversed the procedure and began to set up a great shouting accompanied by the blast of dozens of war trumpets. The effect upon Hannibal's insufficiently-trained elephants was that it was they who panicked and began to break and turn away from what, perhaps, they believed to be the noise of strange beasts considerably larger than themselves.

Some turned about and crashed into their own front line, while others peeled off to the left and stampeded among Hannibal's Numidian cavalry. Masinissa, whose horsemen were perfectly accustomed to elephants, was not slow to profit from the disintegration of the Carthaginian left wing and charged behind the elephants, putting to flight the other Numidians opposing him. The elephant charge ended as Livy describes:

> A few of the beasts, however, being fearlessly driven into the enemy, caused great losses among the ranks of the light-armed, though suffering many wounds themselves. For springing back into the maniples the light-armed made way for the elephants, to avoid being trampled down, and then would hurl their lances from both sides against the beasts which were now doubly exposed to missiles. Nor was there any slackening in the javelins of the men in the front lines until these elephants also, driven out of the Roman line and into their own by missiles showered upon them from all sides, put the right wing, even the Carthaginian cavalry, to flight. Laelius, on seeing the enemy in confusion, increased their panic.

The Carthaginian battle line was now deprived of cavalry on both flanks, Masinissa chasing Hannibal's left wing from the field while Laelius drove in the Carthaginian horse and routed them. The elephant charge upon which Hannibal had been forced to rely had largely deprived him of such cavalry as he had. The disciplined Roman legionaries now forced back the whole of Hannibal's front line upon his second (composed of his better troops), but the disorganised Gauls and other mercenaries were not allowed to pass through, being met by a line of spears, and had to retire on to the flanks of the second line, many of them fleeing the battlefield. For a time the contest now seemed evenly matched; the Carthaginians and African levies, coming up fresh against the legionaries, were able to hold them and even press them back. But gradually the discipline of the Romans began to tell and Hannibal's second line also began to collapse – trying to fall back through the 'Old Guard' in the rear, only to be met with the same reception that they had given the first line.

Seeing that his men were about to come up against Hannibal's finest troops Scipio sounded the recall. It was an example not only of Scipio's genius in war but also of Roman discipline that, even at this moment in the thick of a bloody battle with the plain piled with dead, they responded to their officers. Scipio at once redeployed his troops in one single extended line to face Hannibal's fresh 'Old Guard'. The latter had hardly joined battle and they too, also in a single line, faced the Roman legionaries. This was the beginning of the second phase of the battle, foot soldier against foot soldier, the elephants expended, and the cavalry all away, as Masinissa and Laelius chased the fleeing Carthaginian horse and Hannibal's Numidians. As the two lines closed, Scipio must surely have prayed that Masinissa and Laelius would not stay too long away pursuing the defeated, but would return to give him the victory. While the two lines swayed back and forth, locked in that 'bludgeon work' fighting at which the Romans were always so good, the issue still remained undecided. Then the rising dust and thunder of hooves over the plain told Scipio – and indeed Hannibal – that all was as good as over. Laelius and Masinissa swept back to take the Carthaginians on either wing and in the rear. The horsemen of Numidia, who had served Hannibal so well in the early years in Italy, had finally contrived his ruin. The remnants of the 'Old Guard' broke and fled. The battle was over. The Romans had won the war.

Hannibal himself left the scene of his defeat with a small escort and retired to Hadrumetum. There was nothing he could do now but advise the Carthaginians that further resistance was impossible, and to accept the best terms that they were offered. For the first time in his long career he had met his match as a general, but he had been principally defeated by lack of cavalry. Even now other Numidians, under a son of Syphax, were being mustered in the desert to come to his aid, but by the time that they reached Carthaginian territory all was over. The triumphant Romans and Masinissa's forces annihilated them in what was the last engagement of the Second Punic War – the war which had been initiated by Hannibal sixteen years before, and which ended at Zama.

XXIX

AFTER THE WAR

Hannibal hurried to Carthage from Hadrumetum to tell the council that, whatever some might say, there was no longer any hope of success by prolonging the war. Many of the Carthaginians, conscious that their city was still the richest in the world, and relatively untouched by the war, found it hard to believe that all was lost. A characteristic story is told of Hannibal being present at one meeting when a young noble was urging his fellow citizens to man their defences and to refuse the Roman terms, and of Hannibal mounting the speaker's rostrum and pulling him to the ground. He apologised immediately, saying that he had been so long away, and so accustomed to the discipline of the camp, that he was unfamiliar with the rules of a parliament. At the same time he begged them, now that they were at the mercy of the Romans, to accept 'such lenient terms as they offered, and pray to the gods that the Roman people may ratify the treaty'. For the terms which Scipio had proposed upon his arrival before the walls of Carthage were better than might have been expected from a conqueror who was dealing with a people that had already betrayed an earlier treaty. Polybius adds that the council recognised that Hannibal's advice 'was wise and to the point, and they agreed to accept the treaty on the Roman conditions, and sent envoys with orders to agree to it'.

Seeing that the Carthaginians' great general and their last army were defeated, and that the city lay defenceless – even though the siege would have been hard and long, as the Third Punic War would one day show – Scipio's conditions of peace were reasonable. As before, all deserters, prisoners of war, and slaves were to be handed over, but this time the warships were to be reduced to no more than ten triremes. Carthage, on the other hand, might retain its former territory in Africa, and its own laws within it, but Masinissa was to have complete control of his kingdom, and Carthage must never again make war on anyone, either within Africa or beyond, without Roman permission. (This effectively ensured that the Numidian kingdom would grow at the expense of Carthage, something which would one day lead to the last Punic War.) Since they had broken the truce, the original war indemnity was doubled, although they were allowed to pay in annual instalments over fifty years. All the Carthaginian elephants were to be surrendered, and no more trained, while at the same time one hundred hostages, chosen by Scipio, were to be handed over for deliverance to Rome. In this way he insured against any further attempts at treachery. As before, the Roman army was to be supplied with grain for three months, as well as their pay until such time as the peace treaty was ratified.

It might have been expected that Rome would demand the surrender of Hannibal himself, considering all that he had inflicted upon them over so many years. This would not have been an unusual condition after the conclusion of such a war, and that it was not made can only be ascribed to Scipio himself who, like many generals under somewhat similar circumstances, had conceived a very great admiration and respect for his opponent. In any case it must have been clear to Scipio that the condition of Carthage was such that without a strong man at the helm the whole curious, mercantile edifice would collapse in ruins. The time would come, within little more than fifty years, that such would be the desire of Rome, but at the moment the Republic was too exhausted to pick up the pieces. To ensure that Carthage fulfilled the terms, paid the reparations, and settled down quietly again in North Africa, a man was needed who fully appreciated how fortunate the city was to have been allowed any acceptable terms at all. That man was Hannibal.

There was, indeed, considerable opposition in Rome to the apparently lenient terms accorded to the defeated. This was understandable enough : for Rome, by the spring of 201 when the treaty was finally ratified, had suffered from seventeen years of unremitting war. Scipio, a young man, much disliked by many of his opponents, a man who had achieved his victories in foreign countries far removed from the desolation of Italy, was telling the bereaved and almost bankrupt senators that they should not squeeze Carthage – in the phrase of a centuries-later war – 'until the pips squeak'. But at the instigation of Scipio's supporters the decision was referred from the senate to the popular assembly, and the people, as nearly always throughout history, wanted peace. In Carthage things followed much the same pattern; the rich in the council being appalled when they realised that the money for the first instalment of the reparations would have to come from their own pockets; and the people, feeling that Carthage had suffered enough, wanting above all an end to war. In Hannibal they were lucky enough to have found as incorruptible and able a statesman in peacetime as he had been a great leader in war.

While Scipio and his army embarked for Rome, Hannibal, who had been appointed Chief Magistrate of Carthage, set about his massive task of reconstruction. Despite all the years of war, the city's commercial prosperity had never been deeply imperilled, even after the loss of Spain. One of the reasons for this was that the trade between the Levant and the western end of the Mediterranean had always continued to flow along the North African coast, where the Romans could do little to interfere. Inevitably, from the

beginning of his task Hannibal ran up against the hatred of his enemies –
the former peace faction that had always declared that trade, not war, was
the business of Carthage. They remained deliberately ignorant of the fact
that expanding Rome could never have left their city in peace. Ironically
enough (something that has happened in later wars), the vanquished found
themselves in the position of having nothing to concentrate upon but to re-
build their factories and their fortunes, while the penurious victors were
immediately confronted by a further set of problems that demanded nearly
all their attention. Rome was now to be engaged with a war against Philip
of Macedon, with trouble in Egypt, revolt among many of the tribes of
Spain, and increased resistance from the Gauls in Italy as well as from those
in Gaul itself. They had discovered that an empire, as so many have done
subsequently, is not something that can be easily controlled, but that it is an
expanding volcano, which can never be contained until some weakness in
its sides or substance permits the fires to roar out – only to be followed by
ultimate collapse and inertia.

When Scipio returned to Rome that year he was naturally accorded a
triumph. His achievements in Africa had been outstanding, and not even his
enemies could deny that he had brought the war to a triumphant conclusion.
At the head of his conquering troops he rode through the garlanded streets,
while the war-elephants of Africa, which had been shipped from Carthage,
dazzled the people with their strangeness and their trumpeting. Scipio was
given the cognomen Africanus, 'the first general who was distinguished by
a name derived from the country which he had conquered'. Understandably
he was the hero of the hour and could probably have been made perpetual
consul or even dictator, as Julius Caesar was to become a hundred and fifty
years later. Wisely, he refused any such honours and seems to have been
content to live the life of a gentleman of leisure, indulging in his passion for
Greek literature and for good conversation, both traits which had been evident when he had been at Syracuse, and which had made him suspect to an
older and more dour generation of Romans.

From the end of the war and for seven years afterwards, Hannibal devoted himself to the affairs of his country and to rebuilding the mercantile
prosperity of Carthage. No longer the great expatriate, he devoted himself
exclusively to Carthaginian home affairs and to ensuring that his country
kept faith with the Romans. It can be questioned whether or not he still
harboured any thoughts of revenge, for Carthage's power base in Spain was
lost to her, she had no navy, and the Romans had control of the sea as well
as dominating the Mediterranean basin by land. At the same time he must
have kept an eye on the Roman progress in the east, where the battle of
Cynoscephalae in 197 B.C. gave Rome her great victory over Philip of
Macedon, breaking Macedonian power for ever. Philip was forced to give

up his fleet, his possessions in Greece, and pay a large war indemnity, as Carthage had done and was still doing. It was probably Hannibal's financial skill in ensuring that Carthage could meet these demands – demands which the Romans had expected would go unfulfilled, thus giving them the opportunity to invade – that caused the Roman hatred of him to revive. He had, too, many enemies among the rich citizens at home, for he had denounced a number of highly-placed officials whose peculations he had uncovered.

The Barcid family, for all its services to Carthage, had always had its rivals and enemies, and there were also those who liked to lay the blame for the recent war entirely on Hannibal. The commercial revival of Carthage, inspired and directed by him, had now aroused Roman jealousy and resentment. It was not surprising, then, that these two factions should become allied in the desire to see him removed from office. It was Scipio who intervened on behalf of his former enemy, pointing out that it ill befitted them to meddle in purely Carthaginian affairs, but the feeling against Hannibal could not be permanently contained. In 195 a commission was sent from Rome to Carthage, alleging that he had been helping an enemy of Rome.

This enemy was Antiochus the Great of Syria, whose ambition was to recreate the eastern empire of Alexander the Great, and who had already established his hold over Palestine, Phoenicia and Cyprus. It is more than likely that Hannibal saw in Antiochus the one ruler in the East who might challenge Rome, and restore a balance of power in the Mediterranean that would allow Carthage once again to assert its old supremacy over Spain and Sicily and the other central islands of the sea. Whether there was any correspondence between them is something that will never be known. Certainly the Romans claimed that there was, and it was on this charge that their envoys now proceeded to Carthage. Cato the Elder, who had served under Scipio in Sicily and who was deeply envious of the latter's fame and position, was now consul and he was determined to have Hannibal brought back to Rome.

When the word reached him of what was afoot, Hannibal was under no illusion that his enemies in Carthage would not betray him to the Romans. He managed to leave the country by a series of clever evasions reminiscent of his skill upon the battlefield. Having received the Roman envoys and had them escorted to their quarters on the Byrsa, he was seen about the city as usual during the day. At nightfall, however, on the pretext of going for a ride in the cool of the evening he slipped off to a villa of his not far from Hadrumetum, where he had a ship prepared, his personal belongings and private fortune already embarked, and a faithful crew awaiting him.

Putting in next day at the island of Cercina, not far from the coast, Hannibal was dismayed to find some other ships there on their way to

Carthage, and he was of course recognised by the crews of the vessels. Having invited the captains and crews, flattered by the invitation, to dine with him, he suggested that they bring ashore the sails and spars of their ships so that they could put up awnings as protection against the sun. The entertainment carried on throughout the day and into the night, when Hannibal quietly embarked and got under way. When his guests awoke next morning their host was gone, and, even if they had had any thought of pursuit and had known his destination, it would have taken them some time to re-rig their ships and follow him. Some weeks later Hannibal landed at that ancient home of the Phoenicians, Tyre, the birthplace of Dido and the mother city of Carthage.

The remaining thirteen years of Hannibal's life are sad to contemplate, although not so desiccated as the last years of Napoleon, for Hannibal remained at liberty until the day when he took his own life. It was the year 195 B.C. when the great hero of the eastern Mediterranean world set foot in the cradle of his race, to be acclaimed by all those in the Levant and Asia Minor who saw their freedom threatened by the advancing shadow of Rome. Soon after the defeat of Philip of Macedon, Rome claimed to be the protector of Greece – a judicious move which pleased the Greeks and at the same time ensured their ultimate servitude. It was only in Antiochus that Hannibal could see any hope for the revival of a war against Italy. Antiochus, however, had no wish to be involved in a distant war in the central Mediterranean, he was only concerned to secure and increase his eastern empire. He had ambitions to be recognised in Greece, but a small force which he sent there was soundly trounced at that pass of classic memory, Thermopylae, and he was hard put to it to secure Asia Minor for himself.

Hannibal's reputation did not make him popular among the military men and advisers who surrounded the Syrian king, and he was never given the fleet and the troops which he had asked for in order to invade Italy. Antiochus, indeed, had many men under arms, but they were not of the calibre of the Romans in any respect. In 189 B.C. at the battle of Magnesia he lost conclusively and was compelled to withdraw from most of Asia Minor, leaving it to the Romans and their allies. Previously in a review of the king's army, although it was nearly twice the size of that which his enemy brought onto the battlefield, Hannibal had dryly replied when asked his opinion of this great host: 'Yes, it will be enough for the Romans, however greedy they may be.'

A few anecdotes survive about Hannibal in these years when he moved, an exile from his own country and a declared 'enemy of the Roman people', through the courts and petty kingdoms of the East. His was the laconic style, the *imperatoria brevitas*, revealed earlier in such remarks as 'Rome has her

Hannibal in Fabius' and 'Marcellus was a good soldier but a rash general'. Invited on one occasion by Antiochus to listen to a lecture by an old academic who specialised in military studies he made no comment until his opinion was specifically asked for, when he quietly remarked: 'In my time I have had to listen to some old fools, but this one beats them all.'

There was a second meeting between Hannibal and Scipio some time before Antiochus opened the war in the East. A mission was sent to Ephesus from Rome to try to discover the Syrian ruler's attitude and intentions. Scipio, who was leading it, sent to ask Hannibal if he was willing to meet him, to which the latter readily agreed. The accounts of this describe the two men talking of old times, and Scipio asking Hannibal who he thought was the greatest general in history. 'Alexander the Great,' Hannibal replied, adding that with only a small force he defeated armies many times greater in number than his own, and that he overran the remotest regions of the earth. Asked whom he would put next, Hannibal thought for a moment and said 'Pyrrhus' (the King of Epirus who had invaded Italy in 280 B.C.), citing his brilliant judgement in his choice of ground and his careful disposition of his troops. The Roman (and Scipio was clearly seeking for a compliment) pressed on: 'And the third?' 'Myself without doubt.' Scipio laughed, 'And what would you have said had you beaten me?' 'Then,' replied the Carthaginian, 'I would have placed myself first of all commanders.'

This nicely turned compliment no doubt delighted Scipio, which is probably the reason that we have it reported by both Livy and Plutarch. Of these two great soldier-statesmen Arnold comments that Scipio resembled 'the Achilles of Homer, the highest conception of the individual hero, relying on himself and sufficient to himself. But the same poet who conceived the character of Achilles has also drawn that of Hector; of the truly noble, because unselfish, hero, who subdues his genius to make it minister to the good of others, who lives for his relations, his friends and his country. And as Scipio lived in and for himself, like Achilles, so the virtue of Hector is worthily represented in the life of his great rival, Hannibal, who, from his childhood to his latest hour, in war and in peace, through glory and through obloquy, amid victories and amid disappointments, ever remembered to what purpose his father had devoted him, and withdrew no thought or desire or deed from their pledged service to his country.'

Both these distinguished men, so similar in many respects, so dissimilar in others, ended their lives in exile. Scipio, whom Cato had always hated — for his love of Greek culture almost as much as anything — was charged by the latter and his friends in the senate with defaulting on public funds. Scipio in reply brought his account books into the senate, tore them up, and told his accusers to grovel for proof in the fragments. He then pointed out that thousands of talents of silver had come into the public treasury through his agency, and that his victories had given Rome not only Spain, but also Africa, and now Asia (for he had also served at Magnesia). He left Rome in great bitterness and never returned.

Hannibal, after the defeat of Antiochus and the conclusion of a peace treaty between the King and Rome, no doubt rightly presumed that it would contain a clause relating to the deliverance of the Carthaginian into the hands of the victors. Swiftly and secretly he left by ship for Crete, then a wild and untamed island, the home of pirates and of men who accorded recognition to no monarch or state. Even here he was not to be left in peace. Rome, as she expanded into the east, and as her shipping routes grew more and more extensive, became increasingly concerned about the safety of her merchant marine. It was natural that in due course the Romans should become interested in this great island lying between the Aegean and Egypt, potentially prosperous and useful, but at that moment infested with pirates.

Hannibal had settled at Gortyna, an ancient city, second only to Knossus in importance in ancient times, and situated on a small river about three miles distant from the south coast. An amusing but possibly apocryphal story, tells how when Hannibal made his home here he made a point of openly depositing his treasure in the local temple of Artemis – much as one would in a modern bank. Rightly suspicious of Cretan honesty (as St Paul was to be some centuries later) the 'treasure' that he sent for safety to the temple was no more than a deception; large clay vases being weighted down with lead with a scattering of gold coins visible on the top. The bulk of his remaining fortune was concealed in some hollow bronze statues that stood in the garden of his house. In due course, a Roman squadron visited Crete bent on stamping out piracy and investigating the potential of the island's resources and harbours. Hannibal in his inland retreat was undisturbed, but he knew that it could only be a matter of time before the Romans heard of the wealthy Carthaginian living in retirement at Gortyna, and learned his name. As he had done at Carthage, and as he had done at the court of Antiochus, Hannibal left secretly and swiftly. With him went the statues from his garden. When the Cretan priests of Artemis or Roman soldiers broke open the jars stored in the temple one can imagine his ironic laughter on the wind.

So Hannibal came to remote Bithynia, to the kingdom of Prusias. Even his death did not bring an end to his influence. His memory was to trouble Rome throughout all the centuries of the empire's existence. Once he had stormed at the very gates of their city, once he had been close to overthrowing the state which now commanded nearly all the known world. . . . Historians and poets never forgot him; even the most acerbic such as Juvenal remembered that horrendous cry : 'Hannibal at the gates!'

XXX

CONCLUSION

The war which Hannibal initiated against Rome may be regarded as the last effort of the old eastern and Semitic peoples to prevent the domination of the Mediterranean world by a European state. That it failed was due to the immense resilience of the Romans, both in their political constitution and in their soldiery. Whatever Hannibal might achieve upon the battlefield, the strength that he could not break was the Republic and its association of allies. Had he been fighting against any other nation in the ancient world there is no doubt that his overwhelming victories would have brought them to their knees and to an early capitulation. Livy is right when he says that there was no other people that could have survived a disaster such as Cannae and continued to prosecute a war.

Hannibal's thinking was that of a general of the old school (although there were few except Alexander the Great who were in his category) and his mistake was to believe that victory upon the battlefield secured the victory over a state. He was politically naive. At the same time it must be conceded that no conquering general before in history had encountered a people as dour and rugged as the Romans, who also possessed in their republican institutions, and the flexible strength of their relationship with their allies, so sound a framework for nationhood.

It has often been suggested that if the great Carthaginian had conquered Rome the history of the western world would have been irretrievably changed: there would have been no Graeco-Roman culture permeating the Mediterranean basin and Europe, but instead some Semitic inheritance from Carthage and the East. This is doubtful. Carthage was hardly a nation-state, at least in terms of manpower, and was always reliant upon mercenaries and men of other races to fight her wars. The Carthaginians were not an imperial-minded people but a comparatively small handful of merchants, craftsmen, and seafarers, prosperous and powerful from their trade, but not seeking great tracts of territory to colonise. Their only venture into this area was in Spain where the foundations of empire were laid by Hannibal's father, very largely, it would seem, for an ultimate war of vengeance upon Rome. The idea of attacking Rome overland would never have suggested itself had Carthage retained control of the sea, but Roman seapower prevented this, and in the end this same seapower would strangle Hannibal's lines of communication. He inherited the power-base of Spain and his father's thinking, but it is unlikely that he ever considered his great venture across the Alps as anything other than a massive raid upon the enemy. If Rome had cracked and sought peace from Hannibal, one can be almost certain that the terms imposed upon her would have been sufficient only to ensure a situation in the Mediterranean resembling that which had existed before the First Punic War. Carthage did not have sufficient manpower to colonise in the manner of Rome or other countries in later centuries. Hannibal desired the abasement of a foe that, he felt, had betrayed the terms of the first peace treaty with Carthage and had begun to expand in a manner detrimental to the trading interests of his country.

The Carthaginians were the great entrepreneurs and middlemen of the ancient world : they had little culture of their own to transmit. Although the invention of the alphabet may be ascribed to their ancestors the Phoenicians, there is no evidence that they had any facility for literature, and the only Carthaginian prose work of which we have certain knowledge was a treatise on agriculture. In their architecture, and even in pottery and other artefacts, the predominant influence was that of Greece. Their state, although fairly stable politically – and sometimes admired by Greek writers for this quality – had little to offer the people of other races. They had nothing as durable or as resilient as the Roman republic. If Carthage had triumphed over Rome, and even if Carthaginian influence had permeated Italy, it is unlikely to have been anything distinctive. The influence of the Greeks would still – just as it did with the Romans – have triumphed. The culture of the western world would have suffered a setback if Hannibal had won his war, but it would probably have been only a temporary one. In religious and moral terms the Carthaginians, with their primitive Canaanite beliefs and practices, would soon have been eclipsed by the more sympathetic pantheon of Greece, and inevitably by her philosophers. It is noteworthy that Hannibal himself had a Greek tutor when young, that he took two Greek secretaries with him on his great expedition, that he paid equal reverence to the gods of that country as to those of his own, and that the lost history which he wrote for the people of Rhodes would have been in Greek.

Hannibal's genius in warfare has often and justifiably been acclaimed, for he had all the attributes of a great captain. When it comes to strategy, the movement of great armies and their tactical deployment upon the battlefield, he is almost impossible to fault. Hannibal had been bred for war and the world of the soldier was as natural to him as the sea to a shark or the air to an eagle. In the early years of his campaigns in Italy he enjoyed the benefit of the divided Roman military command and was quick to exploit differences of temperament between the two consuls opposing him. But against the tactics of 'the delayer', the canny Fabius Maximus, Hannibal was compelled to resort to a war of attrition, something for which neither he nor his composite armies were suited.

He was fortunate in possessing so fine an instrument of warfare as his Numidian horsemen, whose speed and adaptability confounded the Romans and, certainly in the early stages, contributed very largely to Hannibal's victories. His handling of his cavalry, whether light or heavy, was masterly, and it was not until Scipio Africanus had learned from this master that the Romans were able to face the Carthaginians with any confidence. Hannibal was fortunate, too, in possessing a fine team of staff officers; between them they taught the world that war is for professionals. Hannibal was a general with a quick adaptable mind, and for him every battlefield was an opportunity to create a new masterpiece. Undulations of the land, scrub or trees, open plain or river valley, each presented to this artist in warfare a completely new canvas. He made the land work for him and drew upon it his grand design – marked always by his distinctive signature.

The man himself eludes us – just as he eluded so many during his lifetime. Married in Spain, about two years before he left that country, to a chieftain's daughter called Imilce (who is said to have borne him a son), the only other mention of his private life is given by the unreliable historian Appian, who writes, long after the events, that during one winter in Italian Lucania 'he abandoned himself to unaccustomed luxury and the delights of love'. Polybius and Livy tell us nothing. Only Silius Italicus, in a long and tedious poem about the Hannibalic War (written at least two hundred years after Hannibal's death), relates a traditional story that Imilce pleaded with Hannibal to allow her to cross the Alps with him, and that he refused. This is not history, but Italian opera.

The man as a soldier and commander we know well enough, and we have a few examples of his laconic wit which allow us to see that a sense of humour never deserted him. Any character analysis of this strange and brilliant Carthaginian might well be called 'The Silences of Hannibal', for it is the taciturnity of his appearance upon the stage of world affairs that marks him out. Scipio Africanus, his great opponent, is a man of flamboyant charm, and enough is known of Alexander who came before him and Julius Caesar who succeeded him among the great generals of the ancient world to make them figures comprehensible in modern times. Hannibal, the boy from North Africa who grows up to dominate European history for sixteen years, seems to vanish like the mist rising off Lake Trasimene on that fateful day; or like the south wind, the sun and the dust that blinded the Romans at Cannae.

If it is true that, as Alfred de Vigny wrote in 'The Military Condition', 'A man who exercises absolute authority is constrained to assume a pose of invariable reserve', then Hannibal is the supreme example. At the same time, many commanders have possessed or cultivated such a distant and withdrawn attitude but not one of them has ever been capable of his mysterious art of 'disappearing'. When, after so many years in southern Italy, he finally leaves for Carthage, the Romans are amazed. They cannot believe that he no longer haunts their land. When the Roman commission comes to Carthage and his own people prepare to betray him he rides out at evening from the city to which he has given his life, embarks on a ship and sails east towards Tyre, the ancient home of his race. When Antiochus of Syria, after his defeat at Magnesia, is prepared to hand Hannibal over to the Romans, it is discovered that the Carthaginian has already gone. When in his remote home in southern Crete the ubiquitous Romans once again arrive and it seems that their routine investigation of the ports, harbours and possibilities of the island is likely to uncover his quiet retreat, he is no longer to be found – he has left the island as if he had never existed. Finally, in distant Bithynia, when King Prusias has been forced to disclose the whereabouts of his aged Carthaginian guest and the soldiers secretly gather round his country home, he escapes yet again – into the eternal silence.

Hannibal was an aristocrat. It is probable that a flinty arrogance was concealed beneath the outward charm and bonhomie that delighted his friends, his soldiers, and even an enemy like Scipio. A member of the Barcid family, he could trace his origins back to the queen who had founded Carthage, and beyond her to a long line of Semitic kings of Tyre. The calm ease and authority with which he handles all the affairs of his life and his campaigns are not those of a man who is no more than a superb general. Scipio, who was clearly fascinated by him, recognised this; and Scipio came from one of the most illustrious patrician families of Rome. The remoteness of Hannibal is in no way a deliberate concealment of his personality, but the remoteness of a man who is, in everything that he undertakes, coolly and clearly in control.

From the days of Polybius onwards many people have endeavoured to follow the tracks of Hannibal: from Spain, across the Pyrenees, into southern Gaul, up the Rhône, eastward to the Alps and then – by as many routes as there are scholars – down into Italy. Centuries before, Juvenal had cried out that he who would follow Hannibal must be a madman, and that his ambition must be insatiable. His strange, dark shadow has haunted European literature over all the centuries and, from Roman wall-paintings, through illuminated manuscripts of the Middle Ages to masters like Tiepolo, the Carthaginian has exercised his curious spell over artists. He is the sphinx whose riddle still eludes us.

SELECT BIBLIOGRAPHY

Allcroft, A. H., & Masom, W. F., *Tutorial History of Rome to A.D. 69*, University Tutorial Press, 1958

Armandi, P., *Histoire militaire des éléphants*, 1843

Arnold, T., *The Second Punic War*, 1886

Beer, Sir Gavin de, *Alps and Elephants: Hannibal's March*, 1955

Beer, Sir Gavin de, *Hannibal*, Thames & Hudson, 1969

Bradford, E., *The Mediterranean*, Hodder & Stoughton, 1971

Colin, J., *Annibal en Gaule*, 1904

Cottrell, L., *Enemy of Rome*, Evans Brothers, 1960

Dorey, T. A., and Dudley, D. R., *Rome against Carthage*, Secker & Warburg, 1971

Hallward, B. L., *Cambridge Ancient History*, vol 8, C.U.P., 1930

Liddell Hart, Sir B. H., *Greater than Napoleon: Scipio Africanus*, Blackwood, 1926

Livy, tr B. D. Foster, Loeb Classical Library, 1922

Mommsen, T., *History of Rome*, tr W. D. Dickson, 1901

Morris, W. O'Connor, *Hannibal*, 1897

Perrin, J. B., *Marche d'Annibal des Pyrénées au Pô*, 1883

Polybius, *The Histories*, tr W. R. Patton, Loeb Classical Library, 1922

Proctor, D., *Hannibal's March in History*, O.U.P., 1971

Rose, J. H., *The Mediterranean in the Ancient World*, C.U.P., 1934

Sanctis, G. de, *Storia dei Romani* (4 vols), vol 3: 1917

Scullard, H. H., *Scipio Africanus: Soldier and Politician*, Thames & Hudson, 1970

Torr, C., *Hannibal crosses the Alps*, C.U.P., 1925

Toynbee, A. J., *Hannibal's Legacy* (2 vols), O.U.P., 1965

Walbank, F. W., *Historical Commentary on Polybius*, vol 1: 1957, vol 2: 1967

Warmington, B. H., *Carthage*, Hale, 1969

Index